UNIVERSITY LIBRARY
UW-STEVENS POINT

MODIFYING
CHILDREN'S BEHAVIOR

MODIFYING CHILDREN'S BEHAVIOR

A Book of Readings

Compiled and Edited by

ALAN R. BROWN

Associate Professor
Department of Special Education
Arizona State University
Tempe, Arizona

and

CONNIE AVERY

Teacher, SPARC Program
Tempe Elementary School District
Tempe, Arizona

CHARLES C THOMAS · PUBLISHER
Springfield · Illinois · U.S.A.

Published and Distributed Throughout the World by
CHARLES C THOMAS • PUBLISHER
Bannerstone House
301-327 East Lawrence Avenue, Springfield, Illinois, U.S.A.

This book is protected by copyright. No part of it
may be reproduced in any manner without written
permission from the publisher.

© 1974, *by* CHARLES C THOMAS • PUBLISHER
ISBN 0-398-02953-9
Library of Congress Catalog Card Number: 74-3338

With THOMAS BOOKS careful attention is given to all details of manufacturing and design. It is the Publisher's desire to present books that are satisfactory as to their physical qualities and artistic possibilities and appropriate for their particular use. THOMAS BOOKS will be true to those laws of quality that assure a good name and good will.

Printed in the United States of America
A-1

Library of Congress Cataloging in Publication Data

Brown, Alan R.   comp.
   Modifying children's behavior.

   1. Classroom management—Addresses, essays, lectures.
2. Behaviorism (Psychology)—Addresses, essays,
lectures. 3. Problem children—Education—Addresses,
essays, lectures. I. Avery, Connie, joint comp.
II. Title. [DNLM: 1. Behavior therapy—In infancy
and childhood—Collected works. 2. Child behavior
disorders—Therapy—Collected works. WS350 B874m 1974]
LB3011.B72   371.9'3   74-3338
ISBN 0-398-02953-9

To
Linda, Lisa and Jennifer Brown
and
Gene and Elizabeth Outcalt

CONTRIBUTORS

Arnold Abramovitz

K. Eileen Allen, Ph.D.
Coordinator of Early Childhood
  Education and Research
Experimental Unit
Mental Retardation Center
University of Washington
Seattle, Washington

Alfred A. Artuso
Superintendent, Santa Monica
  Unified Schools
Santa Monica, California

Saul Axelrod, Ph.D.
Assistant Professor
Department of Special Education
Temple University
Philadelphia, Pennsylvania

Nathan H. Azrin
Director of Behavioral Research
Anna St. Hospital
Anna, Illinois 62906

Wesley C. Becker
Professor of Educational Psychology
Bureau of Educational Research
University of Illinois
Urbana, Illinois

Cedric Benson
Director of Special Education
West Suburban Association for
  Special Education
Oak Park, Illinois

Marcia Broden
Research Assistant
Bureau of Child Research
University of Kansas
Lawrence, Kansas

Harvey F. Clarizio
Assistant Professor of Educational
  Psychology
Michigan State University
Lansing, Michigan

Marilyn Clark
Special Education Teacher
Skyline School
Shawnee Mission, Kansas

Robert Clark
Principal, Bonner Springs Junior
  High School
Bonner Springs, Kansas

Gerald C. Davison
Stanford University

Ronald S. Drabman
Graduate Student
Department of Psychology
State University of New York
Stoney Brook, New York

Ann Dunlap
Teacher, Bonner Springs Junior
  High School
Bonner Springs, Kansas

Paulette M. Everett
Teacher, Experimental Education
  Unit
University of Washington
Seattle, Washington

Steven R. Forness
Special Education Director
Mental Retardation Center
University of California
Los Angeles, California

Marie Gaasholt, Ph.D.
Department of Special Education
University of Oregon
Eugene, Oregon

David K. Giles
Director, Southwest Indian Youth
  Center
Tucson, Arizona

R. Vance Hall
Research Associate, Bureau of Child
  Research
Associate Professor of Education and
  Human Development and Family
  Life
University of Kansas
Lawrence, Kansas

Edward L. Hanley
Assistant Professor of Education
University of Vermont
Burlington, Vermont

Norris G. Haring

Frank M. Hewett
Associate Professor of Education and
  Psychiatry
Chairman, Area of Special Education
University of California
Los Angeles, California

Joseph S. Kaplan
Assistant Professor of Special
  Education
Arizona State University
Tempe, Arizona 85281

Ruth E. Kass
Graduate Student
Department of Psychology
State University of New York
Stoney Brook, New York

Kenneth F. Kaufman
Graduate Student
Department of Psychology
State University of New York
Stoney Brook, New York

Louise A. King
Teacher, Wichita Public Schools
Wichita, Kansas

Richard Kothera
Superintendent of Schools
Rosesland District #92
Shawnee Mission, Kansas

David S. Kuypers
Graduate Student
Department of Psychology
University of Illinois
Urbana, Illinois

Joseph Lachowicz
Director of Research
Southwest Indian Youth Center
Tucson, Arizona

Arnold A. Lazarus, Ph.D.
Department of Psychology
Rutgers University
New Brunswick, New Jersey

Ogden R. Lindsley
Child Rehabilitation Unit
University of Kansas Medical Center
39th Street
Kansas City, Kansas 66103

Thomas Lovitt
Associate Professor

Donald L. MacMillan
Assistant Professor of Education
University of California
Riverside, California

Hugh S. McKenzie
Chairman, Special Education
4814 Skyline Drive
Shawnee Mission, Kansas 66025

K. Daniel O'Leary
Assistant Professor of Psychology
State University of New York at
  Stoney Brook
Long Island, New York

David A. Polefka

Contributors

Frank D. Taylor
Director of Special Services
Santa Monica Unified Schools
Santa Monica, California

Keith D. Turner
Teacher, Experimental Education Unit
University of Washington
Seattle, Washington

Richard F. Whelan
Chairman, Department of Special Education
Professor of Education
Assistant Professor of Pediatrics
University of Kansas Medical Center
Kansas City, Kansas

Montrose M. Wolf
Associate Professor of Human Development
Research Associate, Bureau of Child Research
University of Kansas
Lawrence, Kansas

Steven L. Yelon
144 Highland
E. Lansing, Michigan 48823

Elaine H. Zimmerman

J. Zimmerman
Indiana University School of Medicine
Indianapolis, Indiana 46207

PREFACE

THIS VOLUME REPRESENTS a book of readings on behavior modification with children. It was compiled to disseminate information to special education and regular teachers, but it is our hope that it will have relevance to others who are working with children whose behavior is in need of change.

There is an increasing explosion of articles, books, and knowledge on behavior modification with particular reference to children. Literally hundreds of articles were considered for inclusion in this publication. Those finally chosen were selected for their relevance, readability, uniqueness, and in many instances, general appeal. Many fine articles were excluded for a variety of reasons, not the least being space considerations. We hope, however, that the articles in this volume will stimulate interest and encourage additional pursuits in this area.

There are always many people to thank for their assistance, encouragement, and support in the preparation of any publication. A publication such as this is not completed by the editors alone. Many students and professional colleagues gave freely of their time and made valuable suggestions about the content of this publication and we are appreciative. In addition to this, the support and encouragement of Dr. Willard Abraham, Chairman of the Department of Special Education, Arizona State University was much appreciated. Miss Cathy Pew did the bulk of the secretarial work from this book's inception and she was amply supported by others on the secretarial staff of the Department. Mrs. Eleonore Chadwick, Miss Nancy Bergman and Miss Sandy Weisman also provided valuable ideas and secretarial assistance. A special word of thanks is due to Miss Tammy Miller, who in addition to attending to the numerous details necessary to make this book a reality, she cajoled, teased and badgered when other important issues and tasks delayed the preparation of this publication. Had she not made this book a high priority, it may have been some time until its completion.

Finally, we are, of course, very grateful to those many authors and publishers whose permissions we received to include each of the papers which make up the body of this volume.

ALAN R. BROWN
CONNIE J. AVERY

CONTENTS

	Page
Contributors	vii
Preface	xi

Section I
INTRODUCTION

Chapter

1. THE ORIGINS OF BEHAVIOR MODIFICATION WITH EXCEPTIONAL CHILDREN
   Steven R. Forness and Donald L. MacMillan 5
2. BEHAVIOR MODIFICATION: THE CURRENT SCENE
   Thomas Lovitt 20
3. MODIFICATION AND MAINTENANCE OF BEHAVIOR THROUGH SYSTEMATIC APPLICATION OF CONSEQUENCES
   Richard F. Whelan and Norris G. Haring 28
4. LEARNING THEORY APPROACHES TO CLASSROOM MANAGEMENT: RATIONALE AND INTERVENTION TECHNIQUES
   Harvey F. Clarizio and Stephen L. Yelon 44
5. PRECISION TECHNIQUES IN THE MANAGEMENT OF TEACHER AND CHILD BEHAVIORS
   Marie Gaasholt 57

Section II
CONSIDERATIONS AND ISSUES

6. FREEDOM TO FAIL: THE MORALITY OF BEHAVIORISM IN EDUCATION OR WHY THE BIG FUSS OVER BEHAVIOR MOD?
   Joseph S. Kaplan 71
7. BEHAVIOR MODIFICATION: LIMITATIONS AND LIABILITIES
   Donald L. MacMillan and Steven R. Forness 77
8. HOW TO MAKE A TOKEN SYSTEM FAIL
   David S. Kuypers, Wesley C. Becker and K. Daniel O'Leary   90

Section III
PROMOTING ADAPTIVE BEHAVIORS AND DECREASING PROBLEMATIC BEHAVIOR

Chapter *Page*

9. THE REINFORCEMENT OF COOPERATION BETWEEN CHILDREN
   Nathan H. Azrin and Ogden R. Lindsley 109
10. THE ALTERATION OF BEHAVIOR IN A SPECIAL CLASSROOM SITUATION
    Elaine H. Zimmerman and J. Zimmerman 116
11. THE USE OF "EMOTIVE IMAGERY" IN THE TREATMENT OF CHILDREN'S PHOBIAS
    Arnold A. Lazarus and Arnold Abramovitz 120
12. CLASSICAL AND OPERANT FACTORS IN THE TREATMENT OF A SCHOOL PHOBIA
    Arnold A. Lazarus, Gerald C. Davison and David A. Polefka 128

Section IV
CLASSROOM APPLICATION

13. TOKEN REINFORCEMENT PROGRAMS IN SPECIAL CLASSES
    Saul Axelrod 141
14. BEHAVIOR MODIFICATION OF AN ADJUSTMENT CLASS: A TOKEN REINFORCEMENT PROGRAM
    K. Daniel O'Leary and Wesley C. Becker 158
15. THE EFFECTS OF LOUD AND SOFT REPRIMANDS ON THE BEHAVIOR OF DISRUPTIVE STUDENTS
    K. Daniel O'Leary, Kenneth F. Kaufman, Ruth E. Kass, and Ronald S. Drabman 168
16. THE SANTA MONICA PROJECT: EVALUATION OF AN ENGINEERED CLASSROOM DESIGN WITH EMOTIONALLY DISTURBED CHILDEN
    Frank M. Hewett, Frank D. Taylor and Alfred A. Artuso . 187
17. BEHAVIOR MODIFICATION OF CHILDREN WITH LEARNING DISABILITIES USING GRADES AS TOKENS AND ALLOWANCES AS BACK UP REINFORCERS
    Hugh S. McKenzie, Marilyn Clark, Montrose M. Wolf, Richard Kothera and Cedric Benson 201

Chapter	Page
18. A BEHAVIOR MODIFICATION CLASSROOM FOR HEAD START CHILDREN WITH PROBLEM BEHAVIORS K. Eileen Allen, Keith D. Turner, and Paulette M. Everett	216
19. EFFECTS OF TEACHER ATTENTION AND A TOKEN REINFORCEMENT SYSTEM IN A JUNIOR HIGH SCHOOL SPECIAL EDUCATION CLASS Marcia Broden, R. Vance Hall, Ann Dunlap, and Robert Clark	231
20. THE TIMER-GAME: A VARIABLE INTERVAL CONTINGENCY FOR THE MANAGEMENT OF OUT-OF-SEAT BEHAVIOR Montrose M. Wolf, Edward L. Hanley, Louise A. King, Joseph Lachowicz, and David K. Giles	247

Section V
FUTURE CONSIDERATIONS

21. BEHAVIOR MODIFICATION: WHERE DO WE GO FROM HERE? Thomas Lovitt	257
Index	271

MODIFYING CHILDREN'S BEHAVIOR

SECTION I
INTRODUCTION

Chapter 1

THE ORIGINS OF BEHAVIOR MODIFICATION WITH EXCEPTIONAL CHILDREN

STEVEN R. FORNESS
DONALD L. MACMILLAN

BEHAVIOR MODIFICATION is the "application of the results of learning theory and experimental psychology to the problem of altering maladaptive behavior" (Ullmann and Krasner, 1965, p. 2). It represents a school of thought which focuses on overt behavior and deemphasizes intrapsychic conflicts and similar conceptualizations. To the behaviorist both adaptive and maladaptive behaviors are learned through interaction with stimuli in the environment; thus, stimuli may be manipulated to alter behavior.

The roots of behaviorism can be traced to the temple psychiatry of the Greeks and to the early aversive treatment of the Romans who put eels in the wine cup as a cure for alcoholism (Zilboorg and Henry, 1941). Although behavior modification, as such, was unknown until the present century, many of the techniques in use today had their beginnings in the eighteenth and nineteenth centuries. Its impact on special education, however, was not widely felt until the late 1960's. The present paper attempts to put recent behavior modification programs in historical perspective by documenting the earlier work of selected behavior modification practitioners in and peripheral to the field of special education.

Itard's work in 1800 represents one of the earliest documented uses of positive and negative reinforcement in educational practice. Although his use of reinforcement techniques with Victor is largely overlooked, he employed techniques much as sophisticated researchers do today. For example, Itard, in teachng Victor to spell "milk," would point to the word on the board and pronounce it, rewarding Victor with a drink of milk when he would correctly repeat the word. Once during a lesson, Victor became enraged and scattered his word cards about the room. Itard picked up the boy by the seat of the pants and held him out the fourth floor window (aversive stimulus), whereupon Victor meekly began to pick up the cards.

Seguin, a disciple of Itard, published the results of his work with the mentally retarded in 1866. As with Itard, reinforcement techniques were part of Seguin's methodology. In order to improve coordination and perception, students were required to lower themselves rung by rung from an inclined ladder. However, their hands would often be bruised and scraped by the time they reached the bottom. Seguin's teachers were instructed to place an apple in each pupil's hands after the task was accomplished so that the cooling sensation of the apples, plus the positive reinforcement, would overcome tendencies toward not performing the task the next time.

By the end of the nineteenth and the beginning of the twentieth centuries, Thorndike's (1913) law of effect and Pavlov's (1927) experimentation in respondent conditioning had paved the way for the classical work of Watson and others, which can be regarded as the beginnings of the behavior modification movement as it relates to exceptional children.

Early Beginnings: The Twenties

The work of Watson (Watson and Rayner, 1920) represents the first conditioning of a human emotional reaction in an experimental setting. Watson proceeded on the basis of four assumptions: that the emotional response of fear could be conditioned, that it would transfer to stimuli other than the initial stimulus which evoked the fear, that the fear would last over a period of time, and that it could be unlearned. For his subject, Watson chose Albert, an 11-month-old infant, especially noted for his robust health and apparent lack of fear. The conditioned stimulus was a white rat to which Albert had previously shown no fear and the unconditioned stimulus, a loud noise.

When the rat was first presented, Albert reached for it; but when it touched his hands, the unconditioned stimulus was paired with the conditioned stimulus, causing Albert to whimper. When fear of the rat was eventually conditioned it was still evident days later and generalized to other furry objects.

Watson's findings received indirect support from Haberman's (1917) earlier report of a conditioned response of vomiting in a school child. The child was rushed through breakfast one morning and, on reaching school, vomited because of the anxiety generated over breakfast and being late for school. The next morning, though no rushing ensued, the child again vomited on arriving at school due to the inadvertent pairing of stimuli the previous day—an example of contiguous learning of maladaptive behavior.

In 1924 Jones attempted to take up where Watson left off. She reported her work with Peter, a three-year-old who was afraid of a white rabbit. She attempted desensitization by presenting the rabbit in the far corner of the room while Peter was eating, then gradually moving the rabbit (aversive stimulus) closer and closer until finally it was placed on the tray of food from which Peter was eating (pleasant stimulus). This, coupled with Peter's exposure to children who enjoyed playing with the rabbit, soon overcame the fear. The implications were obvious: Not only is fear learned, it can be unlearned as well.

Burnham's landmark volume (1924) did much to bridge the gap between research and educational application. Burnham felt that the essence of education consisted of (a) the specification of the task to be done, (b) a plan of action to complete the task, and (c) freedom to complete the task according to plan. He insisted on small increments of learning with little chance for failure by the student, for he believed that discipline was a systematic attempt to develop conditioned responses to school tasks. Although Burnham included no systematic research of his own, his assumptions were validated by case studies and a review of the behavior modification literature to that date.

In 1929 English presented a case study on the development of a fear response in a natural home setting, replicating Watson's research in the laboratory. He related the case of Joan who was offered a stuffed toy by her parents while at the same time an older sister, the toy's owner, howled in protest. Joan became frightened by the howl, refused to touch the toy, and, on subsequent occasions, whimpered when it was presented. Through a process of systematic desensitization similar to that used by Jones, the parents were able to overcome the child's fear in a relatively short time.

The Thirties and Forties

The next two decades witnessed a refinement of techniques and a broadened application of the principles established in the 1920's. These studies are prototypes of later works emphasizing operant conditioning and negative practice.

In a study primarily concerned with children's fears, Jersild and Holmes (1935) arrived at conclusions similar to Jones's (1924) and were able to elaborate on earlier findings. They regarded Watson's thesis on the way fear develops as an oversimplification, for they believed it was occasioned by a sudden novel stimulus to which the child had no adequate response. To prevent fear from developing, the use of fearful stimuli should be avoided in activities like teasing or as a disciplinary measure. Promoting skills to cope with fear, such as rough and tumble games, dodge ball, and the like would build stimulus-response associations in which the response would later generalize to fearful stimuli. To overcome fear, the authors suggested such alternatives as instruction in methods of coping with fear, gradual habituation, counterstimuli, and promotion of experience through social modeling.

In 1935 Krasnogorski was able to demonstrate the development of a neurosis under laboratory conditions. A six-year-old boy was trained to give a motor response to a metronome beat of 144 per minute and to inhibit response to a beat of 92. However, as the difference between the metronome beats was decreased, the subject began to show emotional responses, disliked coming to the laboratory, and eventually became disobedient, cried, became overexcited, and even went to sleep. When the differential was increased and the beat was lowered to 120, a stimulus to which the boy had responded earlier, he no longer seemed able to respond. Only when the beat was lowered to 92 was he able to relearn the response. The discrepancy between the child's capacity to respond and the demands of the environment appears not only to explain the development of the disorder but serves to explain the development of classroom behavior disorders as well.

In an article in 1942, Dunlap contributed the concept of negative practice in dealing with stammering and tics. He felt that practicing the stammer or tic led to its control and subsequently to its inhibition. Rutherford (1940) had applied the technique to the extraneous facial and body movements that athetoid subjects make when attempting to speak. She felt that these extraneous movements had developed because of incorrect channelling of the energy to speak and, when finally associated with speaking, had become habit patterns reminiscent of the superstitious behavior observed in animals by Skinner (1938). Her treatment consisted of having the child watch his face in a mirror while the teacher recorded his movements, responding verbally when he observed certain movements, and practicing the sequence of movements until the behavior was brought under conscious control. Rutherford at this point felt that the movements were no longer contingent on speech.

The final study of significance in this era exemplifies the use of positive reinforcement in operant conditioning. Fuller (1949) was able to establish a learned response in an 18-year-old profoundly retarded boy whom physicians diagnosed as incapable of even the simplest learning. The subject lay on his back unable to move, save for random movement of the arms and head, and was totally speechless. Fuller used a syringe filled with sugar milk solution to reinforce and shape movement in one arm. In two sessions he was able to raise the rate of response appreciably, and he also observed anticipatory responses such as opening the mouth to receive reinforcement. Fuller felt that research on vegetative human organisms such as he had used would bridge the gap from animal studies to the study of man.

The Fifties

The 1950's witnessed an amazing upsurge in the area of behavioral research, most of it an outgrowth of Skinner's experimentation and writings. Skinner (1953) provided the impetus for development of ideas and techniques which enabled specialists in many disciplines—psychology, education, medicine, and nursing among them—to change a broad spectrum of deviant behaviors—aggressive, retarded, and phobic, to mention a few.

In 1951 Sheehan applied principles of reinforcement to the behavior of stutterers. He hypothesized that stuttering occurs because the stutterer is reinforced by being allowed to go on to the next word. In the control segment of his study, stutterers read a passage as they normally would with no interference of their stuttering. In the experimental segment, the same subjects read the passage; but whenever they stuttered, they were not allowed to continue until they had pronounced the word once without stuttering. Sheehan's results indicated a lower frequency of stuttering under the experimental condition. An examination of the interpassage quadrants over seven trials also showed a significant decline in stuttering within each passage as trials increased.

In 1956 Azrin and Lindsley were able to condition cooperation between children. Subjects, matched for sex and age, were placed at a special table with a screen separating them. They were given no instructions except that they could play a game with the apparatus. A jelly bean was automatically released in a cup whenever both subjects simultaneously placed metal pens into matching stimulus holes. During the first reinforcement period, subjects usually learned to cooperate within ten minutes. Cooperation gradually declined during extinction, but increased quickly to the preextinction rate in the second reinforcement period. Thus it was demonstrated that cooperative social responses could be controlled by reinforcing contingencies and developed without verbal instructions.

Baer and his co-workers have done considerable work in determining the nature of social reinforcers (Gewirtz and Baer, 1958). Baer studied the effects of deprivation and satiation on social reinforcement. In the deprivation condition, each subject was brought from the classroom by an experimenter who interacted only minimally along the way and left the child alone in the experimental room for 20 minutes. The experimenter then returned and instructed the child to place marbles in two holes. After a baseline period, the experimenter began to verbally reinforce the correct choice. In the nondeprived condition, the experimenter reacted in a similar manner but began the game immediately on entering the experimental room. In the satiation period, the experimenter showed lively interest along the way to the room and interacted in a friendly manner with the subjects for 20 minutes before the game. An analysis of correct marble-placing responses for each group confirmed Baer's hypothesis that social reinforcers were indeed sensitive to deprivation-satiation conditions.

In 1959, Lazarus reported his use of behavior therapy techniques developed earlier by Wolpe (1954). Lazarus used desensitization coupled with positive reinforcement to overcome one child's phobia of cars, resulting from a previous auto accident. He began by reinforcing the child with chocolates each time he mentioned cars in a positive way. Later he reinforced the child for sitting, and eventually riding in a car. Another subject with a phobia of animals was presented with various animals while under tranquilizing medication; the amount of the dosage was gradually decreased each session until the child reacted without fear. A conditioned avoidance response was used to overcome another child's fear of sleeping alone. He was told to imagine his mother's bed and was given a mild electric shock which terminated when he said the words, "my bed." The boy reportedly had not slept in his mother's bed since the initial treatment, and on follow-up, the behavior had continued.

In the same year, Williams (1959) reported a case of the elimination of tantrum behavior through extinction. The subject was a 21-month-old child whose tantrums, developed after a long illness, occurred when he was being put to bed. He would scream and rage, often for two hours, if either parent left the room too soon after he was put to bed. The parents unwittingly reinforced this behavior by remaining in the room. At Williams's suggestion, the parents were instructed to put the child to bed in a casual and loving manner and leave the room, shutting the door behind them. In the first session, the child's tantrum lasted 45 minutes; but the second night (possibly due to the exhaustion in the first session) the child went immediately to sleep. In the third session a tantrum occurred for ten minutes but by the tenth session this behavior was totally extinguished. A week later, an aunt inadvertently reinforced a tantrum which recurred, and it was necessary to extinguish the behavior a second time. No adverse maladjustment or symptom substitution was reported after 1½ years.

The Early Sixties

The work on child development by Bijou and Baer (1961) concentrated professional attention on previously neglected interactions between the child and his learning environment. Systematic techniques now began to replace previously fragmented and haphazard approaches to child management and motivation. The momentum of behavior modification in the early 1960's began to generate programs which stand as prototypes of present day behavior modification efforts with exceptional children.

In the early 1960's Ayllon (Ayllon and Haughton, 1962) pioneered the use of behavior modification techniques on the psychiatric ward. On the wards of Saskatchewan Hospital, many patients had to be coaxed to the cafeteria at meal time, and several who refused to go were unwittingly reinforced for this behavior by being fed in their rooms. Going to the cafeteria was reinforced by the following procedure. The cafeteria was open for entry for only 30 minutes at mealtime, and anyone who failed to arrive during that time was not allowed to eat. This time was gradually decreased to five minutes, with all patients eventually meeting criterion. When criterion was met, patients were further required to obtain a token from the nurses and drop it in a slot in order to enter the cafeteria. Ayllon's "token economy" system served as a model for a later program for adolescent retarded girls at Parsons State Hospital in Kansas (Girardeau and Spradlin, 1964).

In 1962 Ferster and DeMyer developed a technique for analyzing reinforcers. They used a specially designed room containing several types of reinforcing devices, ensuring that at least one of the devices would be relevant to the current deprivation condition of the child. Three autistic subjects obtained a coin by pressing a lever in one device and used the coin in one of the other dispensers to obtain reinforcement: a pinball machine, an electric organ, a phonograph, a picture viewer, an electric train, a food vendor, a trinket vendor, and a compartment in which a trained monkey would perform. Early research indicated that candy and trinket vendors were high frequency reinforcers. However, when reinforcers were dispensed on varying intermittent schedules and when lights over the machines indicated when machines were not dispensing reinforcement, more complex repertoires could be developed, such as delaying gratification (coin saving). Subjects were also taught discrimination learning through a matching device above the coin dispenser. Indications were that normal learning processes in autistics operated at a very basic level but could be gradually shaped through an almost totally automatic environment.

By 1962 Bandura had performed a number of experiments with modeling techniques. One experiment with children focused on Piaget's (1932) concept of the development of moral judgment. In the first seven years, children tend to judge an act as morally wrong in terms of material damages involved. After this age, they tend to judge an act by its intent. By using adults who made evaluative statements contrary to this developmental scheme, it was found that children in the experimental groups actually changed their basis for moral judgments, while children in a control group without adult models did not.

Bandura (1965) presented films to different groups of young children in which models for aggressive responses were portrayed. Children who viewed a film of adults or cartoon characters performing aggressive acts reacted with aggressive responses when placed in a frustrating situation, though control children did not. In a similar experiment, children who had viewed films in which the model was punished for his aggressiveness tended to respond with fewer aggressive acts. Implications were that certain catharsis techniques in dealing with aggression, i.e., viewing films and TV programs of aggressive content, may actually be teaching aggression through reinforcement.

At approximately the same time, Zimmerman and Zimmerman (1962) reported an example of altering classroom behavior by manipulating its consequences. They discussed the case of one boy who appeared to have difficulty in spelling and, when called on, would flounder and have to be urged and prodded by the teacher. The teacher's response (giving attention) was considered to actually reinforce the boy's inability to spell. Therefore the teacher attempted to ignore him unless he spelled correctly. The maladaptive response (misspelling) decreased and was gradually replaced by the adaptive response (spelling achievement) which was reinforced by the teacher's smiling, chatting, and physical proximity. Two years later, systematic teacher attention was used in a similar manner by Wolf (Allen, Hart, Buell, Harris, and Wolf, 1964) in encouraging social behaviors in a nursery school child.

Lindsley (1964) developed and encouraged the use of several means of tailoring environments for the retarded, the brain damaged, and the emotionally disturbed. He felt that retardation was not inherent in the child but was due to the educator's inability to design a suitable environment for such a child. He envisioned the possibility of constructing a synthetic environment with prosthetic devices peculiar to the needs of retarded persons much as physical therapists use artificial limbs, ramps, and elevators for amputees. Lindsley advocated the use of operant techniques because they represented a fresh theoretical approach to educating the retarded, were amenable to experimental description and evaluation, and offered individualized prescriptions for a prosthetic environment.

Such an environment had been created by Birnbrauer (Birnbrauer and Lawler, 1964) at the Rainier School in Washington. It was the first attempt to apply a token reinforcement system to a classroom for retarded children, many of whom had never before functioned productively in a group setting. A variety of techniques were used including individually paced instructional materials, immediate tangible reinforcement for adaptive behavior, and systematic use of teacher attention. Pupils earned checkmarks for completing assignments and were able to delay exchanging checkmark cards for candy till the end of the period or, in some cases, till the end of the week. Subjects were thus taught to work for symbolic reward and to delay gratification, abilities necessary for success in a regular classroom. The Rainier program demonstrated that the classroom environment could be structured to effect studying behaviors in children previously regarded as uneducable.

In 1964 Schwitzgebel reported his use of operant techniques with juvenile delinquents in Boston. Choosing only subjects with notable police records, he went to the subjects' neighborhoods and offered them $1.00 per hour to speak into a tape recorder about their experiences as juvenile offenders. Most were suspicious at first but were intrigued by the opportunity for "easy money." At first they usually showed up late but began to arrive earlier when reinforced by additional money. Subjects at first usually showed hostility toward parents, peers, and the experimenter, but this was later replaced by a developing sense of insight. A three-year follow-up showed that the subjects in the experimental group had a 50 percent reduction in arrests and incarceration when compared with the control group. It would appear that shaping techniques can be used to develop attitudes and desirable behavior in a subject's natural environment as well as in the laboratory and school setting.

That same year at U.C.L.A., Hewett (1964) used operant conditioning to teach reading to a 13-year-old autistic boy who literally had no speech. When he entered the classroom he was reinforced away from hyperactive behaviors and over to his desk with gumdrops. Hewett had devised an upright board with two levels onto which the subject learned to slide a picture card under the appropriate object and to receive a gumdrop reinforcer from behind a glass door. Beginning with concrete objects matched to picture cards, the subject was eventually taught to match picture cards to appropriate words. Hewett was able to teach a 55-word sight vocabulary to the pupil, as well as an understanding of basic principles of classification, letters of the alphabet, and writing of basic phrases. One day when the gumdrops ran out, the subject continued to perform, indicating that the teacher had become a reinforcing stimulus. Also at U.C.L.A., more extensive techniques for dealing with autistic behavior were developed for ward staff and parents by Lovaas (Lovaas, Freitag, Kinder, Rubenstein, Schaeffer, and Simmons, 1964).

A year later, Patterson (1965) reported his work in controlling hyperactive behavior with operant techniques. The subject was a nine-year-old boy, diagnosed as minimally brain damaged. He was hyperactive, academically retarded, and aggressive. Patterson felt that environmental stimuli were responsible for much of the hyperactivity and that one should be able to rearrange the environment to strengthen the child's associations with stimuli in the classroom and specified attending behaviors. Patterson's apparatus was a box on the pupil's desk with a light and an electric counter controlled by the experimenter. Each time the light went on, the student was told that he would be rewarded with a penny. The class was told that the light was part of a "magic teaching machine" which would teach the boy to sit still so he could learn and that they would share in his earnings. At first the pupil was rewarded immediately with candy each time he attended to relevant stimuli (his book or the teacher); later, reinforcement was delayed. A significant decline occurred in the student's hyperactive behavior due largely, perhaps, to his classmates, who dropped by his desk at intervals to see how he was doing and to compliment him on his behavior. Thus, it was illustrated that behavior, even with a supposedly organic basis, can be controlled in the classroom.

Conclusion

Only within the last five years has the impact of behavior modification been widely felt in the education of exceptional children. This brief examination of its origins before that time, however, indicates that its techniques relative to special education have been delineated over several decades and that it has been applied in unsystematic fashion for much longer.

Behavior modification principles have been successfully applied in recent years to several classroom settings for exceptional children: the Experimental Education Unit at the University of Washington for retarded children (Haring and Lovitt, 1967); the Children's Rehabilitation Unit at the University of Kansas Medical Center for emotionally disturbed children (Whelan and Haring, 1966); the Juniper Gardens Project in Kansas City for culturally disadvantaged children (Risley and Hart, 1968); a class for predelinquent children (Quay, Werry, McQueen, and Sprague, 1966); and the Santa Monica City Schools Project for the educationally handicapped (Hewett, 1968). It is noteworthy that behaviorists have also turned their attention to problems of children in regular classroom settings as well (Becker, Madsen, Arnold, and Thomas, 1967). Countless other programs, equally worthy of mention, are operating in institutional, clinical, and public school settings, testimonials to the effectiveness of the behavior modification strategy.

REFERENCES

Allen, K., Hart, B., Buell, J., Harris, F., and Wolf, M.: Effects of social reinforcement on isolate behavior of a nursery school child. *Child Dev,* 35:511-518, 1964.

Ayllon, T., and Haughton, E.: Control of the behavior of schizophrenics by food. *J Exp Anal Behav,* 5:343-352, 1962.

Azrin, N., and Lindsley, O.: The reinforcement of cooperation between children. *J Abnorm Soc Psychol,* 52:100-102, 1956.

Bandura, A.: Behavior modification through modeling procedures. In L. Krasner and L. P. Ullmann (Eds.): *Research in Behavior Modification. New Developments and Implications.* New York, Holt, Rinehart & Winston, 1965, pp. 310-340.

Becker, W., Madsen, C., Arnold, C., and Thomas, D.: The contingent use of teacher attention and praise in reducing classroom behavior problems. *J Spec Educ,* 1:287-307, 1967.

Bijou, S., and Baer, D.: *Child Development, Volume 1: A Systematic and Empirical Theory.* New York, Appleton-Century-Crofts, 1961.

Birnbrauer, J., and Lawler, J.: Token reinforcement for learning. *Ment Retard,* 2:275-279, 1964.

Burnham, W.: *The Normal Mind.* New York, Appleton, 1924.

Dunlap, K.: Technique of negative practice. *Am J Psychol,* 55:270-273, 1942.

English, W.: Three cases of "conditioned fear response." *J Abnorm Psychol,* 24:221-225, 1929.

Ferster, C., and DeMyer, M. K.: A method for the experimental analysis of the behavior of autistic children. *Am J Orthopsychiatry,* 32:89-98, 1962.

Fuller, P.: Operant conditioning of a vegetative human organism. *Am J Psychol,* 62:587-590, 1949.

Gewirtz, J., and Baer, D.: Deprivation and satiation of social reinforcers as drive conditions. *J Abnorm Soc Psychol,* 57:165-172, 1958.

Girardeau, F., and Spradlin, J.: Token rewards in a cottage program. *Ment Retard,* 2:245-251, 1964.

Haberman, J.: Probing the mind, normal and subnormal. *Med Rec,* 92:927-933, 1917.

Haring, N. G., and Lovitt, T. C.: Operant methodology and educational technology in special education. In N. G. Haring and R. L. Schiefelbusch (Eds.): *Methods in Special Education.* New York, McGraw-Hill, 1967, pp. 12-48.

Hewett, F.: Teaching reading to an autistic boy through operant conditioning. *Read Teacher,* 17:613-618, 1964.

―――: *The Emotionally Disturbed Child in the Classroom: A Developmental Strategy for Educating Children With Maladaptive Behavior.* Boston, Allyn & Bacon, 1968.

Itard, J.: *The Wild Boy of Aveyron.* Trans. by G. and M. Humphrey. New York, Appleton-Century-Crofts, 1962.

Jersild, A., and Holmes, F.: Methods in overcoming children's fears. *J Psychol,* 1:75-104, 1935.

Jones, M. C.: The elimination of children's fears. *J Exp Psychol,* 7:382-390, 1924.

Krasnogorski, N.: Conditioned reflex and childhood neurosis. *Am J Disturb Child,* 30:753-768, 1930.

Lazarus, A.: The elimination of children's phobias by deconditioning. *South Af Med Proc,* 5:261-265, 1959.

Lindsley, O.: Direct measurement and prosthesis of retarded behavior. *J Educ,* 147:62-81, 1964.

Lovaas, O., Freitag, G., Kinder, B., Rubenstein, B., Schaeffer, B., and Simmons, J.: Experimental studies in childhood schizophrenia: II. Establishment of social reinforcers. Paper presented to Western Psychological Association, 1964.

Patterson, G. R.: An application of conditioning techniques to the control of a hyperactive child. In L. P. Ullmann and L. Krasner (Eds.): *Case Studies in Behavior Modification.* New York, Holt, Rinehart & Winston, 1965, pp. 370-375.

Pavlov, I. P.: *Conditioned Reflexes.* Trans. by G. V. Anrep (Ed.). London, Oxford University Press, 1927.

Piaget, J.: *The Moral Judgment of the Child.* Trans. by M. Worden. New York, Harcourt-Brace, 1932.

Quay, H., Werry, J., McQueen, M., and Sprague, R.: Remediation of the conduct problem child in the special class setting. *Except Child, 32:* 509-515, 1966.

Risley, T., and Hart, B.: Developing correspondence between non-verbal and verbal behavior of pre-school children. *J Appl Behav Anal, 4:*267-281, 1968.

Rutherford, B.: Use of negative practice in speech therapy with children handicapped by cerebral palsy, athetoid type. *J Speech Hear Disord, 5:* 259-264, 1940.

Schwitzgebel, R.: *Streetcorner Research: An Experimental Approach to the Juvenile Delinquent.* Cambridge, Harvard University Press, 1964.

Seguin, E.: *Idiocy: And Its Treatment by the Physiological Method.* New York, William Wood, 1866.

Sheehan, J.: The modification of stuttering through non-reinforcement. *J Abnorm Soc Psychol, 46:*51-63, 1951.

Skinner, B. F.: *The Behavior of Organisms: An Experimental Analysis.* New York, Appleton-Century, 1938.

———: *Science and Human Behavior.* New York, The Free Press, 1953.

Thorndike, E. L.: *Educational Psychology.* New York, Columbia University Press, 1913.

Ullmann, L. P., and Krasner, L. (Eds.): *Case Studies in Behavior Modification.* New York, Holt, Rinehart & Winston, 1965.

Watson, J., and Rayner, R.: Conditioned emotional reactions. *J Exp Psychol, 3:*1-14, 1920.

Whelan, R., and Haring, N.: Modification and maintenance of behavior through systematic application of consequences. *Excep Child, 32:*281-289, 1966.

Williams, C.: The elimination of tantrum behavior by extinction procedures. *J Abnorm Soc Psychol, 59:*269, 1959.

Wolpe, J.: Reciprocal inhibition as the main basis of psychotherapeutic effects. *Arch Neurol Psychiat, 72:*205-226, 1954.

Zilboorg, G., and Henry, G. W.: *A History of Medical Psychology,* New York, W. W. Norton, 1941.

Zimmerman, E. H., and Zimmerman, J.: The alteration of behavior in a special classroom situation. *J Exp Anal Behav, 5:*59-60, 1962.

Chapter 2

BEHAVIOR MODIFICATION: THE CURRENT SCENE

THOMAS LOVITT

ONLY RECENTLY have behavior modification reports dealing with exceptional children become available. In 1965, Ullmann and Krasner edited the first collection of studies concerned with behavior modification and special education situations. Other collected works followed, among them, those of Ulrich, Stachnik, and Mabry (1966), Bijou and Baer (1967), and Sloan and McCauley (1968). And since 1965, quite a number of the psychological journals have also published articles describing the application of behavior modification principles in school situations.

Coincidental with the increasing appearance of literature on behavior modification has been the growth of academic interest in the training of special educators in behavior modification techniques. Many special education departments now feel obliged to have some part of their staff strongly identified with operant conditioning or behavior modification. This move toward eclecticism, the inclusion of a "behavior modifier" on the staff, is readily apparent by the manner in which the department head introduces a visitor to his staff. It is not unusual for him to single out "our behavior modification man," implying that the colleague is in some way unique—philosophically, methodologically, or in some other way.

Because of this emphasis, one might be led to conjecture, "What is a behavior modifier?" and "If someone is not a behavior modifier, what is he?" It is possible that an individual who is not a behavior modifier might be a behavior maintainer. But this is hardly probable, since educators, particularly those working in special education, are usually not committed to maintaining behaviors. The very fact that children are tagged exceptional or are in a special education setting is an indication that their behavior is not considered normal and is in need of modification. All personnel involved in special education—teachers, school psychologists, speech therapists—are concerned with altering behavior, even though they do not regard themselves as behavior modifiers.

Given that most professionals who deal with exceptional children are committed to modification, regardless of their methodological orientation, how then does a behavior modifier differ from his colleagues? Until recently he was regarded as someone who attempted to alter behaviors with the ubiquitous M&M. He was the one who tried to accelerate reading by giving pupils M&M's contingent on their correct answers and to decelerate temper tantrums by taking away their candies contingent on an outburst. Others thought of behavior modifiers as being "tough rather than tender minded, skeptical rather than credulous, and behaviorally rather than medically oriented" (Krasner and Ullmann, 1966, p. 361).

Today many regard behavior modification as a remediation technique, one method of changing behavior. Specifically, they recognize it as a decelerating tactic for certain undesired behaviors, perhaps because so many behavior modification projects in the past dealt with the deceleration or the elimination of behaviors. There are numerous accounts where operant or behavior modification techniques have been used to attenuate tantrums, thumbsucking, out-of-seat activity, talk-outs, and hitting. A reader of only these studies might easily believe that the term "modification" in behavior modification refers to deceleration rather than to acceleration.

Others regard behavior modification as a useful technique for accelerating or generating fundamental or motoric behaviors. In the field of mental retardation, for example, there are numerous reports on the use of behavior modification in teaching the immobile to walk, the mute to talk, and the incontinent to use the toilet.

The articles in this issue should help allay the belief that behavior modifiers concentrate exclusively on the attenuation of troublesome behaviors or on the generation of fundamental ones. For this issue includes studies dealing with the acceleration of complex processes like reading, writing, and mathematics as well as with the attentuation of such behaviors as tantrums, out-of-seats, and talk-outs. Further diversification is indicated by the broad representation in age, diagnostic category, and setting. The children's ages in these studies range from three to thirteen; their descriptions, from withdrawn to aggressive, from severely retarded to gifted. The various settings represented by these investigations are remedial, regular, experimental, and demonstration classes and an institution. All the studies, however, share common characteristics that should serve to explain the behavior modification label.

Certainly, a major unifying feature of those committed to behavior modification is the individualized nature of their work. In this they differ from those diagnosticians who assess groups of people with the same test, or from rehabilitation personnel who use a single training tactic with most of their patients, or, again, from some of the behavioral assessors and trainers who are committed to group tactics, reporting their findings as relevant to subpopulations where data reflect the general tendency of the groups' scores, range, and variability of performance.

The behavior modifier is inclined to individualize his diagnosis, analysis, and treatment. Ideally, he assesses various behaviors of his subject, behaviors that have generated interest or concern. The behaviors may vary widely from individual to individual, from talking out to creative writing, from hitting others to computing arithmetic problems. Since the behavior modifier *is* concerned with such a broad range of behaviors, no single test or diagnostic contrivance could possibly suffice.

Once an individual diagnosis is made, the behavior modifier designs an individualized treatment regimen. Some behavior modifiers are more creative than others—naturally some do perseverate on a few treatment schemes—but a skilled clinician tailors his training program according to the particular needs of his subject. A behavior modifier does not prescribe a treatment designed for a specific etiological group. He does not, for instance, recommend that all his subjects suspected of cerebral damage use a commercially prepared remedy for the brain injured, nor does he assign all his "dyslexic" patients a standardized teaching method to cure dyslexia.

Finally, after individualized assessment and treatment procedures, the behavior modifier continues his individualized approach by reporting the unique accomplishments of each subject. For the behavior modifier is interested in the effects of his teaching or rehabilitation efforts on a particular subject: whether his subject's behavior was altered positively or negatively, and to what extent.

Behavior modifiers share other characteristics besides their individualized approach. They are concerned with reliable measurement and the discovery of events that alter behaviors. Essentially, operant conditioning, behavior modification, and, more recently, precision teaching comprise three principles: direct observation, continuous measurement, and systematic manipulation.

Behavior modifiers agree that before a behavior can be measured, much less changed, it must be directly recorded. If, for example, the target behavior is tantrums, the outbursts are recorded directly; an indirect approach such as an interview or a standardized adjustment test is not scheduled. If the target behavior is reading, direct measurement on various reading components would be obtained instead of using a standardized reading or achievement test to determine skills.

Among behavior modifiers, however, certain disagreements prevail in regard to the recording of behaviors. Some argue that events should be defined in terms of movement cycles, that the beginning and ending points of a behavior be precisely described.* They would recommend that each complete cycle be recorded, regardless of the time it took to complete the cycle or the time between cycles. Others recommend that time be a component in the definition of a behavior, that crying, for example, be defined as a cry loud enough to be heard at least 50 feet away and of five seconds or more duration (Hart, Allen, Buell, Harris,

---

* See Gaasholt, pp. 129-135.

and Wolf, 1964). For this group, if the duration of the behavior is not as long as the defined length, the behavior is not recorded. Regardless of which observation technique is practiced, all behavior modifiers directly monitor observable events.

Behavior modifiers advocate "continuous measurement"; several samples of the behavior should be obtained during each phase of a project. They recommend that numerous observations be recorded before an attempt is made to alter a behavior, in order to obtain a valid impression of the current frequency of the behavior. If the initial data indicate that a change is warranted, and subsequently an environmental alteration is programed, several additional recordings are taken. These latter measurements reveal to the investigator: (a) whether his training attempt was successful; (b) quantitatively, how successful his procedure was; and (c) when, during treatment, the effects were observable. By maintaining such continuous measures, the teacher or therapist is provided with immediate feedback about the interrelationship between his subject and the treatment.

Just as controversy exists about the recording of behavior, so also is there disagreement among behavior modifiers about the method used to acquire continuous measurement. Some advocate plotting performance rates.* Others record behavior as a ratio or percentage.† When rate is used to describe the dependent variable, an average figure is obtained—frequency of events per unit of time. When percentage is used, a ratio is calculated—what actually happened divided by what might have happened. Although some behavior modifiers select rate per unit of time as the basic datum and others opt for percentage, all agree that several observations of the behavior should be taken before a decision to alter procedures is made.

Once a decision has been made to change a behavior, behavior modifiers agree that conditions be arranged in such a way that efforts employed to effect that change can be evaluated. For be-

---

* See Gaasholt, pp. 129-135; Wolf, Hanley, King, Lachowicz & Giles, pp. 113-117.

† See Allen, Turner, and Everett, pp. 119-127; McKenzie, Egner, Knight, Perelman, Schneider, and Garvin, pp. 137-143.

havior modifiers are not only concerned with effecting change, but with discovering how this change was brought about. In order to obtain such information, the "change tactic" must be systematically manipulated. First, data are obtained to determine a baseline before a new approach is scheduled. During this baseline phase the situational variables that could possibly affect the observed behavior are held constant to ensure that random environmental alterations do not influence the behavior and distort the project's reliability. After the behavior has been measured in the initial condition for a period of time, a change could be made and a second condition scheduled. Generally, this change is the alteration of a single variable. Data continue to be gathered for a number of sessions under this second condition. By comparing the frequency or percentage of the measured behavior from one phase to the next, the investigator can obtain some evidence about the effects of that variable.

A third point of controversy concerns the number of conditions or manipulations required for a project or study. Some behavior modifiers argue that the only way to obtain data which confirm the function of an imposed change is to use an A-B-A or reversal design.* In this before-during-after plan, the first and last conditions are identical while the experimental variable is programed throughout the middle phase. The advocates of this design insist that reliability and generality of data emerge only when the replication maneuvers advocated by Sidman (1960) are practiced. Others maintain that although the A-B-A design is experimentally elegant, it is not educationally relevant. This latter group suggests that often only two experimental phases are required, one before and one during a manipulation.† Both groups agree, however, that the systematic manipulation of events is the basis for an educational technology. They agree, too, that teachers or other managers should not indiscriminately change events within or between experimental conditions. For if rapid and multiple alterations are programed and, as a result,

---
* See O'Leary, Kaufman, Kass, and Drabman, pp. 145-155; Wolf, et al., pp. 113-117.

† See Gaasholt, pp. 129-135; McKenzie et al., pp. 137-143.

a behavior is modified, the teacher has no way of determining which single factor was effective.

Certainly, other disagreements exist between behavior modifiers and clinicians of other methodologies, as well as among behavior modifiers. Generally, however, the behavior modifier (a) is committed to individual diagnosis, treatment, and analysis; (b) is concerned with observable events and the direct measurement of their occurrence; (c) obtains several measures of a designated behavior before arriving at a decision or adjusting the environment; and (d) if change is warranted, manipulates systematically some aspect of the environment in order to reliably evaluate the effects of that variable.

The fundamentals of behavior modification, then, are neither new nor unique. These principles—direct observation, continuous measurement, and systematic manipulation of the environment—are at least as old as Bernard (1865).

The fact that behavior modification comprises these three elements and is a scientific process eludes many of its critics. This is particularly obvious when some erstwhile behaviorists have used a favored tactic or procedure only to find it wasn't universally successful. Following such an experience, some hastily abandoned the total process because of their disillusionment. They failed to discriminate *principles* from *techniques*.

Certainly no universal stimuli or reinforcers exist. Some people learn best when information is visually presented; others, aurally. For some individuals M&M's serve to accelerate performance, for others, self-counting, the opportunity to record one's own behavior, is a reinforcing event. None of these techniques is a panacea. Assuredly, were one to advocate the use of self-counting as the universal reinforcer, he would eventually be as disappointed as his predecessors who attempted to make a science of M&M's. People do behave uniquely, and if procedures found successful with some are advocated for all, failure will naturally ensue. The failure, however, is with the techniques, not with the principles.

The reader of behavior modification reports should use the same appraisal guidelines to evaluate them that he uses to judge studies representing different methodologies. He should first ask, is the topic relevant, important, or interesting? If the report is of little relevance or the topic is so shopworn that no new information emerges, then the investigation should be criticized, regardless of the author or the methodology. The reader then must judge the credibility of the study and determine whether the author's data are valid and his interpretation rational. The reader must also decide whether the procedures and design of the study have been adequately explained so that future replication, hence generalization, is possible.

The reader should judge each behavior modification study on its own merits, neither accepting nor rejecting any investigation because of its methodological insignia. The studies included in this issue were selected to illustrate the basic principles of behavior modification with a wide variation of topics, designs, and populations. Therefore, the reader can appraise each study from his own viewpoint as a practitioner—is the topic relevant and important? And as a scientist—has there been enough procedural rigor to make the data believable?

REFERENCES

Bernard, C.: *An Introduction to the Study of Experimental Medicine.* New York, Dover, 1957 (originally published in French, 1865).

Bijou, S. W., and Baer, D. M.: *Child Development: Readings in Experimental Analysis.* New York, Appleton-Century-Crofts, 1967.

Hart, B. M., Allen, K. E., Buell, J. S., Harris, F. R., and Wolf, M. M.: Effects of social reinforcement on operant crying. *J Exp Child Psychol,* 1: 145-153, 1964.

Krasner, L., and Ullmann, L. P.: *Research in Behavior Modification.* New York, Holt, Rinehart & Winston, 1966.

Sidman, M.: *Tactics of Scientific Research.* New York, Basic Books, 1960.

Sloane, H. N., and McCauley, B. D.: *Operant Procedures in Remedial Speech and Language Training.* Boston, Houghton Mifflin, 1968.

Ullmann, L. P., and Krasner, L.: *Case Studies in Behavior Modification.* New York, Holt, Rinehart & Winston, 1965.

Ulrich, R. E., Stachnik, T., and Mabry, J.: *Control of Human Behavior.* Glenview, Ill., Scott, Foresman, 1966.

Chapter 3

MODIFICATION AND MAINTENANCE OF BEHAVIOR THROUGH SYSTEMATIC APPLICATION OF CONSEQUENCES

RICHARD F. WHELAN
NORRIS G. HARING

IT HAS OFTEN BEEN ASSERTED that a 50-year gap exists between knowledge gained in basic research laboratories and application of that knowledge to problems which exist in classrooms. Educators are confronted with an evergrowing fund of scientific knowledge from the learning laboratories. The assignment for educators is as follows: Reliable scientific knowledge must be applied to classroom situations; it is only through such applications that information concerning behavioral principles discovered in laboratories can be validated. Educators should no longer have to answer or defend themselves against the indictment of not utilizing known discoveries in classroom settings.

The Educational Challenge

Ferster (1964) completed a study concerned with teaching the meaning and use of mathematical symbols to very young subjects. The results of this study are cited to emphasize the importance of applying laboratory data directly to classroom settings. Two subjects, Dennis, age three and one-half, and Margie, age three, were selected for the study. Ferster chose the language of arithmetic because it describes environmental relationships in a clear, systematic, and consistent manner. The symbol three describes a set of objects which exhibits the quality of "threeness," and it does this precisely. Arithmetic symbols also provide the experimenter with simple, distinct stimuli which can be reliably presented and controlled. "Moreover, the language of numbers gets around the obstacle of vocal limitations" (Ferster, 1964, p. 98).

Using a binary number system, the subjects learned to write or say numbers by pushing buttons which turned lights on or off. The binary system was chosen because its two digit base, zero and one, was most amenable to presenting symbolic material in a light-on, light-off fashion. Also, by presenting problem solving tasks in this way, verbal communication between subject and experimenter was totally curtailed. Presentation of learning tasks and recording of responses were fully automated; the learner and the environment interacted without the variable of experimenter presence.

Behavioral responses which constitute an understanding of mathematical fundamentals are a very complex process. Therefore, the subjects were presented tasks which were sequential, ordered, and reduced to very small steps. The subjects first learned to match colors accurately and subsequently learned to match binary numbers. From that point, Dennis and Margie learned to match binary numbers to correct numbers of objects, i.e., three triangles were matched to appropriate light-on, light-off sequences. To ensure that the subjects were attending to numerosity concepts and not making matching responses because of consistent stimuli arrangements, the experimenter substituted other objects for triangles, and rearranged size and location of objects on the stimuli presentation panel. When the subjects could match binary numbers to objects correctly, the experiment moved into the final phase. The subjects learned to respond to objects by writing, in lights, a symbol which represented numbers.

Each phase of the experiment was mastered before the subjects moved onto the next step. Correct responses resulted in a subsequent consequence which increased such responses; in this experiment, food was the consequence. Food was delivered to the subject as a consequence for making a correct response. This consequence acted as an environmental event which increased the frequency of correct responses in comparison to the frequency of error responses. For the subjects in this study it was

---

From *Exceptional Children*, Vol. 32, 1966, pp. 281-289. Reprinted with the permission of the Council for Exceptional Children and the senior author.

determined prior to the initiation of the experiment that the consequence (food) would increase the frequency of behavior occurring immediately prior to the delivery of the consequence.

The consequence of an error was a time-out period; all of the lights on the stimuli presentation panel were darkened. Responses which the subjects wrote during the time-out resulted in subsequent consequences which decreased the frequency of error responses. Under time-out conditions, or after an error response had been made, the subjects could not receive the consequence (food) because it was provided only after correct responses were made. An error response removed the subjects from conditions where only correct responses received consequences which served to increase the frequency of these correct responses. Any response, then, which removed the presentation of the consequence (food) was virtually eliminated from the subject's behavior. After a lapse of time, the panel was relighted and the subjects were again in a position to receive consequences for correct responses. Increasing correct responses, small learning sequences, and eliminating incorrect responses resulted in practically errorless learning (Ferster, 1964).

What is the significance of this experiment? The results are not too surprising even though the subjects were quite young. Bruner (1963) believes that highly abstract concepts can be learned at a very early age if they are presented simply and with materials appropriate for subjects being taught. If Bruner is correct, the type of learned behavior illustrated by Ferster's experiment should be considered as well within the behavioral repertory of most young children. This is highly significant information, but of even more importance is the introduction of Ferster's subjects. Dennis and Margie were chimpanzees. Ferster stated: "We have developed in these animals forms of behavior that bear a much more complex relation to the environment than chimpanzees normally show" (Ferster, 1964, p. 106).

Learning through verbal interaction is often emphasized in classrooms. That is, the children are expected to receive auditory stimuli, interpret them with understanding, process them, and then respond in the manner dictated by the verbal stimuli. Normal children who have, over a period of years, learned to control their behavior as a result of consequences contingent upon verbal emissions, usually function adequately in such classroom situations. Stated another way, their behavior is under the control of environmental consequences.

What relevance does the preceding discussion have to the behavioral management of an emotionally disturbed child? What possible connection can animal research and verbal interactions between pupil and teacher have with behavioral management methods? If a teacher were asked to teach mathematical concepts similar to those in Ferster's experiment to a severely disorganized child, the comments to that request might be as follows:

1. That is impossible; the child could not possibly understand what he is to do.
2. The child would only be confused if he were presented with such material.
3. He just would not understand a word said about the task.
4. Because the child would be confused, he would be unable to respond appropriately.

The teacher may also assert that the child is too disturbed to learn such information; when he becomes more amenable to verbal instruction, work may begin on such topics.

What is the explanation for this discrepancy between educators' perception of the learning process and reported results of well-designed learning experiments? Michael stated: "The basis of this misunderstanding seems to involve the assumption that most learning takes place by processes requiring an ability to verbalize the requirements of the learning situation, or to profit from verbal instructions" (Michael, 1963, p. 4). If this condition is accurate, then nonverbal organisms would not learn at all. Of course, this is not a true state of affairs; nonverbal organisms do learn. Behavioral principles apply to the management of children as well as to lower animals. Even severely emotionally disturbed children possess more complex behavior repertoires than chimpanzees, rats, or dogs. The challenge for educators is to utilize behavioral principles to modify undesirable and maintain desirable behavior in emotionally disturbed children, and also to apply these principles to prevent children from becoming candidates for special education classes.

Behavioral Principles

There is a small but rapidly expanding accumulation of data which indicate that behavioral principles, reliably demonstrated in learning laboratories, are also applicable to managing, modifying, building, and maintaining the behavior of children who function in special education classrooms (Haring and Phillips, 1962; Bijou, 1964). The fundamental concept upon which these principles rest is that behavior, abnormal as well as normal, is learned.

Educators are interested in the behavior of children, or more specifically, the effects of behavior upon the environment. Furthermore, educators study "the connection between a response and its consequences" (Skinner, 1963, p. 505). Analysis of these connections has demonstrated behavioral principles which account for a major portion of human activity. Behavior is maintained by its effect on the environment, and it consists of those activities which change the external environment, which in turn changes the subsequent state and behavior of the individual (Nurnberger, Ferster, and Brady, 1963).

There are some environmental consequences which increase the frequency or rate of behavior. These environmental events may be defined as accelerating consequences since their effect is to increase the emission frequency of behavioral responses (Lindsley, O., 1965). If accelerating consequences are provided only after the occurrence of a correct response, then that behavior will increase in frequency. For example, in our society an accelerating consequence for increasing work rate may be additional salary. Increasing the salary as a consequence of higher work rate may result in even higher work rate.

There are also some environmental consequences which decrease the frequency or rate of behavior. Such environmental changes may be defined as decelerating consequences. The presentation of a decelerating consequence subsequent to a behavioral response will decrease the frequency of that response. If, in our example cited above, work rate is below minimal standards, a decelerating consequence may be less salary. Decreasing salary because of low work rate may decrease the emission or occurrence of such a low rate.

These two examples are highly simplified in order to convey the meaning of some behavioral principles. Actual application of these principles to children in a classroom is a very complex process. Additional examples concerned with the precise and systematic applications of behavioral principles are discussed in subsequent sections of this paper. A comprehensive presentation of behavioral principles (Holland and Skinner, 1961), application to behavioral modification (Eysenck, 1960; Ayllon and Haughton, 1962; Barrett, 1962), and utilization of these principles in academic learning situations (Hewett, 1964; Staats, Minke, Finley, Wolf, and Brooks, 1964) are beyond the scope of this paper. The reader will experience positive consequences for exploring procedures used in the functional analysis of behavior.

Behavioral Modification Techniques

Of particular importance to educators is Lindsley's statement regarding behavioral modification. It is as follows: "There is a great tendency today to confuse the acquisition of behavior with its maintenance" (Lindsley, 1964, p. 65). For example, a teacher may wish to change the behavior of a child from running to her desk with questions, to holding up his hand and remaining at his desk until the teacher can come to him. The teacher, through discovery of effective consequences, may use these to accelerate remaining in the seat and holding up a hand. At first, consequences would be applied after every correct response. Such a procedure is utilized to assist the child in the acquisition of appropriate behavior. Along with this, the teacher would apply decelerating consequences for getting out of the chair and running to the teacher's desk; that is, the teacher may not verbally interact with the child or give him attention until he remains seated. For this example, the assumption is made that the teacher's attention is meaningful to the child, and this is certainly not true in every case.

After the child has acquired the desired behavior, the teacher need not apply accelerating consequences to him for each and every response; she may only need to do so for every fifth or tenth correct response. By using aperiodic consequences, the teacher maintains the desired behavior. At this point of the behavior management program, maintenance procedures would be utilized to strengthen appropriate behavior which had already been acquired.

One goal of education is to enable children to work and learn independently in the classroom. The teacher's task is to arrange the environment in such a way that when children interact with it, learning is maximized. When a child has acquired a behavior, and that behavior is being maintained, the teacher can devote more time and skills to other children who need to acquire specific behaviors. Many teachers, because they experience gratification for helping children grow and learn, often find it difficult to use maintenance techniques, or to allow children to learn independently. Teachers may use techniques which are vitally important for the acquisition of behavior, but these techniques are not necessary for ensuring a continuous maintenance of positive behavior.

When behavior needs to be maintained, then it is no longer necessary to provide accelerating consequences to each behavioral response. Maintaining behavior requires that the teacher reduce considerably the number of accelerating consequences provided; indeed, it is a necessity if a child is to develop independent learning skills and self control. It is during this maintenance process that appropriate behavior is accelerated by consequences which are intrinsic to completion of tasks, social approval, feelings of self-worth, and the satisfaction of assuming self-responsibility. Therefore, dependence upon numerous teacher applied consequences gradually loses significance to a child.

Zimmerman and Zimmerman (1962) demonstrated the use of behavioral modification techniques to alter specific behavior in a classroom situation. One subject, when asked to spell a word which he had previously studied, would make faces, mumble, and pause for a few seconds. Because of this behavior, the teacher spent considerable time in helping the boy sound out the word, and gave other cues until the word was spelled correctly. Even though the teacher was making extra time and effort available to the boy, spelling behavior did not improve. It was postulated that teacher attention might actually be maintaining this undesirable behavior, since over a period of several class sessions it required increasing amounts of time to elicit the correct response.

To check the accuracy of the postulate, the teacher asked the child to go to the blackboard to take a quiz over ten spelling words. The boy misspelled the first word ten times, but the teacher ignored this behavior by attending to other work at her desk. Each time the boy misspelled the word, he would look at the teacher. However, the teacher did not respond to this behavior. This procedure was followed for the rest of the spelling test. With the presentation of each word, the boy exhibited fewer incorrect responses, and the time required to write the word correctly was decreased. Teacher attention immediately followed each correct response; inappropriate responses did not receive teacher attention. When the ten words were spelled correctly, the boy received an A grade and social attention from the teacher. After a month of exposure to this technique, the frequency of undesirable responses decreased to near zero, and the boy continued to make academic progress.

A similar procedure was utilized in working with a child who received staff attention whenever he displayed tantrum behavior. The tantrums were ignored, and staff attention was made dependent upon appropriate behavior. In several weeks, tantrum behavior disappeared (Zimmerman and Zimmerman, 1962).

Equally successful results were obtained when crying, emitted or maintained, depending upon its effects on the environment, was brought under control of social consequences. Teachers ignored children's crying and gave social attention and approval for non-crying behavior. To prove that the crying was a function of adult social consequences, the teachers reversed procedures and gave added attention to crying episodes. The results indicated that when adult attention was given to crying, crying increased in frequency. When such crying was ignored, episodes decreased from ten times a morning to zero or one. It was further noted that the children, when their crying did not receive teacher attention, became absorbed in constructive activity (Hart, Allen, Buell, Harris, and Wolf, 1964).

Baer (1962) used movie cartoons to bring thumbsucking under the control of environmental consequences. When the child put his thumb in his mouth, the cartoon was turned off; withdrawal of thumb from mouth resulted in continued presentation of the cartoon. During initial learning sessions thumbsucking decreased in frequency, but it recovered quickly upon termination of experimenter controlled consequences. After further sessions, thumbsucking decreased in areas other than the experimental room. This study readily demonstrates one application of behavioral modification techniques to the alteration of specific behaviors. However, it must not be concluded that cartoons would be equally effective with all thumbsuckers.

Application of Behavioral Modification Techniques

The Children's Rehabilitation Unit, University of Kansas Medical Center, is a training, demonstration, and research center housed in a medical center complex. The schools of education, medicine, and related disciplines join to provide comprehensive behavioral modification programs for most categories of exceptional children. Unit staff are currently investigating the results emanating from the application of behavioral modification techniques to a wide variety of behavioral deviations and learning disabilities.

Staff members are investigating and demonstrating efficiency of utilizing behavioral modification techniques with individuals, small class groups, and classes of 15 to 20 children. Validity of these techniques will be achieved only if they can be practically applied to groups of children by one teacher. It is most unreasonable to expect school districts to staff special classrooms with a teacher, assistants, and expensive automated equipment. Instead, the concept of staging seems to offer a more efficient approach.

Staging refers to adding children one at a time to groups until the class size reaches a point where the teacher can still comfortably plan task assignments, schedule appropriate consequences, record and measure behavior, and evaluate behavioral progress. Staging is closely related to the acquisition and maintenance phases of behavioral modification. Given appropriate materials and knowledge of behavioral modification techniques, there may be no reason why one teacher could not plan remediation programs for ten to fifteen children with emotional problems. When one child's behavior has been brought under the control of environmental consequences (his behavior is being maintained), then another child could be added to the class. The adding of children one by one could be continued until the maximum size for efficient programming is reached.

A specific example selected from our collection of data illustrates the effectiveness of correctly applying behavioral modification techniques. Bob is in a class for boys with emotional problems. He has a history of yelling, running about the room, tearing up his work, and not accomplishing assigned tasks. The teacher assigned Bob fifteen arithmetic problems to complete within 30 minutes, which was the time lapse before another task was to be initiated. Bob spent fifteen minutes of that time looking around the room, tapping his feet, and playing with his pencil. The teacher had noted that Bob consistently tried to get her to stand by his desk and watch him work. Taking this cue, the teacher instituted a systematic schedule of consequences. That is, Bob did one problem without the teacher being present; then the teacher watched him do one. Within fifteen minutes Bob had his work completed, and the teacher in that space of time had successfully raised the number of problems done independently, compared to those completed with teacher present, to a ratio of three to one. Bob completed three problems without the teacher observing his work and then worked a problem with the teacher observing the process.

For this example, an accelerating consequence (teacher presence) was used to aid Bob in acquiring a specific behavior. However, in a very brief time lapse, the teacher assisted Bob in maintaining the behavior by reducing the number of accelerating consequences provided for the completion of problems. In this case, teacher presence was an effective consequence for Bob. Precise scheduling of consequences, systematic application of behavioral modification techniques, and environmental manipulation have combined to bring Bob's behavior under better control. The goal with Bob is to modify his behavior to the extent that it can be maintained by the environmental consequences present in regular classes; when he reaches that stage he will return to a regular class placement.

A statement of caution is certainly indicated at this juncture. Teacher's presence and verbal praise served as accelerating consequences for Bob. Teachers who work with such youngsters know that praise is not effective in all cases. Levin and Simmons (1962a, 1962b) demonstrated that praise was actually aversive for some emotionally disturbed children; it did not serve as an accelerating consequence. When given verbal praise for responses, the frequency of responding decreased rapidly and dramatically. Of course, using praise as an accelerating consequence is a goal; teachers must attempt to modify children's behavior so that it will come under the control of normal social consequences.

The best planned classrooms for children with behavioral problems experience episodes when children become obstreperous. On occasion, these episodes may reach proportions which necessitate physical restraint. Unit staff have demonstrated that an effective technique for decreasing this type of behavior is to provide time-out contingent upon the emission of this behavior. Time-out is simply removing a child from a situation in which he has been receiving accelerating consequences for appropriate behavior. The child is placed in a small room next to the classroom until the deviant behavior subsides. When this occurs, the child may leave the time-out area and return to the classroom. However, the technique of time-out is effective only when the classroom provides so many accelerating consequences for the child that he would rather spend his time there than in the time-out room.

Premack (1959) has added a relevant dimension to the task of formulating empirical behavior modification techniques. Stressing the importance of behavioral consequences, Premack stated the following principle: "**Any response A will [accelerate] any other response B, if and only if the independent rate of A is greater than that of B**" (Premack, 1959, p. 220). Briefly interpreted, the Premack principle simply states that any behavior is strengthened or accelerated when followed by behavior which occurs at a high frequency or rate (Homme and de Baca, 1964).

This principle has been effectively utilized in one experimental study (Haring and Phillips, 1962) and is presently being demonstrated at the Unit. Once the teacher has observed any child for a period of time, she is able to list high frequency behaviors and low frequency behaviors; for one child, reading a paragraph may be low frequency behavior, but making a model airplane may be high frequency behavior. It becomes relatively easy for the teacher to plan a reading lesson immediately before the child builds the model. Building the model becomes the consequence for engaging in reading behavior.

Task assignments, such as in reading or arithmetic, are arranged on a ratio basis, while engaging in high frequency behavior is scheduled on an interval basis. For example, the child may have to complete a ratio of five problems before he can engage in five minutes of model building. The ratio of problems completed is gradually increased, but the time interval devoted to model building can remain relatively constant. It may be discerned that larger and larger ratios of work can be required until more time is spent on what was originally low frequency behavior than on high frequency behavior. In fact, a reversal is often noted; arithmetic or reading may become high frequency behavior because the successes accumulated in such activity may be self-maintaining. Expressed in another manner, the child has learned self-control.

The possibilities for utilization of these techniques in classrooms are practically limitless. Again, caution must be mentioned. What is high frequency behavior for one child may not be true for another. The teacher must discover this information for each individual and apply it correctly. Evaluation of application must be demonstrated by subsequent behavior modification; that is, did the child's responses closely approximate the responses necessary for the successful completion of a task or a specific behavioral movement? These procedures make it possible to refrain from making value judgments about the child. When a planned program does not bring about desired changes of behavior, the teacher revises or modifies the program, instead of saying that the child cannot learn because he is emotionally disturbed. Successful modification of deviant behavior depends upon the refined applications of these techniques. This approach negates the necessity of labeling behavior; and even more important, it avoids the possibility that a label can be used to explain behavior, such as stating that the reason a child cannot learn is because he is schizophrenic.

Discussion

Initial responses to the presentation of behavioral principles and behavioral modification techniques might be as follows: I use these procedures in my classroom everyday; they are not new at all. Homme and Tosti (1964) have the most adequate reply to this response.

> If it is not the lack of [consequences] which makes behavioral control difficult, one might reason, it must be the lack of knowledge of the principles of behavioral control. If one attempts to verify this, he will find that this, too, is incorrect. If given a test on the principles so far discussed, most people would score very high. It is not a lack of [consequences] or a lack of knowledge about how to use them. The difficulty can be primarily traced to a failure to *systematically* apply what is known. It is not only that [behavioral] principles are not systematically applied, they are, if applied at all, only sporadically applied (Homme and Tosti, 1964, p. 4).

This quote and the prior cautions concerning applications of behavioral modification techniques are vitally important. It is only through correct, efficient application that children's behavior can be changed to the extent that they can subsequently contribute to the real world in which they live.

There are advantages inherent in using behavioral modification techniques in classroom situations. Teachers have traditionally been assigned to change or modify the behavior of children entrusted to them for several hours a day. Causes of deviant behavior, while important for some disciplines, are not of primary concern for educators. Educators must work with exhibited, overt behavior, and not with general, dynamic causes of that behavior. Behavioral responses can be measured and analyzed quantitatively. Precise, observable measurements are directly related to the application of appropriate behavioral modification techniques. Behavior can be observed; postulating unobservable causes that attempt to explain behavior leaves educators with esoteric concepts which cannot be arranged or manipulated in classrooms designed to modify behavior.

Educators often express concern about motivating children. Motivation is often referred to as drive, need, and such other terms which imply that motivation is internally based. Perhaps a more practical explanation of motivation is in asking what consequences are available to control behavior. High rates of responding in problem solving situations, such as in working arithmetic problems, because such responses have accelerating consequences, is in reality what many label motivation when they view occurrence of that behavior. When one states that a child is motivated, what is really being observed is a child who is responding under the control of environmental consequences.

Behavioral modification techniques may possibly provide precise aids which the teacher can utilize in assisting children to learn the desirable consequences of organized, appropriate behavior. Children who exhibit deviant behavior cause pain to themselves and also to others who interact with them. Teachers must not only modify or remove specific deviant behaviors, but must also develop socially acceptable behavior patterns in children. Behavioral modification techniques provide teachers with systematic skills which can be utilized to modify children's behavior to the extent that when it is emitted in a variety of situations, it is consistently more appropriate than inappropriate.

While behavioral modification is not antagonistic to any professional concerned with such problems, an individual more concerned with unconscious behavioral determinants might claim that removing inappropriate behaviors is merely changing the surface signs of emotional disorders. This individual might also assert that the underlying conflicts which caused the behavior have not been resolved; therefore, the individual will merely substitute other, and possibly more, deviant behaviors. A review of cases where behavioral modification techniques have been applied to removal of deviant behaviors indicates that effort "directed at elimination of maladapted behavior ('symptoms') is successful and long lasting" (Grossberg, 1964, p. 83). Knowledge concerning behavioral principles "has clarified the nature of the relation between behavior and its consequences and has devised techniques which apply the methods of a natural science to its investigation" (Skinner, 1963, p. 515).

Information presented in this paper reviews behavioral modification techniques which have been practically and efficiently applied with individuals and groups of children; the results of such application have been reported. Whether these techniques achieve satisfactory results when compared to behavioral systems that have different orientations can only be known by observing and recording behavioral changes in children. The proof of which system is the most efficient for solving behavioral problems will be discerned only when such problems are solved.

Behavioral modification techniques provide systematic procedures and tools which teachers may implement to change or modify deviant behavior and encourage more acceptable, appropriate growth behavior. Skeptical, cautious acceptance and application of behavioral modification techniques are certainly indicated. Data reported from laboratory experiments and a few studies with small groups of children have demonstrated a high degree of reliability. However, these data must be validated in regular and special classroom situations. This validation may or may not be forthcoming; it has yet to be demonstrated.

REFERENCES

Ayllon, T., and Haughton, E.: Control of the behavior of schizophrenic patients by food. *J Exp Anal Behav*, 5:343-352, 1962.

Baer, D.: Laboratory control of thumbsucking by withdrawal and representation of reinforcement. *J Exp Anal Behav*, 5:525-528, 1962.

Barrett, B.: Reduction in rote of multiple tics by free operant conditioning methods. *J Nerv Ment Dis*, 135:187-195, 1962.

Bijou, S.: Application of behavioral principles to normal and deviant young children. Paper read at American Psychological Association, Los Angeles, September, 1964.

Bruner, J.: *The Process of Education.* Cambridge, Harvard University Press, 1963.

Eysenck, H. (Ed.): *Behavior Therapy and the Neuroses.* New York, Pergamon Press, 1960.

Ferster, C.: Arithmetic behavior in chimpanzees. *Sci Am, 210*:98-106, 1964.

Grossberg, J.: Behavior therapy: a review. *Psychol Bull, 62*:73-88, 1964.

Haring, N., and Phillips, L.: *Educating Emotionally Disturbed Children.* New York, McGraw-Hill, 1962.

Hart, B., Allen, E., Buell, J., Harris, Florence R., and Wolf, M.: Effects of social reinforcement on operant crying. *J Exp Child Psychol, 1*:145-153, 1964.

Hewett, F.: Teaching reading to an autistic boy through operant conditioning. *Read Teacher, 17*:613-618, 1964.

Holland, J., and Skinner, B.: *The Analysis of Behavior.* New York, McGraw-Hill, 1961.

Homme, L., and de Baca, P.: Contingency management on the psychiatric ward. Unpublished manuscript, Behavioral Technology Department, Westinghouse Research Laboratories, Albuquerque, 1964.

Homme, L., and Tosti, D.: Some consideration of contingency management and motivation. Unpublished manuscript, Behavioral Technology Department, Westinghouse Research Laboratories, Albuquerque, 1964.

Levin, G., and Simmons, J.: Response to praise by emotionally disturbed boys. *Psychol Rep, 11*:10, 1962 (a).

Levin, G., and Simmons, J.: Response to food and praise by emotionally disturbed boys. *Psychol Rep, 11*:539-546, 1962 (b).

Lindsley, O.: Direct measurement and prothesis of retarded behavior. *Journal of Education, 147*:62-81, 1964.

Michael, J.: Relevance of animal research. In R. Schiefelbusch and J. Smith (Editors), *Research in Speech and Hearing for Mentally Retarded Children.* Conference report, Bureau of Child Research, University of Kansas, 1963.

Nurnberger, J., Ferster, C., and Brady, J.: *An Introduction to the Science of Human Behavior.* New York: Appleton-Century-Crofts, 1963.

Premack, D.: Toward empirical behavior laws: I. Positive reinforcement. *Psychol Rev, 66*:219-233, 1959.

Skinner, B.: Operant behavior. *Am Psychol, 18*:503-515, 1963.

Staats, A., Minke, K., Finley, J., Wolf, M., and Brooks, L.: A reinforcer system and experimental procedure for the laboratory study of reading acquisition. *Child Dev, 35*:209-231, 1964.

Zimmerman, E., and Zimmerman, J.: The alteration of behavior in a special classroom situation. *J Exp Anal Behav, 5*:59-60, 1962.

Chapter 4

LEARNING THEORY APPROACHES TO CLASSROOM MANAGEMENT: RATIONALE AND INTERVENTION TECHNIQUES

HARVEY F. CLARIZIO
STEPHEN L. YELON

TODAY, MORE THAN EVER before, there is acute concern about the mental health of children. Traditionally, we have modeled intervention efforts after the clinical concept of treatment. Dissatisfaction with the limitations of psychotherapeutic intervention (Levitt, 1957) together with the professional manpower shortage in the mental health field has led, however, to suggestions, e.g., Redl (1962), that we need new modes of treatment, closer to real life situations, if we are to tackle children's problems more effectively.

When psychodynamic models were the preferred method of treatment, teachers were accorded at best a second-string status on the clinical team helping emotionally handicapped children. The increasing popularity of behavior therapy and other approaches based on learning theory now offers teachers opportunities for an integral role in the quest for better mental health for children. Indeed, it might well be the mental health specialist who will now assume the supportive role (Gallagher and Chalfant, 1966) in the "treatment" of children.

In the application of learning theory principles to the modification of deviant behavior, the emphasis is on the changing of behavior with little attention devoted to the etiology of the behavior. Why should teachers focus primarily on the behavior rather than on its causes? There are several reasons:

From the *Journal of Special Education*, Vol. 1, 1967, pp. 267-274. Reprinted with the permission of the Editor of the *Journal of Special Education,* and the senior author.

1. First, teachers by virtue of their orientation are not trained to probe the causes of behavior that even mental hygiene specialists often consider obscure and uncertain. Hence, is it really helpful to ask the teacher to understand the causes underlying children's disturbed behavior?
2. Teachers in any case are rarely in a position wherein they can directly manipulate the causes so as to modify their influence on the child's classroom adjustment. For example, if the problem lies in the parent-child relations or in a brain lesion, there are few if any constructive intervention techniques that the teacher can employ. Yet the child's troublesome behavior persists and must be handled as effectively as possible when it occurs in the classroom.
3. Even in such occasional cases where the causes can be identified and manipulated directly, the maladaptive behaviors may persist. Thus, despite the discovery and correction of the contributing role of poor vision and faulty child-rearing practices in a reading disability case, a pupil may continue to experience difficulty with his reading until attention is *specifically* devoted to his reading behavior, and unless he can experience success in this specific area, his mental health will continue to be impaired.
4. Behaviors or symptoms or habits may in their own right be incapacitating and disturbing, and current persisting symptoms may themselves be producing emotional disturbance (Franks, 1965) above and beyond the core disturbance from which the child is suffering. And, as research indicates (White and Harris, 1961), it is difficult to disentangle educational and emotional maladjustments in the school-age child (Gallagher and Chalfant, 1966).
5. There is little substantial evidence to indicate that if the teacher assists the child in modifying his behavior or symptoms, other undesirable behaviors will inevitably take their place in the manner of symptom substitution (Grossberg, 1964).
6. Finally, and most importantly, as already implied, the teacher most commonly has no resort other than to deal with the

pupil's behavior as it appears in the here and now. As Lewis (1965) attests:

> If we cannot aspire to reconstruction of personality that will have long range beneficial effects, we can modify disturbing behavior in specific ways in present social contexts. This more modest aspiration may not only be more realistic but it may be all that is required of the child-helping professions in a society that is relatively open and provides a variety of opportunity systems in which a child can reconcile his personal needs with society's expectations of him.

Having argued that the teacher should be primarily concerned with behavior per se rather than with its causes, let us turn to techniques emanating from learning theory which have relevance to the modification of deviant behavior in the classroom (see Glossary of Terms at the end of this reading). Although the techniques to be presented are discussed separately for the sake of clarity, it should be recognized that more than one of them may be operating at any given time in real life attempts to modify behavior. Moreover, common to all of these techniques is the use of "systematic environmental contingencies to alter the object's responsiveness to stimuli" (Krasner and Ullman, 1965).

The Techniques

EXTINCTION. There is a growing body of research demonstrating that simple withdrawal of reinforcers can reduce or eliminate such troublesome behavior as excessive talking, tantrum behavior and academic errors (Warren, 1965; Williams, 1959; Zimmerman and Zimmerman, 1962). Extinction is not always, however, the most economic and effective means of producing behavioral change (Bandura and Walters, 1963). Certain cautions should be recognized:

1. Spontaneous remission—the return of undesirable behavior —may occur following the extinction trials, thus necessitating additional extinction sessions.
2. When behavior is maintained on a partial reinforcement schedule, removal of the reinforcers may actually produce

an increase in the frequency and intensity of the deviant responses. Moreover, it is sometimes extremely difficult not to reinforce maladaptive behaviors in a school setting, since circumstances may be beyond the teacher's control. The aggressive youngster who kicks the teacher or a classmate cannot help but be reinforced by the look of pain on the victim's face. The needed cooperation of classmates in the application of extinction procedures may also be difficult to secure, so that by necessity the deviant behavior is established on a partial reinforcement schedule.

3. General observation suggests that certain behaviors do not diminish and disappear simply because reinforcers are withdrawn, and sometimes teachers cannot or will not wait long enough to permit the completion of the extinction process. These limitations are particularly acute in situations in which emotional contagion is a distinct possibility. Behaviors seriously injurious to the self would also seemingly not lend themselves well to this technique. In brief, this method of behavior change has proven to be of value with acting-out as well as inhibited youngsters. Yet, its limitations suggest that other methods of behavioral modification are at times more economical and effective (see also Ausubel, 1957; Bandura, 1965).

POSITIVE REINFORCEMENT. Operant conditioning techniques constitute one of the main tools of behavior modification. In this technique, emphasis is placed on the response made by the individual, and only minimal attention is given to the stimuli eliciting the response. Essentially, the teacher presents a reward whenever the child emits the desired response. While teachers have been cognizant of the value of positively reinforcing "good" behavior, there is ample evidence to suggest that even "good" teachers not uncommonly reinforce undesirable behavior. One of the merits of the positive reinforcement technique stems from its applicability to antisocial youngsters as well as to withdrawn children (Bandura and Walters, 1963).

There has been a dearth of psychotherapeutic approaches designed for the conduct of a problem child, despite such pupils typically being the most disruptive of classroom procedures. The application of positive reinforcement principles to seriously aggressive children involves the manipulation of three variables: the schedules of reinforcement, the interval factor and the type of reward. With respect to the concept of reinforcement schedules, a distinction must be enforced between the acquisition and the maintenance of behavior. For the former, continuous or full-schedule reinforcement or reward after each appearance of the desired behavior is most effective, whereas for the latter, partial or intermittent reinforcement is most economical and effective. The interval variable merely refers to the passage of time between the production of a response and the presentation of the reward or reinforcer. The delay factor should usually be quite short initially, because acting-out children typically have difficulty in postponing gratification. Step by step, the interval can be lengthened as the child acquires more adequate behavioral controls.

The rewards for such pupils, at the start, may have to be tangible or physical in nature but should always be paired with verbal social reinforcers, e.g. "You handled yourself well in that situation today" (Quay, 1963). Gradually, the reinforcers can be shifted away from the concrete into language and other symbolic forms of reward until the child can respond satisfactorily to them. In deciding upon the most suitable reinforcers, consideration should be given to such factors as the child's developmental level and sociocultural background.

The main unresolved question with the technique of positive reinforcement centers around the question of how to make the child initiate the response in the first place so that he can be rewarded (Franks, 1965). The technique of social modeling may well provide at least a partial answer to this problem (Baer, 1963; Ferster, 1961; Hewett, 1964; Slack, 1960; Wolf, Risley and Mees, 1964).

MODELING. Modeling is based on the premise that a child will imitate the behavior of others. Modeling is important in that children commonly acquire social skills through imitation of and identification with examples of socially approved behaviors presented by suitable models. School teachers thus have a unique opportunity to influence the behavior of entire groups of children. However, this technique has been typically overlooked in the management or modification of deviant behavior in schools. Modeling procedures may represent a more effective means than positive reinforcement of establishing new response patterns in children (Bandura, 1965). Moreover, a behavior pattern, once acquired through imitation, is often maintained without deliberate external reinforcement, because human beings learn to reinforce themselves for behaving in certain ways. Teacher training institutions have long recognized the importance of modeling procedures in the training of future teachers and, accordingly, attempt to provide adequate models in the form of critic teachers. However, attention should now be devoted to the teacher's use of modeling procedures in influencing the behavior of the pupils.

There are three effects of exposure to models: the *modeling effect,* the *inhibitory* or *disinhibitory effect,* and the *eliciting effect* (Bandura, 1965). Through the *modeling effect* children come to acquire responses that were not previously a part of their behavior. As noted earlier, modeling procedures may be considerably more economical in establishing new responses than the method of operant conditioning based on positive reinforcement, especially when a combination of verbalizing models and demonstration procedures are used. The strengthening or weakening of inhibitory responses already existing in the observer (the *inhibitory* or disinhibitory effect) can also be accomplished through modeling procedures. Children, for example, who see a model punished or rewarded for aggressive behavior tend to decrease or increase their aggressive behavior accordingly. The *eliciting* or *response facilitation effect* refers to the teacher's eliciting responses that precisely or approximately match those exhibited by the model. Thus, observation of the teacher's response provides discriminative clues that trigger similar responses already in the pupil's behavior repertoire. This eliciting effect is distinguished from the modeling and the disinhibiting effects in that the imitated behavior is neither new nor previously punished.

The probability that a child will imitate a model is a function of several variables. Modeling is partly dependent upon the reinforcing consequences of the model's behavior. Thus, if a model is rewarded for his socially approved behavior, the likelihood that the observer will behave in a socially approved manner is increased. Other factors include the process of attending to the model's behavior, e.g., previous training in observation, and various environmental stimuli, e.g., the complexity of the stimuli (Baldwin, 1967; Bandura, 1962b; Bandura and Hutson, 1961; Bandura and Kupers, 1964; Bandura, Ross and Ross, 1963).

PUNISHMENT. Aversive conditioning or punishment is an intervention technique which has been used primarily to discourage undesirable behavior. This technique consists in the presentation of either physically or psychologically painful stimuli or the withdrawal of pleasant stimuli when undesirable behavior occurs. The use of punishment as a technique for behavioral modification has been contraindicated for the following reasons:

1. Punishment does not eliminate the response; it merely slows down the rate at which the troublesome behaviors are emitted.
2. This technique serves notice to stop certain negative behaviors; it does not indicate what behaviors are appropriate in the situation.
3. Aggressive behaviors on the teacher's part may provide an undesirable model for the pupil.
4. The emotional side effects of punishment, such as fear, tenseness and withdrawal are maladaptive.
5. Punishment serves as a source of frustration which is apt to elicit additional maladaptive behaviors.

Some psychologists, who are currently reconsidering the concept of punishment, contend that it can have a beneficial effect if applied to specific responses rather than to general behavior (Marshall, 1965).

Teachers, whatever their motivations, use verbal reprimands

and other forms of correction in their approach to classroom management, and the judicious use of punishment as an intervention technique is most likely necessary in that it is impossible to guide behavior effectively with positive reinforcement and extinction alone. As Ausubel (1957) asserts, "It is impossible for children to learn what is *not* approved and tolerated simply by generalizing in reverse from the approval they receive for the behavior that *is* acceptable." Thus, punishment of specific responses can have an informative and beneficial effect. A particular positive value that may accrue from the use of punishment is that undesirable behaviors are held in abeyance, thus permitting the teaching of desirable modes of behavior through such intervention techniques as social imitation or positive reinforcement. Although punishment techniques have been used primarily with acting-out pupils, they have also been found to be of value in certain cases of withdrawn behavior (Bandura, 1962a; Church, 1963; Lovaas, 1965; Meyer and Offenbach, 1962; Redl, 1965; Sears, Maccoby and Levin, 1957; Solomon, 1964).

DISCRIMINATION LEARNING. Children sometimes engage in maladaptive behavior because they have transferred behaviors acceptable in one setting to a second setting where these behaviors are considered inappropriate and maladaptive. Thus, for example, the child who is overly dependent upon his mother may behave in a very dependent way toward his teacher. Such cases of inappropriate generalization can sometimes be remediated through the use of discrimination learning. Essentially this process consists of labeling given behaviors as appropriate within a specific environmental context. The teacher in the above case, for example, may inform the child in a nonpunitive way that she is not his mother but his teacher and that as such she will require him to become more self-reliant. This labeling by the teacher makes the child more aware of both inappropriate and appropriate behaviors. Interestingly, children do not always have to be able to express such discriminations verbally in order to achieve "insight" into their behavior. It is rather required, to insure effective results, that appropriate responses be rewarded and undesirable responses discouraged. Discrimination learning thus may be of service in conjunction with most other techniques in managing conduct and personality problems in the classroom (Ayllon and Michael, 1959; Barrett and Lindsley, 1962; Brackbill and O'Hara, 1958; Penny and Lupton, 1961; Stevenson, Weir and Zigler, 1959).

DESENSITIZATION. Desensitization as an intervention technique has been used principally with the fearful and phobic child. The basic objective is to have the child achieve a relaxed response in the presence of what were previously anxiety producing stimuli. To accomplish this relaxed response, the subject is encouraged to perform approximations of previously punished acts within nonpunishing or actually rewarding situations. Or through gradual exposure to the feared object or situation, a subject may become able to perform a formerly feared act or approach the feared object in a relaxed manner (Bentler, 1962; Garvey and Hegrenes, 1966; Jersild and Holmes, 1935; Lazarus, 1960; Wolpe, 1958).

Concluding Remarks

As evidenced by our discussion of the limitations of each technique, we do not envision management techniques emanating from learning theory as a panacea, but these intervention techniques do have certain potential advantages:

1. The fruitfulness of these techniques in modifying human behavior has been demonstrated in laboratory settings as well as in natural settings.
2. They are consistent with the teacher's role whereby she must reflect cultural expectations and set standards for her pupils' academic and social behavior.
3. Behavioral approaches offer specific and practical techniques for use in day-to-day classroom problems. While teachers already use some or all of these techniques, they frequently do so intuitively or inconsistently thereby reducing their efficacy.
4. These techniques enable the teacher to strive toward more realistic and obtainable goals relative to their pupils' mental health.
5. One of the most important attributes of these techniques

is the fact that they can be taught to teachers. While there are few if any teacher training institutions currently offering didactic and practice training in such techniques, one can envision the time when teachers will acquire such skills through laboratory courses taken in conjunction with their formal course work or through in-service meetings and workshops.

GLOSSARY OF TERMS

Behavior Therapy. A therapeutic process in which the primary goal is to change overt behavior rather than to restructure an individual's personality makeup. The process uses principles of learning for its methodological source.

Extinction. The decrease and eventual disappearance of a response learned under conditions of reinforcement when the reinforcement is withheld.

Reinforcement. Whatever serves to maintain the occurrence or increase the strength of a response, e.g., food, water or the avoidance of punishment.

Partial Reinforcement. A condition in which subjects receive reinforcement only at various time intervals or after a certain number of responses.

Positive Reinforcement. Much the same as reinforcement, i.e., *presenting* a pleasant stimulus when a response occurs, as opposed to negative reinforcement where an unpleasant stimulus is *removed* when a response occurs.

Modeling. A condition where the behavior to be acquired is demonstrated for the learner.

Punishment. A condition where a learner is made to feel uncomfortable by being presented an unpleasant stimulus, e.g., the infliction of pain by hitting, and/or a condition where a pleasant stimulus is withdrawn so that the learner is made to feel discomfort, e.g., having treats withdrawn.

REFERENCES

Ausubel, D.: *Theory and Problems of Child Development.* New York, Grune and Stratton, 1957.

Ayllon, T., and Michael J.: The psychiatric nurse as a behavioral engineer. *J Exp Anal Behav,* 2:323-334, 1959.

Baer, D.: Effect of withdrawal of positive reinforcement on an extinguishing response in young children. *Child Dev, 32*:67-74, 1961.

———: Social reinforcement and behavior change. *Am J Orthopsychiatry,* 591-633, 1963.

Baldwin, A.: Theories of child development. *Critique of Social Learning Theory.* Chapter 16. New York, Wiley, 1967.

Bandura, A.: Punishment revisited. *J Consult Psychol, 26*:289-301, 1962a.

———: Social learning through imitation. In M. Jones (Ed.): *Nebraska Symposium on Motivation.* Lincoln, Nebraska, University of Nebraska Press, 1962b, pp. 211-269.

———: Behavioral modification through modeling procedures. In L. Krasner and L. Ullman (Eds.): *Research in Behavior Modification.* New York, Holt, Rinehart and Winston, 1965.

Bandura, A., and Hutson, A.: Identification as a process of incidental learning. *J Abnorm Soc Psychol, 63*:311-318, 1963.

Bandura, A., and Kupers, C.: The transmission of patterns of self-reinforcement through modeling. *J Abnorm Soc Psychol, 69*:1-19, 1964.

Bandura, A., Ross, D., and Ross, S.: Imitation of film mediated aggressive models. *J Abnorm Soc Psychol, 66*:3-11, 1963.

Bandura, A., and Walters, R.: *Social Learning and Personality Development.* New York, Holt, Rinehart and Winston, 1963.

Barrett, B., and Lindsley, O.: Deficits in acquisition of operant discrimination and differentiation shown by institutionalized retarded children. *Am J Ment Defic, 67*:424-436, 1962.

Bentler, P.: An infant's phobia treated with reciprocal inhibition therapy. *J Child Psychol Psychiat, 3*:185-189, 1962.

Brackbill, Y. and O'Hara, J.: The relative effectiveness of reward and punishment for discrimination learning in children. *J Comp Physiol Psychol, 51*:747-751, 1958.

Church, R.: The varied effects of punishment on behavior. *Psychol Rev, 70*:369-402, 1963.

Ferster, C.: Positive reinforcement and behavioral deficits of autistic children. *Child Dev, 32*:437-456, 1961.

Franks, C.: Behavior therapy, psychology and the psychiatrist: contribution, evaluation and overview. *Am J Orthopsychiatry, 35*:145-151, 1965.

Gallagher, J., and Chalfant, J.: The training of educational specialists for emotionally disturbed and socially maladjusted children. In *N.S.S.E. Yearbook 1966, Social Deviancy Among Youth.* Chicago, University of Chicago Press, 1966, pp. 398-423.

Garvey, W. and Hegrenes, J.: Desensitization techniques in the treatment of school phobia. *Am J Orthopsychiatry, 36*:147-152, 1966.

Grossberg, J.: Behavior therapy: a review. *Psychol Bull, 62*:73-88, 1964.

Hewett, F.: Teaching reading to an autistic boy through operant conditioning. *Read Teacher, 17:*613-618, 1964.

Jersild, A., and Holmes, F.: Methods of overcoming children's fears. *J Psychol, 1:*75-104, 1935.

Krasner, L., and Ullman, L.: *Case Studies in Behavior Modification.* New York, Holt, Rinehart and Winston, 1965.

Lazarus, A.: The elimination of children's phobias by deconditioning. In H. Eysenck (Ed.): *Behavior Therapy and the Neuroses.* New York, Pergamon Press, 1960, pp. 114-122.

Levitt, E. E.: Results of psychotherapy with children: an evaluation. *J Counsel Psychol, 25:*189-196, 1957.

Lewis, W.: Continuity and intervention in emotional disturbance: a review. *Except Child, 31:*465-475, 1965.

Lovaas, I.: Building social behavior in autistic children by use of electroshock. *J Exp Res Personal, 1:*99-109, 1965.

Marshall, H.: The effect of punishment on children: a review of the literature and a suggested hypotheses. *J Genet Psychol, 106:*108-133, 1965.

Meyer, W., and Offenbach, S.: Effectiveness of reward and punishment as a function of task complexity. *J Comp Physiol Psychol, 55:*532-534, 1962.

Penny, R. O., and Lupton, A.: Children's discrimination learning as a function of reward and punishment. *J Comp Physiol Psychol, 54:*449-456, 1961.

Quay, H.: Some basic considerations in the education of emotionally disturbed children. *Except Child, 30:*27-31, 1963.

Redl, F.: Crisis in the children's field. *Am J Orthopsychiatry, 32:*759-780, 1962.

———: The concept of punishment. In N. Long, W. Morse, and R. Newman (Eds.): *Conflict in the Classroom.* Belmont, Calif., Wadsworth, 1965.

Sears, R., Maccoby, E. and Levin, H.: *Patterns of Child Rearing.* Evanston, Ill., Row Peterson, 1957.

Slack, C.: Experimenter-subject psychotherapy: a new method for introducing intensive office treatment for unreachable cases. *Ment Hyg, 44:*238-256, 1960.

Solomon, R.: Punishment. *Am Psychol, 19:*239-253, 1964.

Stevenson, H., Weir, M., and Zigler, E.: Discrimination learning in children as a function of motive-incentive conditions. *Psychol Rep, 5:*95-98, 1959.

Warren, A.: All's quiet in the backroom. Paper read at the Council for Exceptional Children, Wichita, Kans., Oct., 1965.

White, M., and Harris, M.: *The School Psychologist.* New York, Harper, 1961.

Williams, C. D.; The elimination of tantrum behavior by extinction procedures. *J Abnorm Soc Psychol*, 59:269, 1959.

Wolf, M., Risley, T., and Mees, H.: Application of operant conditioning procedures to behavior problems of an autistic child. *Behav Res Ther*, 1:305-312, 1964.

Wolpe, J.: *Psychotherapy by Reciprocal Inhibition*. Stanford, Calif., Stanford University, 1958.

Chapter 5

PRECISION TECHNIQUES IN THE MANAGEMENT OF TEACHER AND CHILD BEHAVIORS

MARIE GAASHOLT

PARENT-TEACHER CONFERENCES and report cards require teachers to evaluate pupil progress. Unfortunately, these appraisals are often inadequate because the observation periods are too short, the tests imprecise, and the goals undefined (Zimmerman, 1969). Lack of time, heavy class loads, and inadequate materials too often result in the acceptance of less than precise measuring techniques and evaluation.

Important as the measurement of pupil performance is the evaluation and measurement of teacher performance. Yet, systematic evaluations of teacher performance as it influences pupil performance are rarely carried out. Precision teaching, a system of continuous and direct recording of a pinpointed movement (Lindsley, 1969), is a technique whereby teachers can efficiently and economically evaluate both pupil performance and their own instructional endeavors. Precision teaching involves five basic steps:

1. Pinpointing a pupil behavior.
2. Recording this behavior daily, computing the rate (number of responses over elapsed time), and charting it on a 6 cycle behavior chart.
3. Recording teacher behavior in relation to pupil behavior.
4. Analyzing data to decide what change in teacher performance might affect pupil performance, if a pupil performance rate needs to be changed.
5. Making only one change in teacher performance at a time and then reevaluating.

Method

Children and Setting

Six or seven children were referred to the Engineered Learning Project (ELP) experimental classroom every eight weeks. The ELP, a unique teaching situation (Walker, Mattson, and Buckley, 1969), is sponsored by the Department of Special Education, University of Oregon. The students, of average or above average intelligence, were behavior problems in their respective classrooms. Twenty-five children (24 boys and 1 girl) in grades three through seven received instruction during the 1968-69 school year. All the children were below grade level in one or more subjects, as indicated by the Gates McKillop Reading Test, Stanford Diagnostic Arithmetic Test, and daily performance rates.

The goal of the project was to alter teacher defined deviant behaviors of the students. Within this primary focus, the instructional goals were to pinpoint each child's deficit areas and to teach the needed skills as effectively as possible while searching for materials and motivators which could be used in the regular classroom.

Charting

Performance rates were charted on equal proportion 6 cycle chart paper with units ranging from .001 to 1000 over 6 logarithmic cycles (see Figs. 5-1 to 5-6). This standardized chart is specifically designed for recording broad ranges of behavior, a great advantage when two very different behaviors are being charted. A teacher concerned with a behavior, e.g., temper tantrums, which might occur only once a day and a teacher concerned with oral reading rates which could occur at a rate of 200 words per minute could use the same type of chart paper to record either behavior.

Data Collection

Direct observation of academic behavior was made by the teacher, the teacher aide, and the students. Students recorded their start and stop times, while either the teacher or the teacher aide recorded and charted the rate on the 6 cycle chart paper.

Since the children attended the ELP classroom for only eight weeks, immediate daily feedback was needed if the teacher's classroom planning was to be effective. The following teacher questions were typical: "Should Robert advance to 3-place multiplication, or does he need additional instruction and practice on basic facts and 2-place multiplication problems?" "Will Mark read better if I say 'good' for every three sentences he reads correctly?" "Am I giving equal instruction, time, and effort to each child?" By direct recording and charting, the teacher had a firm basis for the decisions she would have to make in program planning.

Teacher-Pupil Interaction

It is generally assumed that help and encouragement will accelerate pupil performance. However, without data teachers have no way of knowing how often interaction occurs between pupil and teacher or whether the contact is pupil- or teacher-initiated. To obtain such data, a sheet of paper taped to each child's desk was used to record the times a teacher or teacher aide went over and spoke to the child. The sheet also indicated whether the contact was student- or teacher-initiated and noted in which subject area it occurred.

Figure 5-1 shows the teacher-pupil interaction data for one group. The vertical lines indicate the range of teacher interactions with the seven pupils, while the short horizontal lines show the daily median or middle rate. These pupil-teacher interactions were recorded daily for 166 minutes. The record floor at .006 on the chart was determined by dividing 1 by the time of the observation ($1 \div 166 = .006$). The record floor indicates the time of the observation period and indicates the lowest rate (other than zero) at which a behavior could occur.

As illustrated on the figure, the first day's range extended from .1 to .3 with a median at .2. Multiplying these rates by the observation time determines frequency of interaction. On the first day the range of interaction was from about 17 to 50 with a median of 33. These data indicated that over a 22-day period the

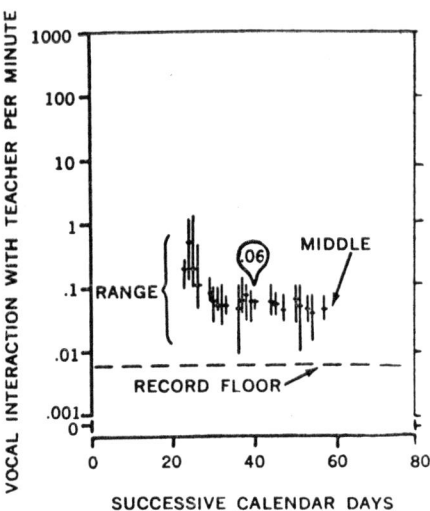

Figure 5-1. Range and middles of interactions between teachers and seven students during individualized instruction periods.

range of interactions remained about the same but the median rate of interacting had decelerated.

When the individual data were analyzed, it was revealed that on some days one child was asking for and receiving teacher attention at a rate eight times higher than the other six students. When the pattern persisted on the fourth day it was decided to cut down on teacher-initiated contacts, and this decision was successfully implemented.

The data also revealed that one child rarely received any teacher attention. What little interaction was made was initiated by the student. Although it was decided to pay more attention to the pupil and a conscious effort to give him equal time was made, the chart showed that the previous pattern recurred.

When the teacher-pupil interaction records of various groups of children were compared, it was obvious that variation was great between groups and among individuals within groups.

Effect of Teacher Behaviors on Pupil Performance

Filling out an IS Description is the first step of a teaching plan. The IS Description is a list of the environmental components which could have an influence upon the behavior, the specific effects of which have not been determined. With a lesson plan based on an IS Description (Lindsley, 1969), teacher behaviors, like instruction or verbal praise, are specified and can, therefore, be independently measured. The IS Description has two sides, one describing acceleration and the other, deceleration. The following is an explanation of a child's reading session planned on the IS Description:

1. Program: The activity was scheduled between 9:30 and 10:00 A.M. The child's oral reading rate was sampled for 2 minutes.
2. Programed events: The classroom events used to elicit Mark's reading responses were the book *Smashup* and verbal instructions such as "Remember to look at the ends of the words" and "Try not to repeat so many passages today."
3. Movement cycle: Oral words read correctly was the behavior to be counted.
4. Arrangement: The ratio between the movement cycle and the arranged event was 3 to 1, the first number referring to the movement cycle, the second to the arranged event.
5. Arranged event: After Mark read three sentences correctly, the teacher said "Good!"

The program and programed events for the deceleration portion of Mark's IS Description were identical to the acceleration side. Incorrect words were counted, rated, and charted as the movement to decelerate but no arranged event, hence, no arrangement, was contingent on that behavior.

Consistency in following a lesson plan is important, but often difficult to maintain. Therefore, the teacher's responses, which formed the programed and arranged events for the child, were monitored. For example, if the teacher said "good" after three correct sentences, her response was counted as correct. If the teacher failed to say "good" or said "good" regardless of the number or the quality of the sentences that the pupil read, her response was incorrect and so tallied. Teacher errors declined from 3.0 per minute the first five days to zero the last five days during the charting.

Since teacher errors were reduced, the project was considered successful. However, the function of the change on pupil progress could be determined only by consulting the student's chart. These latter data indicated that as the teacher adhered more closely to her teaching plans, the pupil's correct reading rate accelerated.

In a similar project, "teacher helps" and a pupil's oral reading rate were simultaneously measured. Teacher helps consisted of teacher statements such as "Think hard," "What's the beginning sound?" or pointing to a particular word or to part of a word. These data revealed that for a period of about five weeks the median rate of teacher helps in a 30-minute reading period was one per minute. During this same time, the boy's median correct oral reading rate was about fifteen per minute. During the final phase of the project, when the teacher attempted to reduce the helping rate, her median rate was zero and the pupil's 45. Apparently, teacher helps were hindering the boy's performance.

An analysis of the teacher's actions indicated that some helps like "come on" were program events (preceding or not contingent on pupil behavior) whereas others such as pointing to a mispronounced word were arranged events (followed by or contingent on pupil performance). On the teacher's IS Description or plan sheet she had not included coaxing as a programed event or pointing as an arranged event. She had written out a plan, but had not followed it consistently. This information would not have been available without measurement of teacher behavior.

Setting Proficiency Levels in Math

Teachers have many questions which are not answered by curriculum guides or teacher manuals: "Should the student be able to do basic facts (add, subtract, multiply, and divide) at 10, 30, or 60 answers per minute before advancing to more difficult problems?" "Will acquisition of new material vary when different proficiency levels are used?" "How can classroom data indicate when a child is most likely to succeed at a new task?"

In an attempt to find answers to such questions, performance rates of two children in the ELP classes were examined. To obtain these data the pupils were provided with a ditto sheet of 60 problems involving one or two movements. A sum requiring one written numeral, 2 × 3 = ——, was counted as one movement, while a solution requiring two written numerals, such as 6 × 9 = ——, was considered two movements. Five different dittos containing a mixed arrangement of the same 60 basic facts were used daily. To avoid positional memorization, no child received the same ditto two days in succession.

Both students, Robert and Sam, began on multiplication facts where the multiplier and multiplicand were from 0 to 5. According to Robert's chart (Fig. 5-2) his correct and error rates throughout the first 17 days generally accelerated. His median correct rate was seven and his median error rate was .2 answers per minute.

In the second phase of the study more difficult problems were programed. The multiplication program throughout this phase included problems whose multipliers and multiplicands were

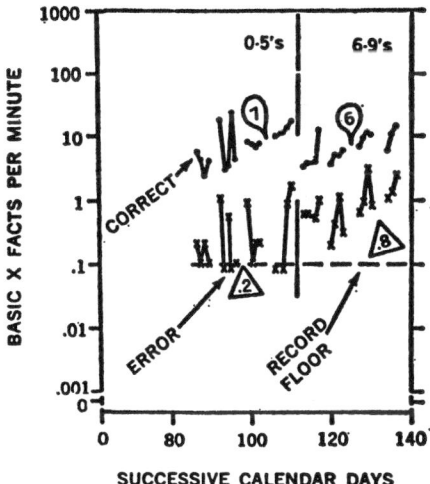

Figure 5-2. Robert's correct and error rates of basic multiplication facts. He had not reached a proficiency level in the first phase. Correct rate decelerated while error rate accelerated when the second phase (more difficult problems) was begun. The x's on the record floor indicate a rate of one, those x's placed immediately below the record floor indicate a zero error rate.

from 6 to 9. The data throughout this phase also revealed that correct and error rates were generally accelerated. It may be additionally observed, however, that an immediate correct rate drop and error rate increase were noted when the more difficult materials were scheduled. These performance changes continued to be noted as Robert was advanced to successively more difficult materials. Probably, Robert's initial correct rate of seven and error rate of .2 were not proficient, since he experienced more and more difficulty as he was advanced to more difficult material.

Sam's performance on multiplication facts is illustrated by Figure 5-3. As noted throughout the first phase of ten days when the 0 to 5 type problems were scheduled, his median correct rate was 20 and his median error rate, zero. When the more difficult problems were scheduled throughout the second phase, his correct median rate rose to 30 per minute, while his error rate remained generally at zero.

When still more difficult multiplication problems were subsequently scheduled, Sam's performance continued to improve.

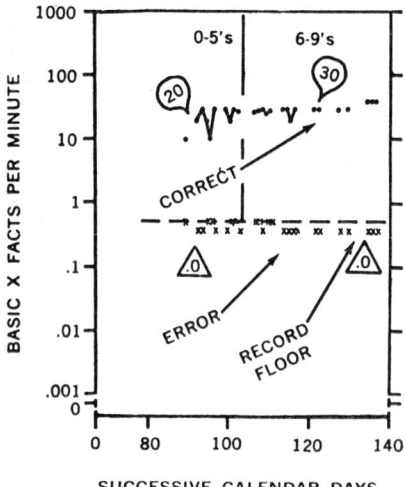

Figure 5-3. Sam's correct and error rates of basic multiplication facts. During the first phase a proficiency level had been reached. In the second phase, when more difficult problems were scheduled, his performance continued to be satisfactory.

Unlike Robert, Sam probably reached a proficiency level on the first set of multiplication facts, since his rates on successive problems were always satisfactory.

One way to set a proficiency level in math is to have children write numbers for one minute. If the numbers are correctly formed and the child has worked efficiently, the number writing rate indicates the highest possible response rate (Haughton, 1969). Basic facts rates may be set just below the written number rate since the goal is complete mastery; however, solving complex problems may produce a slightly lower performance rate.

Multiple digit problems require more movement cycles per problem than one or two digit basic facts problems. The problem 608 × 2, for example, has five movements when all written numbers and the process of carrying to the tens place are counted. All movements must be counted to give equal credit for performance on more difficult problems. When all movements are tallied, a fairly consistent digit per minute rate is maintained whether complex problems or basic facts are involved.

Setting Proficiency Levels in Writing

This project attempted to set reasonable proficiency levels for cursive writing, and to assess the effects of student self-charting on individual writing rates. According to studies by Kunzelmann (1969), some pupil performance rates are about half that of adults. With this information in mind, the teacher calculated her own writing rate for several days. She observed that her rates were about 100 letters per minute, and she therefore established a writing rate of 50 letters per minute as a proficiency level for her pupils.

To obtain the pupils' writing rates, a mimeographed sheet containing paragraphs of cursive writing, penmanship paper, and pencil were distributed each day. At the signal, everyone, including the teacher, wrote as quickly and as neatly as possible for one minute. Then everyone corrected his own paper by circling any incorrectly formed letters. A brief discussion concerning the formation of letters occasionally preceded this correction period.

Although not all the children had reached the assumed proficiency level, every child, on the twelfth day of the project, was given his correct and error charts and told how to chart his own rate.

In the first phase, before self-charting was introduced, the middle group rate was 28 correct letters per minute and was accelerating. After student charting began, the middle rate was slightly higher. The data suggest that charting may have hindered the rate of cursive writing, since, as a group, performances during the second phase were decelerating (see Fig. 5-4).

A further analysis of the relationship between proficiency level and charting was possible when the rates of individual students were examined. Mark's middle rate for the first 11 days was 53, slightly above the assumed proficiency level. After he began to chart, his middle rate continued to rise to 60 words per minute. Mark's self-charting could therefore be interpreted as an aid to his writing rate (see Fig. 5-5).

On the other hand, Robert's chart showed a middle rate of 17 for the first ten days, considerably below proficiency level, but

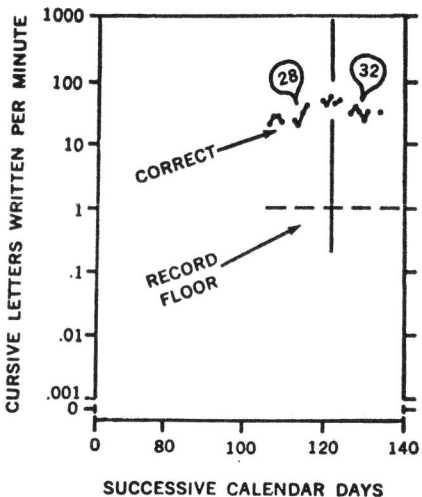

Figure 5-4. This group summary contains the students' daily middle (median) rates before and after the students began charting their own writing rates.

Precision Techniques 67

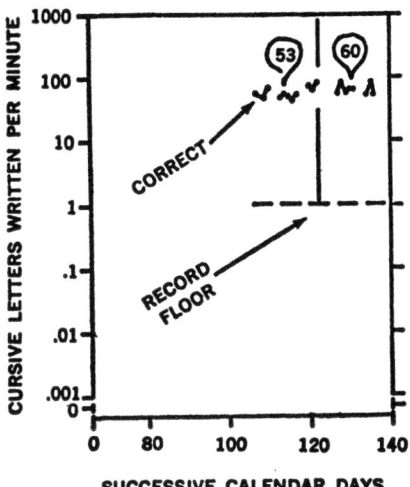

Figure 5-5. Mark reached proficiency level of writing cursive letters during the first phase. His writing rate continued to accelerate after personal charting.

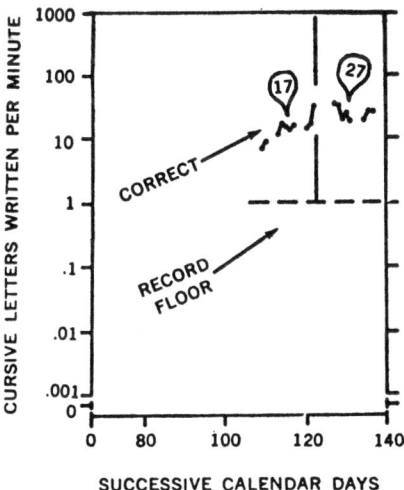

Figure 5-6. Robert did not reach proficiency level of writing cursive letters in the first phase. After personal charting was initiated in the second phase his rates begin to decelerate.

accelerating. When self-charting was initiated, Robert's rates decelerated sharply, indicating that self-charting may have hindered a continued acceleration of his writing rate (see Fig. 5-6).

These writing data, like those in math, seem to indicate that when a child has reached a proficiency level, new tasks and program events are less likely to cause a rate decrease, and some new program events, such as self-charting, may actually increase the rate. When the behavior is in the acquisition stage, new program events may slow down acceleration.

Conclusions

A thorough study of performance data can improve teaching skills. This study suggested the following conclusions: (a) Teacher behavior differs with different children. Direct recording immediately clarifies these trends, allowing teachers to give parents and administrators interaction data objectively and accurately, and measures the effectiveness of attempted alterations of teacher or pupil behavior. (b) What a teacher plans and what she does often differ. When planning is based on an IS Description and the teacher's performance is recorded, possible strengths or weaknesses in the plan and the implementation show up. (c) The attainment of a proficiency level before altering events seems necessary for optimum growth. A child should not struggle with new tasks until he is proficient in basic ones.

REFERENCES

Haughton, E.: University of Oregon. Personal communication, 1969.

Kunzelmann, H.: Research and interpretation. Paper presented at the Precision Teaching Workshop, Eugene, Oregon, August, 1969.

Lindsley, O.: Direct measurement and prosthesis of retarded behavior. Revised edition, *University of Oregon Curriculum Bulletin*, Eugene, Oregon, 1969, p. 25.

Walker, H., Mattson, R., and Buckley, N.: Special class placement as a treatment alternative for deviant behavior in children. In F. A. M. Benson (Ed.): *Modifying Deviant Social Behaviors in Various Classroom Settings*. Eugene, University of Oregon Press, 1969.

Zimmerman, C.: Classroom academic feedback and elementary administrator and staff behavior. Unpublished doctoral dissertation, University of Oregon, 1969.

SECTION II
CONSIDERATIONS AND ISSUES

Chapter 6

FREEDOM TO FAIL: THE MORALITY OF BEHAVIORISM IN EDUCATION OR WHY THE BIG FUSS OVER BEHAVIOR MOD?

JOSEPH S. KAPLAN

WHEN SKINNER INTRODUCED operant conditioning to the world in 1939, few educators would have predicted the controversy such a development would lead to in the 1970's. If Skinner is correct in stating that behavior is shaped and maintained by its consequences, then the day of autonomous man (if he ever had his day) is over. For all that is necessary to shape and maintain desired behavior is to arrange the environment so that certain consequences are made contingent upon it. A problem then arises: Who does the manipulating? Skinner, himself, asserts that often the man who builds the environment, whether it be physical or cultural, is not the man who is controlled by it (Skinner in Evans, 1968). Thus we have one of the controversial issues facing contemporary education: whether or not we, as teachers, have the right to "build the environment" for our students. Are we not infringing upon their freedom by deciding which behaviors are appropriate (i.e., acceptable) and which are inappropriate (i.e., unacceptable) in the classroom? Do we have the right to control their behavior? To ask such questions is to make the following assumptions:
1. Students are (as is 20th Century man) self-autonomous.
2. No one has ever tried to control a student's behavior and in so doing limit his self-autonomy.
3. Every student has the responsibility to use his freedom in such a way that he will never infringe upon the rights or harm the person of another individual.

How many of us in education honestly believe any of these assumptions to be true. Let us examine each more closely.

First, as to the assumption that students are free, it is the writer's contention that no one is completely self-autonomous. Freedom, like everything else in life is on a continuum; it is a relative concept. Some learning environments are more "free" than others and some students are more "free" than their peers. Certain teachers may boast, "My classroom is very democratic." What this usually means is that their students get to vote on whether they want to study astronomy or geology in science. True, there are learning environments where kids decide such things as curriculum, but these are few and far between in the public schools.

I am not convinced that students in the public schools are, or ever have been, "free." Moreover, I am not convinced that public school teachers are or ever have been "free." Some would argue that they are free in the sense that they create the environment which ultimately controls them. Therefore, indirectly they do exercise some control over their destiny. However, how many of us can say that we are the innovators of our environments? How many first year teachers have found their creativity stifled by administrators supporting the policies of Boards of Education? There is not as much freedom in the public schools as we would like to think. Kids are controlled (albeit ineffectively) by teachers who are controlled by principals who are controlled by Boards of Education who are controlled by parents who, besides being controlled by their kids (effectively), are controlled by political and/or religious ideologies, the economy, the media and their own self-doubts, among others.

Control is very much a part of the 20th Century. To say that it is not and that contemporary man is self-autonomous is to avoid the truth. Nowhere is control more evident and nowhere is 20th Century man less free than in the public schools. Even the Humanist teacher in our society seeks to control his or her students. Using persuasion, argument, inducement, emulation, or enthusiasm to get a student to learn, they are controlling the student just as surely as the Behaviorist who designs the token system or the programmed materials.

The assumption that teachers have never tried to control their students' behavior is equally as ridiculous as saying we are all "free" men in the truest sense of the word. In the past we have relied most heavily upon aversive forms of control even when the evidence suggested that these were not the most effective in the long run. According to the data up to now, aversive methods of control have been shown to generate escape and avoidance reactions in others which can turn into effective opposition (Reese, 1966). Nowhere have such reactions been more common than in the public schools where the process of education for the child may be more likely to proceed because of the threat of failure or punishment to which the child is exposed rather than the promise of success or reward. Considering this history of attempting to control behavior, why then, do many educators find behavior modification so subversive? It is as if all of a sudden man has developed a conscience and decided that controlling the behavior of others is not moral. It is the writer's contention that educators are threatened by the use of behavior modification in their classrooms because it may prove to be an effective means of controlling behavior. This raises the question: Do teachers really want to control the behavior of their students or are they subconsciously pleased to be ineffectual? A more important question at this point may be: Should teachers control the behavior of their students? This leads us to the third assumption: Everyone is responsible for his actions and external controls are not necessary, i.e., all kids will be "good" because they just naturally want to be.

We would all agree that freedom implies personal responsibility on the part of man. However, one must ask these questions: Are children responsible enough to determine their own destiny? Should a five-year-old decide when he should go to sleep? Should a three-year-old be allowed to explore his neighborhood unsupervised including the playground across the street? Should a teenager be free to experiment with drugs? Should any man be free to drink as much alcohol as he wishes and then drive home? Does everyone who desires self-determination have the personal responsibility to exercise his freedom in such a way that he will not do himself or others any harm? I do not think so and as an educator, I am especially concerned with certain children in our schools who need someone to manipulate their environments in order to shape and maintain their behavior. I am referring to the handicapped child.

I find it interesting that the Ancient Greeks, who gave birth to the concept of freedom so cherished by modern Western man, had no problems regarding the development of responsibility and initiative in their citizens. All those individuals who couldn't think for themselves were left to die in mountain caves. Contemporary man has not seen fit to follow this practice and as a result, we find ourselves with a dilemma. Because we live in a democratic society, we believe in the freedom and dignity of each individual regardless of his I.Q. or ability to communicate his feelings to others. Self-autonomous man should be free to express himself and determine what his behavior should be. Does this include the delinquent who "expresses himself" through vandalism or the retardate who, through lack of skills, lives out his days as the ward of the state in some institution? What about the acting-out child whose dislike for himself is exceeded only by his peers' dislike for him due to his aggressive, unprovoked physical attacks on everyone in his immediate environment? What about the schizophrenic child who decides that banging his head against the wall until it bleeds is more "fun" than reading a book. Are these examples of autonomous man free to choose their own destiny or are these individuals not saying, "Control me for I cannot control myself"?

In the past, this "control" has been given in the form of psychodynamic therapy, chemotherapy and/or large doses of punishment, among others. We have tried unsuccessfully to control the behavior of the socially deviant through group and individual therapy, tracing the delinquent's problems to his alcoholic father or promiscuous mother and, in the process, given him an excuse to continue his antisocial behavior. When he outgrew the therapy, we were willing to call him a juvenile delinquent; later we labeled him a "criminal" and sent him to prison. Jail becomes the ultimate "solution" to the problem of controlling his behavior.

We have tried to control the behavior of the acting-out child through the application of a medical model which emphasizes labeling him brain damaged (another excuse for his behavior) and prescribing different amounts and types of medication until the magic potion is found. By the time he has alienated everyone (including his parents) or his pediatrician has run out of pills, he is exiled to a private school where his deviant behavior is tolerated by the teachers and encouraged (i.e., reinforced) by his equally deviant peers; another ultimate "solution." The process isn't any different for the child who is labeled retarded or schizophrenic. Control of their behavior is accomplished through segregation from the mainstream of education by placing them in a special class or an institution.

Perhaps, before the end of this article, the writer should clarify his view (i.e., definition) of freedom since everyone seems to have his own concept. Webster defines freedom as the exemption or liberation from the control of some other person or some arbitrary power (Webster, 1958). To Carl Rogers, freedom is a fulfillment by the person, of the ordered sequence of his life (Rogers, 1962). B. F. Skinner views freedom as an illusory concept invented by man as a result of his need to be given credit for his "good" behavior and achievements (Skinner, 1971). As an educator, I feel the most practical definition of freedom is expressed by Reese who writes:

> A man who has a limited behavioral repertoire and whose behavior produces a limited variety of reinforcers may be considered a man with very little freedom. On the other hand, a man who can read and write and speak effectively—who has, perhaps, artistic or athletic or mechanical skills—such a man has far more freedom. Freedom defined in these terms is indeed a function of behavioral control, but the relation need not be inversive. We can produce an environment which favors a large number of available responses and thereby increase man's freedom, or we can produce an environment which restricts his response repertoire and his freedom. (Reese, 1966).

To illustrate Reese's definition of freedom, let me cite a personal example. My father, having gone up to the fifth grade, is limited in terms of academic skills, while I have a wider variety of more highly developed skills. As a result, I have a greater number of vocational and avocational choices open to me. Thus, if one follows Reese's definition of freedom, I am freer than my father because the quality and quantity of my skills place more choices at my disposal and I am freer to behave in a greater variety of ways. I am less under the control of some other person or some arbitrary power than my father is. Therefore, it is the writer's opinion that the amount of freedom one enjoys increases proportionately with the number of marketable skills one possesses.

What I have suggested in this paper is that certain individuals not only need others to control their behavior, but that we have been trying to do this all along and have not been very effective. It is the writer's contention that we have a responsibility to control the behavior of these individuals in our society *for the present*, so that they may have more self-autonomy *in the future*. To refuse to control is to leave control not to the person himself, but to other parts of the social and nonsocial environments (Skinner, 1971).

REFERENCES

Evans, Richard I.: *B. F. Skinner: The Man and His Ideas*. New York, E. P. Dutton, 1968.

Reese, Ellen P.: *The Analysis of Human Operant Behavior*. Dubuque, Iowa, Wm. C. Brown, 1966.

Rogers, Carl: (in a tape of a debate with B. F. Skinner at the University of Minnesota). American Academy of Psychotherapists Tape Library, Vol. 10, 1962.

Skinner, B. F.: *Beyond Freedom and Dignity*. New York, Alfred A. Knopf, 1971.

Chapter 7

BEHAVIOR MODIFICATION: LIMITATIONS AND LIABILITIES

Donald L. MacMillan
Steven R. Forness

Within recent years the application of behavior modification techniques in classrooms of exceptional children has inceased greatly. Evidence abounds regarding the efficacy of behavior modification with retarded children (Bijou and Orlando, 1961), learning disabled children (Hewett, 1965; Lovitt, 1968), autistic children (Ferster and DeMeyer, 1961; Hewett, 1964; Lovaas, Freitag, Gold, and Kassorla, 1965), emotionally disturbed children (Levin and Simmons, 1962a; Levin and Simmons, 1962b), brain damaged children (Patterson, 1965), and assorted behavior problems in the classroom (Hively, 1959; Hewett, 1966; Valett, 1966; Whelan and Haring, 1966). Hence, the contention that behavior modification is an effective technique with atypical children appears to be well documented.

Hewett (1968) contends that behavior modification assigns the teacher the role of a learning specialist, the role she is best prepared to assume. Alternate strategies (i.e., psychoanalytic, sensory neurological) place the teacher in the role of psychotherapist or diagnostician, roles which teachers are generally ill-prepared to assume. In light of successes in teaching atypical children with behavior modification techniques, Bijou (1966) contends that one can no longer categorically explain the failure to learn in terms of a child's deficiencies, but rather must consider the tutorial inadequacies of the teacher. The combination of the factors above—teachers in roles of competence and the emphasis on what the child can do with properly sequenced and correctly reinforced material—provides a more positive approach to the education of exceptional children than did previous approaches which attributed the failure to learn to the child's defect.

By focusing on the consequences of altering and maintaining behavior, certain long standing assumptions of educators have been questioned. One such assumption is that certain rewards, such as letter grades and teacher approval, have universal applicability. For certain children, the above rewards are ineffective. In attempts to identify rewards for children who do not respond to the traditional ones, investigators have utilized rewards considered unconventional by some (candy, check marks, tokens) with considerable success.

Research has further sensitized teachers to the power of their attention, and how their attending to misbehavior may have the effect of increasing its occurrence (Zimmerman and Zimmerman, 1962). Premack (1959) describes the use of activities the child prefers (high probability behavior) as an accelerating consequence for less preferred behavior (low probability behavior). Hence, if the child enjoys building model planes, the teacher can use this behavior as a reward for his performing tasks he enjoys less. Such evidence has had an impact on the ongoing practices in the special education classroom.

Enthusiasm over the reported successes of behavior modification with atypical children coupled with teachers' desperation for something that works may blind us to what behavior modification does not, or cannot, do. Mann and Phillips (1967) point out that a number of practices presently operative in special education are designed to fractionate global or molar areas of behavior. While their discussion did not include mention of behavior modification, their contention may also be valid with regard to this strategy. It is important that behavior modification be put in perspective with respect to the overall picture of education. Three limitations in the application of behavior modification to exceptional children will be discussed. Some of the limitations are inherent in the theoretical paradigm itself; others lie in the application, or misapplication, of that theory by

practitioners. Specifically, the three limitations to be discussed are:
1. Learning theory does not guide the teacher in determining educational goals.
2. A view of motivation as exclusively extrinsic in nature is limiting in scope.
3. The operational definition of reinforcement ignores certain cognitive aspects of reinforcement.

Educational Goals
Behavioral Goals

Ullmann and Krasner (1965) state that the first question asked by the behavior analyst is, "What behavior is maladaptive, that is, what subject behaviors should be increased or decreased?" (p. 1). To the experimental psychologist this is a question answered only through objective analysis of behavior. Too often, however, the real question that gets answered is "What behavior manifested by the child most annoys me as his teacher," regardless of whether or not that behavior is interfering with the child's learning or development.

The behavior modification strategy does not determine educational goals for the child. This is not to suggest that the behavior modification strategy claims to determine goals, but in its inability to do so may lie the reason for its lack of acceptance in public school programs. Hewett, Taylor, and Artuso (1969) discuss the lack of balanced emphasis on goals and methods. They write:

> In general, selection of these goals is based on a desire to aid the child in changing maladaptive behavior to adaptive behavior. At best, these concepts of "maladaptive" and "adaptive" provide only the broadest of guidelines for selection of specific behavioral goals. In this sense the powerful methodology of the behavior modification approach is not matched by concern with goals in learning. Teachers are provided with an efficient means of taking emotionally disturbed children someplace but are not substantially aided in the selection of where to go.
> It is this lack of balanced emphasis on goals and methods that

may preclude the acceptance of behavior modification in the field of education, particularly in the public school, and thereby may greatly limit its usefulness. (p. 523)

Once the teacher has determined what the child is to be taught, the behavior modification techniques can be employed to achieve that end. Alternate developmental theories (e.g., Erikson, Piaget) may be more helpful for determining goals in that they suggest to the teacher the developmental tasks that the child must master, and what skills he must acquire in order to achieve subsequent levels. Lacking a developmental framework, the teacher rather arbitrarily decides what the child must learn.

Wood (1968) expressed concern over the possibility that teachers are provided with a powerful tool in behavior modification techniques without simultaneously developing an understanding of its implications and potential misuse. In light of evidence suggesting that teachers, in general, are more concerned with maintaining power over students than in transmitting knowledge and skill, his concern seems well founded (Eddy, 1967; Henry, 1957; Landes, 1965; Moore, 1967). Implicit in the application of behavior modification techniques with children is the right of the behavior modifier to define what represents adaptive or appropriate behaviors. Wood (1968) described the teacher's role in such a relationship as follows: Having defined the child's present behavior as inappropriate *he* plans to shape it toward behavior *he* has defined as appropriate. In describing the teacher most likely to misuse this tool without considering the child's rights to participate in defining the goal behavior, Wood states:

> These teachers may often be those against whose already abusive application of their authority pupils have the greatest need to be protected. Like many "tools," behavior modification techniques are themselves morally blind. Like a stout sword, they work equally well in the hands of hero or tyrant. Any person of moderate intelligence can, with assistance if not independently, apply them with great effectiveness for good or ill. (p. 14)

In the case of many exceptional children, a number of their rights were abridged at the time of classification or labeling, thus making them more susceptible to abuse than had they not been so labeled.

Academic Goals

When the educational goal is related to the teaching of subject matter, and the teacher employs a strict behaviorist strategy to achieve this goal, certain limitations inherent in the paradigm should be realized. The usual learning situation is much more complex than is suggested by the behavioristic paradigm. Enthusiastic proponents of behaviorism tend to be blinded by the framework and deny other possible explanations for human learning. The analysis of human learning in terms of discrete operational steps may ignore or violate the inherent logic in the material to be learned. Flavell (1963) explains Piaget's theory that schemata (organized information) develop as a consequence of assimilation and accommodation, and learning is facilitated by presenting materials in a manner amenable to reorganization of previously existing cognitive structures (schemata). In addition, Gagné (1962), operating within a different theoretical framework than Piaget, states that the nature and structure of the task to be learned is of greater importance than the behavioristic principles of learning, for example, reinforcement and practice.

It may be that behavior modification strategy fails to adequately consider the goals to which the shaped behavior is related. Determination of goals is left to the teacher who may, or may not, be a good judge of appropriate behavior. When the principles of behavior modification are applied to the teaching of subject matter the reductionistic conception of the learning process is a definite limitation. Autoinstructional techniques suffer from many of the same limitations, which are elaborated upon by Stafford and Combs (1967).

Motivation

Extrinsic

From the behavioristic point of view, motivation is seen as extrinsic to learning. Bijou and Baer (1961) stress the importance of behavioral scientists concerning themselves only with events which can be observed and quantified. In the application of reinforcement theory to behavioral management an attempt has been made to observe the suggestions of Bijou and Baer. In attempts to get children to read, sit in their seats, attend to materials, and develop other school appropriate behavior, the emphasis has been placed on the use of tokens, check marks, and candy in association with the desired behavior. In programs developed to shape behavior through extrinsic rewards or consequences which are observable and able to be quantified, it is postulated that the child will ultimately want to engage in these appropriate behaviors because he will pair the social rewards of teacher or peer approval with the extrinsic rewards used during the shaping program. Inherent in such an approach is the belief that desire or motivation can be manipulated by simply applying consequences when the organism behaves in a desired fashion. The theoretical approach described above is extremely limited, ignores much of the available evidence, presented in summary below, and discounts alternative explanations of motivation.

Intrinsic

Piaget describes the equilibration process, wherein cognitive adaptation and growth result from the dynamic functioning of the processes of assimilation and accommodation. Exploratory behavior is inherently interesting and rewards the child if it relates to the child's existing mental structures (schemata). Not only is it important to present material in a fashion commensurate with the child's previous level of cognitive development, but material thus presented can become a source of intrinsic motivation to the child (Hunt, 1961). There is no observable or quantifiable "pay-off" for such behavior; however, when a match between schemata and task exists the child finds the task inherently interesting.

Stimulation-seeking behavior appears to be another source of intrinsic motivation in higher order organisms. Festinger's (1957) "theory of cognitive dissonance," concludes that when incoming stimulation differs from existing perceptions or conceptions one is motivated to resolve the discrepancy. Festinger (1957) postulated that cognitive incongruities are a primary source of motivation in human beings, a source which is intrinsic in nature, and one which cannot be observed or quantified.

Although working outside of the two preceding theoretical frameworks, Harlow (1949, 1953) suggests that there may be an innate drive of curiosity, which is more likely to operate when the learners' primary needs have been satisfied (Maslow, 1943). Harlow (1953) explained that children and monkeys can enjoy exploration for its own sake. He cites the monkey who continues to solve problems despite the fact that his cheeks are full of food with which he was rewarded for correct or incorrect responses. Despite such unsystematic schedules of reinforcement, the monkeys increased their ability to learn how to learn (Harlow, 1949).

White (1965) offers another framework within which one can consider motivation. He contends that it is in studying the satiated child that one is truly able to understand human nature. In his paper critical of the traditional Freudian position which views motivation in terms of need reduction, White suggests that such a framework is unable to explain satisfactorily the apparent play behavior of the infant, or the one year old who tries to spoon feed himself despite the fact that he could gain greater oral satisfaction by allowing his mother to feed him. It may be added that neither can the reinforcement theory explain this behavior in terms of the observable events. Rather, White contends, the child is concerned with achieving mastery over his environment. Regarding play behavior, he writes:

> It is directed, selective, and persistent, and it is continued not because it serves primary drives, which indeed it cannot serve until it is almost perfected, but because it satisfies an intrinsic need to deal with environment. (p. 15)

The goal of behavior which White sees as an attempt to achieve competence may be to effect familiarity with the environment, or in more global terms, autonomy. In other words, the "payoff" is a feeling or sense of competence.

The point to be made with regard to motivation is that the behavioristic viewpoint is not the only framework within which one can consider motivation. In fact, the behavioristic paradigm is unable to explain adequately the behaviors described by Piaget, Festinger, Harlow, and White. One is unable to observe the consequences for behaviors that result from exploration, cognitive dissonance, curiosity, and competence as motives. Yet these sources of motivation must not be ignored or discounted as one attempts to reach the atypical child, or any child for that matter. Certain programs, such as Hewett's (1968), which are essentially behavior modification oriented, have altered their initial approaches and now attempt to utilize intrinsic sources of motivation. To the extent that this is practiced, however, such programs violate the pure approach suggested by Bijou and Baer (1961).

Reinforcement

Within the behavior modification framework, reinforcement is commonly defined as "a stimulus which increases the probability of a response." The reinforcement does not have to be directly related to the behavior, and often the separation is intentional. An example of this separation is the use of candy to reinforce problem solving or seat sitting. Theoretically, such a definition does not adequately explain the verbal confirming response discussed by Jensen (1968). In addition, certain practical ramifications should be considered by the practitioner prior to the application of reinforcers which are unrelated to the behavior they are reinforcing.

Verbal Confirming Response

Jensen (1968) describes the "verbal confirming response" (V_c) or feedback, which is a type of self or symbolic reinforcement used by humans. It is extremely limited in lower forms of animals and young children. V_c is more than merely a secondary reinforcement. A secondary reinforcer is a previously neutral stimulus which has gained reinforcing power through being paired with a primary or biologically relevant reinforcer. Secondary reinforcers are known to extinguish very rapidly in animal studies. Such is not the case with V_c which has the effect of strengthening behavior even though the verbal confirming response itself has no reinforcing properties in the biological sense. "The V_c response is most often covert, especially in adults, and may even be unconscious. It consists, in effect, of saying to oneself *Good* or *That's right* or *wrong*" (Jensen, 1968, p. 124). The function of language in the above manner has been demonstrated by several Russian psychologists (Razran, 1959). An interesting feature of the V_c is that it must be self initiated. To the extent that it is necessary in efficient problem solving, the use of extrinsic reinforcers that are unrelated to the specific behavior they are reinforcing preclude the necessity for developing the V_c. In depriving the child of the opportunity of this V_c, are we hindering his development as a problem solver?

Arbitrary vs Natural Reinforcers

Turning to more practical considerations, Ferster (1966) distinguished between arbitrary and natural reinforcers in a paper on aversive stimuli. He pointed out that arbitrary reinforcers differ from natural reinforcers in two ways: (a) when arbitrary reinforcers are used, the performance that is reinforced is narrowly specified rather than broadly defined, and (b) in the case of arbitrary reinforcers, the individual's existing repertoire of responses does not influence his behavior nearly as much as is the case with natural reinforcers. Therefore, natural reinforcers lead to more integrated, general learning.

In the first case, a positive consequence is promised for a specific behavior, seat sitting, and a child can obtain that consequence only by conforming to specific demands. He sits in his seat to obtain the reward, but learning does not necessarily generalize to global behaviors, that is, adequate classroom behavior. In the second case, arbitrary reinforcers benefit the controller, not the controlled. The teacher who says, "If you sit in your seat, I'll give you five check marks" is arbitrarily reinforcing seat sitting, which is reinforcing to the teacher for employing the strategy. But the child is not being reinforced by a consequence that naturally exists in his environment. His natural environment has never reinforced his sitting in his seat with a check mark, nor is it likely to in the future. In fact nonsitting has probably been rewarded through satisfying the curiosity drive.

While check marks, tokens, M&M's, and the like may be justifiable as initial means of bringing behavior under control, they must not represent an end in themselves. In several instances, teachers employing the behavior modification strategy, as they interpret it, have had their children on check marks for an entire year. When asked the reason the children were still functioning at this low reward level, the teacher indicated, "I'm not about to change something that is working." This teacher has failed in her responsibility to bring the child's behavior under the control of reinforcers that will exist in the child's natural environment (e.g., social praise). Whelan and Haring (1966) distinguished between the acquisition of behavior and its maintenance. The arbitrary reinforcers are useful in the acquisition stage, but in the maintenance stage they suggest:

> When the behavior needs to be maintained, then it is no longer necessary to provide accelerating consequences to each behavioral response. Maintaining behavior requires that the teacher reduce considerably the number of accelerating consequences provided; indeed, it is a necessity if a child is to develop independent learning skills and self control. It is during this maintenance process that appropriate behavior is accelerated by consequences which are intrinsic to completion of tasks, social approval, feelings of self worth, and the satisfaction of assuming self responsibility. Therefore, dependence on numerous teacher applied consequences gradually loses significance to a child (Whelan and Haring, 1966, p. 284).

It is interesting to note that the above authors, two of the most commonly cited behavior modification advocates, refer to intrinsic consequences, feelings of self-worth and satisfaction of assuming self-responsibility. It may be that the problem lies with the practitioner who has learned the *how* of behavior modification and rigidly adheres to its doctrines. In training teachers to utilize the strategy, it seems essential that the instruction should include a heavy dosage of the possible misuse of this potentially useful strategy.

Conclusions

In conclusion, the behavior modification strategy has tremendous potential for work with atypical children. Its use with these children is promising; however, its misuse could be terrifying. It is not a panacea. It gives no direction in determining educational goals; it reduces constructs of learning, motivation, and reinforcement of simplistic terms on occasion. To the unsophisticated practitioner, it may be blinding to broader frames of reference regarding the constructs listed above. Furthermore, it may preclude children from learning how to learn and thus becoming independent of teachers as such—a major goal of education. It is time we admitted the shortcomings and limitations of the approach as well as extolling its virtues. In an address to a group of autoinstructional technique enthusiasts, Howard Kendler at the 1964 American Psychological Association Convention said the following: "You have a system called Socrates, but you don't have one called God." This statement applies to the present discussion, and should be heeded by the rigid behaviorist.

REFERENCES

Bijou, S. W., and Baer, D.: *Child Development*. New York, Appleton-Century-Crofts, 1961, vol. I.

Bijou, S. W., and Orlando, R.: Rapid development of multiple-schedule performances with retarded children. *J Exp Anal Behav*, 4:7-16, 1961.

Bijou, S. W.: A functional analysis of retarded development. In N. R. Ellis (Ed.): *International Review of Research in Mental Retardation*. New York, Academic Press, 1966, vol. I.

Eddy, E. M.: *Walk the White Line: A Profile of Urban Education*. New York, Doubleday Anchor, 1967.

Ferster, C., and DeMeyer, M.: The development of performances in autistic children in automatically controlled environments. *J Chronic Dis*, 25: 8-12, 1961.

Ferster, C. B.: Arbitrary and natural reinforcement. Paper delivered at the meeting of the American Association for the Advancement of Science, Washington, D. C., 1966.

Festinger, L.: *A Theory of Cognitive Dissonance*. Evanston, Ill., Row, Peterson, 1957.

Flavell, J. H.: *The Developmental Psychology of Jean Piaget*. Princeton, N. J., Van Nostrand, 1963.

Gagné, R. M.: Military training and principles of learning. *Am Psychol, 17:* 83-91, 1962.
Harlow, H.: The formation of learning sets. *Psychol Rev, 56:*51-65, 1949.
———: Mice, monkeys, men, and motives. *Psychol Rev, 60:*23-32, 1953.
Henry, J.: Attitude organization in elementary school classrooms. *Am J Orthopsychiatry, 27:*117-133, 1957.
Hewett, F.: A hierarchy of education tasks for children with learning disorders. *Except Child, 31:*207-214, 1965.
———: Teaching reading to an autistic boy through operant conditioning. *Read Teacher, 17:*613-618, 1964.
———: The Tulare experimental class for educationally handicapped children. *Calif Educ, 3:*608, 1966.
Hewett, F. M.: *The Emotionally Disturbed Child in the Classroom.* Boston, Allyn & Bacon, 1968.
Hewett, F. M., Taylor, F. D., and Artuso, A. A.: The Santa Monica project: Evaluation of an engineered classroom design with emotionally disturbed children. *Except Child, 35:*523-529, 1969.
Hively, W.: Implications for the classroom of B. F. Skinner's analysis of behavior. *Harvard Educ Rev, 29:*37-42, 1959.
Hunt, J. McV.: *Intelligence and Experience.* New York, Ronald Press, 1961.
Jensen, A. R.: Social class and verbal learning. In M. Deutsch, I. Katz, and A. R. Jensen (Eds.): *Social Class, Race, and Psychological Development.* New York, Holt, Rinehart & Winston, 1968.
Landes, R.: *Culture in American Education.* New York, John Wiley & Sons, 1965.
Levin, G., and Simmons, J.: Response to food and praise by emotionally disturbed boys. *Psychol Rep, 11:*539-546, 1962(a).
———: Response to praise by emotionally disturbed boys. *Psychol Rep, 11:*10, 1962(b).
Lovaas, O. I., Freitag, G., Gold, V. J., and Kassorla, I. C.: Experimental studies in childhood schizophrenia: Analysis of self-destructive behavior. *J Exp Child Psychol, 2:*67-84, 1965.
Lovitt, T. C.: Operant conditioning techniques for children with learning disabilities. *J Spec Educ, 2:*283-289, 1968.
Mann, L., and Phillips, W. A.: Fractional practices in special education: A critique. *Except Child, 33:*311-317, 1967.
Maslow, A. H.: A theory of human motivation. *Psychol Rev, 50:*370-396, 1943.
Moore, G. A.: *Realities of the Urban Classroom: Observations in Elementary Schools.* New York, Doubleday Anchor, 1967.
Patterson, G. R.: An application of conditioning techniques to the control of a hyperactive child. *Behav Res Ther, 2:*217-226, 1965.

Premack, D.: Toward empirical behavior laws: I. Positive reinforcement. *Psychol Rev, 66*:219-233, 1959.

Razran, G.: Soviet psychology and psychophysiology. *Behav Sci, 4*:35-48, 1959.

Stafford, R. R., and Combs, C. F.: Radical reductionism: A possible source of inadequacy in autoinstructional techniques. *Am. Psychol, 22*:667-669, 1967.

Ullmann, L., and Krasner, L.: *Case Studies in Behavior Modification.* New York, Holt, Rinehart & Winston, 1965.

Vallett, R.: A social reinforcement technique for the classroom management of behavior disorders. *Except Child, 33*:185-189, 1966.

Whelan, R. J., and Haring, N. G.: Modification and maintenance of behavior through application of consequences. *Except Child, 32*:281-289, 1966.

White, R. W.: Motivation reconsidered: The concept of competence. In I. J. Gordon (Ed.): *Human Development: Readings in Research.* Glenview, Ill., Scott, Foresman & Company, 1965.

Wood, F. H.: Behavior modification techniques in context. *Newsletter of the Council for Children with Behavioral Disorders, 5*(4):12-15, 1968.

Zimmerman, E. H., and Zimmerman, J.: The alteration of behavior in a special classroom situation. *J Exp Anal Behav, 5*:59-60, 1962.

Chapter 8

HOW TO MAKE A TOKEN SYSTEM FAIL

David S. Kuypers
Wesley C. Becker
K. Daniel O'Leary

Token systems of reinforcement have usually been implemented in classrooms when the available social reinforcers such as teacher praise and approval have been ineffective in controlling the behavior of the children. Token systems involve the presentation of a "token" (e.g., a checkmark) following the emission of specified responses. When the child has accumulated a sufficient number of tokens, he is then able to exchange them for "back up" reinforcers (e.g., candy, toys). The tokens initially function as neutral stimuli, and they acquire reinforcing properties by being exchangeable for the back-up reinforcers. Teacher praise and approval are often paired with the tokens, in order to increase the effectiveness of praise and approval as conditioned reinforcers. A general goal of token systems is to transfer control of responding from the token systems to other conditioned reinforcers such as teacher praise and grades.

Different investigators have reported upon the success of token systems in controlling the behavior of children in classrooms where the usual social reinforcers were ineffective (Birnbrauer, Bijou, Wolf, and Kidder, 1965; Birnbrauer and Lawler, 1964; Birnbrauer, Wolf, Kidder, and Tague, 1965; O'Leary and Becker, 1967).

Teachers operating successful token programs in these studies have usually been explicitly trained in the systematic use of principles of operant behavior, and much of the success of the programs is most likely due to the general application of principles other than those governing the use of tokens per se. The central aspect of a token system is the pairing of teacher praise with tokens which are backed up by an effective reinforcer. In most effective studies, however, many other procedures have also been used. For example, praise for appropriate behavior and ignoring of disruptive behavior are used at times when tokens are not being dispensed. Time out (or isolation) is often used when intensely disruptive behaviors occur. Systematic contingencies in the form of privileges are often applied throughout the day. The children following the rules are the ones who get to help teacher, to be first in line, to choose an activity, etc. The principle of shaping is also systematically applied. Praise, privileges, and tokens are not administered for achieving an absolute standard of performance, but for improving behavior or for maintaining a high level of acceptable behavior.

The present study is one of several aimed at clarifying the important components of effective token systems. The authors' objective is primarily to make clear to those who might adopt such systems where things can go wrong if a token system is attempted without full consideration of the many variables important to success. The study uses a general procedure which was shown to be very effective when coupled with training in behavior theory, a time out procedure, shaping, and differential social reinforcement throughout the day (O'Leary and Becker, 1967). The present study, however, examines the effectiveness of the token system by itself in a classroom in which no other modifications were made in the teacher's handling of the class. The study approximates what might happen if a teacher read about a token system and tried to use it mechanically without a fuller understanding of those basic principles and supplementary procedures which are often used in successful studies but which are not emphasized or made explicit.

The study was planned to include additional phases to train the teacher in behavior principles; following this, a more effective program would have been established. However, at the request of the teacher, it was necessary to terminate the study prior to its completion. We will come back to this point in the discussion.

Method

The subjects who participated in this study were six third grade and six fourth grade children who were described as socially maladjusted. The children were typically assigned to an adjustment class when they showed such behaviors as temper tantrums, fighting, failure to pay attention in class, inability to work on their own, and academic retardation. While the token system of reinforcement was in effect for the entire class, observations were conducted on only three of the children at each grade level—six children in all. Four of the children were selected because they engaged in a high rate of inappropriate and disruptive behavior, and two were selected because the teacher reported a low incidence of highly disruptive behavior in relation to the other class members. Two of the children had previously attended a classroom at another school in which a token system of reinforcement had been used (O'Leary and Becker, 1967).

Observations

The incidence of inappropriate classroom behaviors of the four highly disruptive children was recorded by two undergraduate students during the morning between 9:30 and 11:30. Between 1:00 and 2:00 in the afternoon, three undergraduate observers recorded the behavior of six children which included the four observed in the morning plus two children who were reported by the teacher not to show much disruptive behavior. Deviant behaviors were defined as behaviors likely to be incompatible with group learning conditions. Definitions used for six classes of deviant behaviors, and one class of relevant behavior, are as follows:

Coding Categories for Children

Deviant Behavior

GROSS MOTOR BEHAVIORS. Getting out of seat, standing up, walking around, running, hopping, skipping, jumping, rocking chair, moving chair, knees on chair. Include such gross physical movements as arm flailing, feet swinging, and rocking.

DISRUPTIVE NOISE. Tapping feet, clapping, rattling papers, tearing papers, throwing book on desk, slamming desk top, tapping pencil or other objects on desk. Be conservative, rate what you hear, not what you see, and do not include accidental dropping of objects or noise made while performing gross motor behaviors.

DISTURBING OTHERS. Grabbing objects or work, knocking neighbor's books off desk, destroying another's property, throwing objects at another without hitting, pushing with desk. Only rate if someone is there.

CONTACT. Hitting, pushing, shoving, pinching, slapping, striking with objects, throwing object which hits another person, poking with object. Do not attempt to make judgments of intent. Rate any physical contact.

ORIENTING RESPONSES. Turning head or head and body to look at another person, showing objects to another child, attending to another child. Must be of four seconds' duration to be rated and is not rated unless seated. Any turn of 90 degrees or more from desk while seated is rated.

VERBALIZATIONS. Carrying on conversations with other children when it is not permitted, calling out answers to questions or comments without being called on, calling teacher's name to get her attention, crying, screaming, singing, whistling, laughing, coughing, or blowing nose. Do not rate lip movements. Rate what you hear, not what you see.

Relevant Behavior

Time on task, e.g., answering questions, listening, raising hand for teacher attention, working at assigned task, reading. Must include whole ten second interval except for orienting responses of less than four seconds' duration.

The children were observed in a fixed order for 22 minutes each session, three times a week. Observations were made on a 20 second observe, 10 second record basis. Each observer had a clipboard with a stop watch and a recording sheet. Simple symbols were used to indicate the occurrence of a particular class of behavior. A given class of behavior could be rated only once in an observation interval.

Percentage of deviant behavior was defined as the percentage of intervals in which one or more deviant behaviors occurred. Reliability was checked on the average of once a week, and was calculated by dividing the number of agreements on behavior code and time interval by the number of agreements plus disagreements.

Class Activities

For most of the day the children were in a single classroom with one teacher. During the morning the children's activities consisted of group reading lessons and individual seat work. During the afternoon the first 40 minute period consisted of a group arithmetic lesson and the second 40 minute period consisted of either art or music in another room for the fourth graders and art or spelling for the third graders.

Experimental Phases

BASELINE. During the baseline phase, the teacher was asked to handle the children according to her usual techniques and procedures. Observers had recorded the children's behavior for approximately three weeks before the collection of baseline observations was begun. This initial period was instituted in order to allow the children to adapt to the observers' presence in the classroom.

TOKEN REINFORCEMENT PHASE. The following written instructions were given to the teacher and discussed with her. These instructions were used as the basis for the token reinforcement stage.

A. *Instructions for initial introduction of token program.*

1. Prior to the explanation of the token economy to the children, a list of rules should be written on the blackboard and left there while the program is in effect. (The rules worked out with the teacher were: *stay in seats, raise hand, quiet, desk clear, face front,* and *work hard.* For the art period for the third graders the rules were: *quiet, work hard,* and *be polite.*)
2. Explain to the children that they will be rated on how well they follow the rules from 1:00 to 2:30. Spiral notebooks

will be attached to their desks, and every rating period the teacher will put a number from 1 to 10 in their notebooks. The better a child follows the rules the higher the number he will receive.
3. By earning points in this way, the children will be able to win prizes. They must have a certain number of points in order to win a prize. Show the children the prizes and explain that 10 points earns a prize from this box (show an example) and 25 points earns a prize from this box. Do not let the children handle the prizes.
4. Emphasize that at all other times when the children are not being rated their behavior will not affect their rating during the afternoon period.
5. Explain to the fourth graders that their other teachers will rate them when they leave the classroom, and that they will have to bring back a slip with their number on it signed by their teacher. If they do not bring back this slip, they will not receive any points that day. Also explain that the other children in the art and music class will not be told about their point system.
6. Emphasize that they will not receive prizes every day, and that sometimes they will have to collect points over two or more days in order to obtain prizes. However, they will be told how long they have to work to earn a prize.

B. *General instructions for operation of token program.*
1. Each day before the rating period, go over the rules with the children. Point out that they can earn prizes, tell them how many points they must have to win different types of prizes, and then show them some of the prizes they can win.
2. When rating a child, point out the rules he followed in order to receive the points he did. "I'm giving you 8 points because . . . ," "I'm not giving you 10 points because. . . ." Also indicate what behaviors could be improved on to earn full points.
3. At all times, except when prizes are being shown to the class

or when the children are picking out the prizes they have earned, the prizes should be stored in a location where the children cannot reach them.
4. If the children mention certain types of prizes they would like to be able to earn or if they do not appear interested in any of the prizes available, please notify the investigator as soon as possible.
5. Record points on two pages. One will be picked up each day. Enter ratings from art and music teachers into the book also.
6. Except for the first day of the token program, prizes should be given out at the end of the school day. On the first day give out prizes after the third rating period.
7. The children will be rated from 1 to 10 on how well they follow the classroom rules and behave in class. Rules can be modified or changed, but if this is done, notify the class and put the change on the blackboard.
8. The value of the prize will be changed as the children are required to earn more points to win prizes. The number of points required will be indicated on the appropriate boxes.
9. A child should be very well behaved to earn the highest value prizes. Do not allow the children to try to talk you into giving them more points. Make a judgment and then explain that he earned only so many points, but he can earn more by behaving better.

Two values of prizes were used—one group in the 5¢ to 10¢ range, and one group in the 15¢ to 19¢ range. They included such things as candy, gliders, balls, pencils, and clay.

For third graders ratings were given after each 30 minute period. Since the fourth graders left for art or music during the second 30 minute period, the problem was initially handled by doubling the points earned in the first period and by having the art or music teacher give a rating for that period. After four days the system was changed so that both third and fourth graders were rated after two 40 minute periods. During the first four days prizes were distributed each day. After that they were distributed every other day. The number of points required to earn prizes was gradually increased from 10 to 30 for lower value prizes and 25 to 35 for higher value prizes.

The teacher used her own judgment in making ratings within the guidelines given above. She was informed of how the observers rated the children the first few days of the program, but no attempt was made to determine her ratings. In all other aspects of her behavior, the teacher was expected to continue as she had before.

BASELINE TWO. The token system was withdrawn for two weeks and baseline conditions reestablished. It was during this period that the teacher decided not to continue with the study.

Results

Reliability

During the afternoon observations, interobserver reliability for individual children for the thirteen day baseline period ranged from 64 to 98 percent agreement with an average of 80 percent. During the token period the interobserver reliability ranged from 69 to 100 percent with an average of 87 percent. For the second baseline, the range was 68 to 100 percent with an average of 82 percent. The reliabilities for morning observations ranged from 52 to 100 percent with an average of 85 percent.

Group Data

For all six children in the afternoon, the average percentage of deviant behavior during the baseline period was 54. During the token period the average decreased to 27.8 percent and then increased to 41.5 percent when the tokens were removed. The daily averages for the different periods have been plotted graphically in Figure 8-1. If fewer than four children were observed on any day, then that day was eliminated from the analysis. The single day that a substitute teacher was in the classroom was also eliminated. An analysis of variance, using the average percentage of deviant behavior for each child during each period, indicated

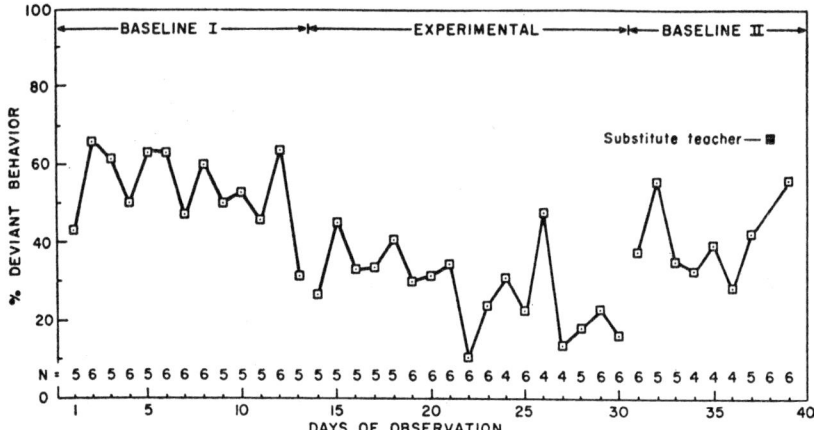

Figure 8-1. Percentage of deviant behavior as a function of experimental conditions for children observed during the afternoon.

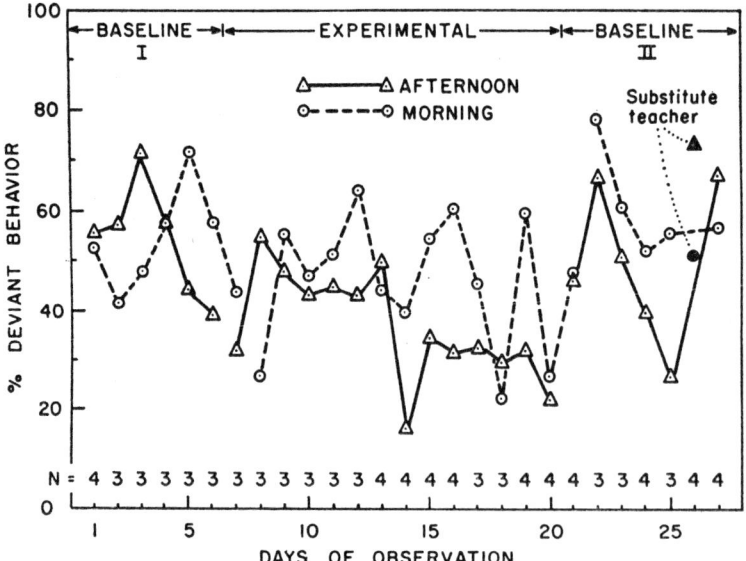

Figure 8-2. Percentage of deviant behavior as a function of experimental conditions for children observed during morning and afternoon.

that the effects of periods were significant beyond the .01 level ($F = 11.27, df = 2$).

The average daily percentage of deviant behavior for the four children observed both in the morning and afternoon is plotted graphically by days for the different periods for both the morning and afternoon observations (see Fig. 8-2). A child had to be observed in both the morning and afternoon for his percentage of deviant behavior to be included in the analyses, and if fewer than three children were observed on any day, then that day was eliminated from the analysis. The average percentage of deviant behavior for the first baseline period was 53.2 for morning and 54.3 for afternoon observations. For the token periods the percentages were 45.0 (A.M.) and 35.5 (P.M.); and for the second baseline they were 58.5 (A.M.) and 50.4 (P.M.). These data show little, if any, generalization of improved behavior from the afternoon period when the token system was in effect to the morning period when the token system was not in effect. No statistical tests were carried out on the generalization data because of wide individual variations in effect. The important results of the study are made clear by examination of the individual graphs.

Individual Data

The individual graphs show that four children (1 through 4, Fig. 8-3) improved considerably under the token system, and two showed at best occasional good days. No consistent individual gains occurred during the morning period when individual data were examined (these graphs are not presented). Of interest is the fact that children 4 and 6 had participated in the earlier program by O'Leary and Becker (1967). Child 6 rarely responded to the new program, and often would not even keep his point book on his desk.

Discussion

Although an average significant effect of the token program was demonstrated, it is quite clear from the individual graphs and the generalization measures that the program was only mar-

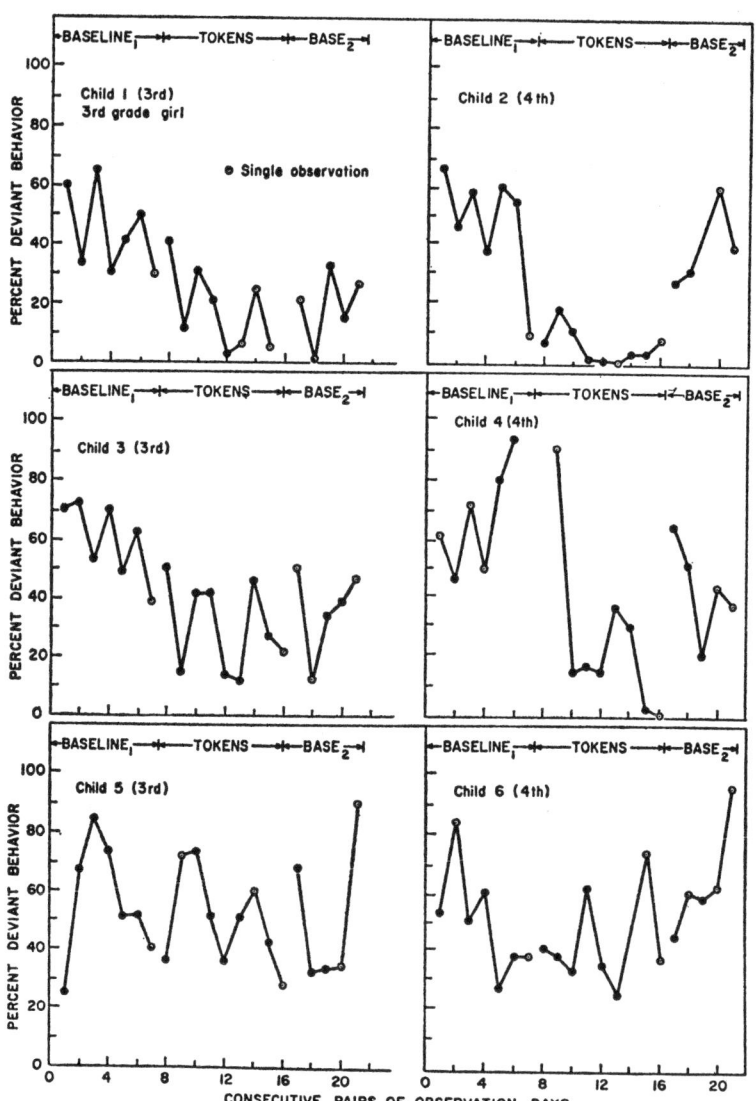

Figure 8-3. Percentage of deviant behavior for individual children based on afternoon observations.

ginally effective. Many interpretations are always possible when there is a failure to establish experimental control over behavior; however, a number of the findings when compared with those from the earlier study by O'Leary and Becker (1967) suggest some reasonable conclusions. The reader should first keep in mind that the formal token system was very similar to that used by O'Leary and Becker, including the shift to a two day delay in backup reinforcers after the first four days. The programs were carried out at similar times during the day, on similar children in adjustment classes. In the first study (O'Leary and Becker, 1967) there were more Negro children and the general level of deviant behavior was higher during baseline. The token system in the first study produced a dramatic shift from approximately 80 percent deviant behavior to under 10 percent, and it was effective for all children. Furthermore, although generalization measures were not taken, repeated reports by diverse observers indicated a dramatic change in the behavior of the children throughout the day. Some of the keys to the differences in findings include the following:

1. Tokens or points were given for meeting an absolute standard in the present study, rather than for improvement. A shaping procedure was not used by the teacher. Under these conditions, the two children who were considered by the teacher to be less troublesome to begin with (children 1 and 2) responded very well to the program. While these two children had an average percentage of deviant behavior during baseline approximating that of the other children, it was qualitatively different behavior. Their behaviors involved talking and turning around in their seats rather than fighting, making loud noises, and wandering around the room. It was easy for the teacher to give them high ratings and for them to respond to the reinforcement system. The children who could not as easily meet the standards set by the teacher could have been punished for improved behavior by receiving low point scores. The high degree of vari-

ability over days and between children is precisely what would be expected when an absolute standard is applied.

2. No attempt was made to have the teacher systematically apply differential social reinforcement in between the times when points were awarded or at other times during the day. This aspect of the earlier program was probably responsible for much of its effectiveness. Points which are awarded 30 or 40 minutes later are not enough to help a child learn more appropriate behaviors. With effective and continuous use of praise for good behaviors and ignoring of deviant behaviors, immediate consequences can be brought to bear on such behavior, especially when praise has been made important to the children through its pairing with tokens. The lack of generalization effects are most likely due to this difference in procedures. (We had hoped to clearly show this by introducing systematic social reinforcement in the next stage of the experiment.) Observations of the teacher throughout the day indicated that she would intermittently pay attention to deviant behaviors and would often ignore the children when they were behaving well. If paying attention is reinforcing and if ignoring amounts to an extinction condition, these teacher behaviors would be affecting the children in a way opposite to that desired.

3. The teacher in this study was not trained through a workshop in the systematic application of behavioral principles. Such training may be important in knowing how to shape behavior and how to effectively use differential social reinforcement.

4. Some initial difficulties were encountered in getting the fourth graders to respond to the program (children 2, 4, and 6, Fig. 8-3). They typically received high ratings (appropriately given) by their art and music teachers which made it less necessary for them to behave in the classroom to earn points. The point system was eventually changed so that good behavior in both periods was essential (in the

move to 30 points for a lower prize and 35 for a higher one).
5. Another potential problem was that during baseline the teacher considered the level of deviant behavior to be close to an acceptable level. She had a great capacity for tolerating disruptions in the class as long as they did not interfere with her work with an individual child. Also, in making judgments about following the rules, she was much more lenient than our judgment would deem appropriate. Her frame of reference would likely foster the reinforcement of deviant behaviors, as defined in the present study, and leave the level of improvement at a low level.

The authors titled this paper, "How to make a token system fail." In actuality, the system functioned as expected—as far as it went. The minimal token system employed was statistically effective and could not have been much more effective, if differential social reinforcement and shaping must be a central part of a workable system. The real failure in this experiment was the failure to give the teacher sufficient support and information to keep her working with the researchers so that subsequent phases of the study could demonstrate more definitively the importance of additional procedures. The behavior of the morning observers was a particular source of irritation for the teacher. Although instructed to fade into the background, two of them did not. Chewing and cracking gum, talking, and obviously watching the children were among their behaviors found irritating by the teacher. Her warnings were not responded to soon enough, although eventually one of the observers was fired. By then it was too late to save the study. There were other failures in the administration of the study which produced unnecessary irritations for the teacher, such as intruding on her evening and weekend time to discuss problems.

We explicitly point out these problems so that others may profit from our mistakes. Great care should be exercised in selecting and training observers, in providing guidelines for the supervisory staff, and in preparing the teacher for what is coming. While the teacher emphasized the role of the observer's behavior in her decision to stop the study, the study was not stopped until we had withdrawn the token system for about four days. Problem behavior as well as the concerns of the teacher had increased. Although the teacher agreed to let us finish the second baseline period, better preparation of the teacher on our part could have saved the study.

Implications

A token system is usually designed to make more usual social reinforcers effective for children and lead to an elimination of the token system. These objectives involve the use of a complex set of procedures. The findings of this study when contrasted with those from O'Leary and Becker (1967) should suggest to the reader who is interested in applying a token system some of the important procedures which may be missed or not thought important in looking at the literature on token systems. If the token system involves delays in giving tokens or points (to simplify the procedure for the teacher), it is probably very important to use differential social reinforcement at all times. Explicitly, this involves giving praise and privileges for improvement in behavior, and ignoring (rather than criticizing or distracting) children showing deviant behaviors—unless someone is being hurt. In the latter case, withdrawal of all social attention and loss of the opportunity to earn tokens by isolating the child (time out) is the procedure of choice. It is also important to use tokens and praise to shape improved behavior, so that all children can be affected by positive reinforcement. Catch the child being good. Focus on that aspect of behavior which is an improvement (e.g., in seat rather than out, even if not yet working) and reinforce it. Look for sequential steps toward improvement which can be successively reinforced (in seat, not turning and talking to neighbors, desk cleared of excess materials, paying attention, working, working diligently).

A token system is not a magical procedure to be applied in a mechanical way. It is simply one tool within a larger set of tools available to the teacher concerned with improving the behavior of children. The full set of equipment is needed to do the job right.

REFERENCES

Birnbrauer, J. S., Bijou, S. W., Wolf, M. M., and Kidder, J. D.: Programmed instruction in the classroom. In P. L. Ullman and L. Krasner (Eds.): *Case Studies in Behavior Modification.* New York, Holt, Rinehart and Winston, 1965, pp. 358-363.

Birnbrauer, J. S., and Lawler, J.: Token reinforcement for learning. *Ment Retard,* 2:275-279, 1964.

Birnbrauer, J. S., Wolf, M. M., Kidder, J. D., and Tague, C. E.: Classroom behavior of retarded pupils with token reinforcement. *J Exp Child Psychol,* 2:219-235, 1965.

O'Leary, K. D., and Becker, W. C.: Behavior modification of an adjustment class: A token reinforcement program. *Except Child,* 33:637-642, 1967.

SECTION III
PROMOTING ADAPTIVE BEHAVIORS AND DECREASING PROBLEMATIC BEHAVIOR

Chapter 9

THE REINFORCEMENT OF COOPERATION BETWEEN CHILDREN[1]

NATHAN H. AZRIN
OGDEN R. LINDSLEY

MOST METHODS for the development and experimental analysis of cooperation between humans require specific instructions concerning the cooperative relationship between the individual responses. Peters and Murphree have developed one of the most recent of these methods (1954). Skinner has suggested (1953), and shown with lower organisms (1952), that cooperation between individuals can be developed, maintained, and eliminated solely by manipulating the contingency between reinforcing stimuli and the cooperative response.

The advantages of eliminating instructions concerning cooperation are that (a) the initial acquisition of cooperation can be studied, (b) subjects (Ss) that learn by demonstration and instruction with difficulty (i.e., infants, certain classes of psychotics, and lower organisms) can be studied, and (c) no problems involving the effects of instructions upon the behavior of the Ss are involved.

Some more general advantages of operant conditioning techniques are (a) a more continuous record of the cooperative process is obtained, (b) extraneous environmental variables are minimized, and (c) relatively long periods of experimental observation are possible.

Problem

Can cooperation between children be developed, maintained, and eliminated solely by the presentation or nonpresentation of a single reinforcing stimulus, available to each member of the cooperative team, following each cooperative response?

---

1. *Journal of Abnormal and Social Psychology*, 52:100-102, 1956.

Cooperative Teams

Twenty children, seven to twelve years of age, were formed into ten cooperative teams of two children. The children in each team were matched as to age and sex. Seven teams were boys and three were girls.[2] Selection was made via the request, "Who wants to play a game?" The first two volunteers of the same age and sex were chosen for each team. The age given by the children was verified against available community center records. No information concerning the game was given during the selection. No teams were rejected.

Cooperative Response

Cooperation was assured by designing an apparatus that (a) could not be operated by one individual alone (assuring group behavior), and (b) demanded that one individual respond to the behavior of the other individual in order to produce reinforcement (assuring cooperation).

Procedure

The two children of each cooperative team were placed at opposite sides of a table with three holes and a stylus in front of each child (see Fig. 9-1). A wire screen down the center of the table prevented each child from manipulating the other child's stylus, which was on the other side of the table.

The following instructions were given: "This is a game. You can play the game any way you want to or do anything else that you want to do. This is how the game works: Put both sticks (styli) into all three of the holes." (This sentence was repeated until both styli had been placed in the three available holes.) "While you are in this room some of these" (the experimenter (E) held out several jelly beans) "will drop into this cup. You can eat them here if you want to or you can take them home with you." The instructions were then repeated without reply to

---

[2] We wish to thank the Harriet Tubman House and the South Bay Union of Boston, Mass., for providing the subjects and the use of their facilities.

Figure 9-1. Apparatus used for the reinforcement of cooperation between children.

any questions, after which E said: "I am leaving the room now; you can play any game that you want to while I am gone." Then E left the room until the end of the experimental session.

If the styli were placed in opposite holes within 0.04 seconds of each other (a cooperative response), a red light flashed on the table (conditioned reinforcing stimulus) and a single jelly bean (reinforcing stimulus) fell into the cup that was accessible to both children.[3] Cooperative responses were recorded on counters and a cumulative response recorder in an adjoining room.

Experimental Design

Each team was studied for one continuous experimental session divided into the following three consecutive periods without experimental interruption:

1. FIRST REINFORCEMENT PERIOD. Every cooperative response was reinforced for over 15 minutes. If the rate of response was not steady at this time, the reinforcement was continued until five minutes passed with no noticeable change in the rate of cooperation.

2. EXTINCTION PERIOD. The cooperative responses were not re-

---

[3] Skinner (1952) presented two reinforcing stimuli (one to each pigeon) following each cooperative response.

inforced for a period of at least 15 minutes and until a steady rate of response for at least five minutes was observed.

3. SECOND REINFORCEMENT PERIOD. The cooperative responses were again reinforced until at least three minutes of a stable rate occurred. This was done to determine whether a reduction in rate during the extinction period was due to extinction, satiation, or fatigue.

Results

All teams learned to cooperate without specific instructions in the first ten minutes of experimentation. Observation through a one-way vision screen disclosed that leader-follower relationships were developed and maintained in most cases. Almost immediately eight teams divided the candy in some manner. With two teams, one member at first took all the candy until the other member refused to cooperate. When verbal agreement was reached in these two teams, the members then cooperated and divided the candy. Most vocalization occurred during the initial acquisition period and throughout the extinction period. This vocalization was correlated with a higher variability in rate during these periods (see below).

N 10	*First three mins. of first reinf. period*	*Last three mins. of first reinf. period*	*Last three mins. of extinction period*	*Last three mins. of second reinf. period*
Median	5.5	17.5	1.5	17.5
Range	1–26	6–26	0–7	6–27

NUMBER OF COOPERATIVE RESPONSES PER MINUTE

Table 9-I. The Median and Range of the Number of Cooperative Responses per Minute for the Critical Experimental Periods.

Figure 9-2 contains cumulative records of the cooperative responses of the three teams with the highest, the median, and the lowest number of cooperative responses for the experimental

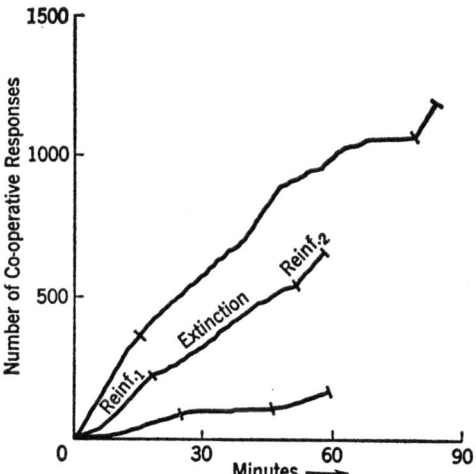

Figure 9-2. Cumulative response records for the teams with the highest, median, and lowest rates of cooperation.

session. These curves show a large difference in the rate of acquisition of cooperation. One team took almost ten minutes to acquire a high cooperative response rate. Stable rates of cooperation can be observed during the latter parts of the first reinforcement period. The gradual, rather than immediate, decline in cooperation during extinction suggests an orderly extinction of cooperative behavior as is found with individual extinction curves. In all cases the variability of rate was greater during extinction than during reinforcement. Skinner has found this increased variability in rate during extinction with lower organisms and has described it as emotional behavior (1953, p. 69). The high rate of response following the first reinforcement of the second reinforcement period shows that reacquisition is almost immediate.

Table 9-1 contains a quantification of the records for statistical analysis. The median and range of the number of cooperative responses per minute for all ten teams during the critical periods of the experiment are given. The number of cooperative responses per minute for the first three minutes of the first reinforcement period was significantly lower than the rate during the last three minutes of the first reinforcement period ($p <$

.02).[4] This shows that the rate of cooperation was significantly lower during initial acquisition than during maintenance of cooperation. The number of cooperative responses per minute during the last three minutes of extinction was significantly lower than the rate during the last three minutes of the first reinforcement period ($p < .001$). This shows that the removal of reinforcement during extinction significantly lowered the rate of cooperation between these children.

The number of cooperative responses per minute during the last three minutes of the second reinforcement period was significantly above the rate during the last three minutes of the extinction period ($p < .001$). This shows that the rate of cooperation was significantly increased during the second reinforcement period and that the drop in rate during extinction was due to the absence of the reinforcing stimulus rather than satiation or fatigue. The rates of cooperation during the second reinforcement period and the last three minutes of the first reinforcement period were not significantly different and show that the rate was almost immediately restored to its preextinction value upon the presentation of reinforcement for the second time. The rate of cooperative responding during the first three minutes of the second reinforcement period was significantly higher than during the first three minutes of the first reinforcement period ($p < .02$). This again shows that the reacquisition of cooperation was not gradual, as was initial acquisition, but occurred almost immediately.

Conclusions

Operant conditioning techniques can be used to develop, maintain, and eliminate cooperation between children without the use of specific instructions concerning cooperation. The rate of a cooperative response changes in much the same way as a function of single reinforcements as does an individual response. In the reinforcement of cooperative responses, a reinforcing stimulus need not be delivered to each member of the

---

[4] Wilcoxon's nonparametric T for paired associates was used in all statistical treatments (1949).

cooperative team following each cooperative response. The presentation of a single reinforcing stimulus, available to each member of the cooperative team, is sufficient to increase the rate of cooperation. The cooperative response gradually increases in frequency when reinforced and gradually decreases in frequency when no longer reinforced (extinction). Cooperative responses are maintained at a stable rate during reinforcement but occur in sporadic bursts during extinction. Reinforcement following extinction results in an almost immediate restoration of the rate of cooperation to its preextinction value.

REFERENCES

Peters, H. N., and Murphree, O. D.: A cooperative multiple-choice apparatus. *Science, 119:*189-191, 1954.

Skinner, B. F.: *Science and Human Behavior.* New York, Macmillan, 1953.

———: Classroom demonstration. Personal communication, 1952.

Wilcoxon, F.: *Some Rapid Approximate Statistical Procedures.* New York, American Cyanamid Co., 1949.

Chapter 10

THE ALTERATION OF BEHAVIOR IN A SPECIAL CLASSROOM SITUATION

ELAINE H. ZIMMERMAN
J. ZIMMERMAN

THE CLASSROOM BEHAVIOR of two emotionally disturbed boys was altered by arranging and manipulating its consequences.

The boys, in-patients in a residential treatment center (LaRue D. Carter Memorial Hospital), attended the first author's English class daily for one hour as part of an educational therapy program. There were three boys in the class, each receiving individual attention.

Case I

Subject 1 (S-1) was 11 years old. He appeared to have no organic disorder and was of normal intelligence. In early class sessions, whenever S-1 was called upon to spell a word which had previously been studied and drilled, he would pause for several seconds, screw up his face, and mutter letters unrelated to the word. Following this, the instructor (E) consistently asked him to sound out the word, often giving him the first letter and other cues, encouraging him to spell the word correctly. Only after E had spent considerable time and attention would the boy emit a correct response. The procedure was inefficient and profitless for improving the boy's spelling behavior. In fact, it may have been maintaining the undesirable pattern, since over the first 10 or 15 class sessions, consistently more time and attention were required of E to obtain a correct spelling response.

While "studying" in class, S-1 would obtain sheets of paper, wrinkle them, and throw them away, laughing as he caught E's eye or that of one of the other students.

Reprinted with permission from the *Journal of the Experimental Analysis of Behavior*, 1962, Vol. 5, No. 1, 59-60, Copyright 1962 by the Society for the Experimental Analysis of Behavior, Inc., and with the permission of the authors.

The Change in Approach

After several weeks in class, S-1 was quizzed via paper-and-pencil test on a lesson based on ten spelling words, with time alloted for study and review. He handed in a paper with a muddled combination of barely legible letters. Immediately, E asked him to go to the blackboard. Her instructions were simply: "We will now have a quiz. I will read a word and you will spell it correctly on the board." She read the first word, and the subject misspelled it ten or more times on the board. During this time, E sat at her desk, ignoring S-1, apparently busy reading or writing. Each time S-1 misspelled the word, he glanced at E; but she did not respond. The boy erased the word and tried again, several times repeating "I can't spell it," or "I can't remember how," etc. Although ignored, the boy made no effort to sit down or leave the room. After approximately ten minutes, he spelled the word correctly; E looked up at him immediately, smiled, and said, "Good, now we can go on." She read a second word; and after a similar series of errors and verbal responses, S-1 spelled the word correctly. With each successive word (through 10 words), the number of inappropriate (unreinforced) responses decreased, as did the latency of the correct response. At the end of the quiz, E took the boy's spelling chart, wrote an "A" on it, and praised him. She then asked the subject to help her color some Easter baskets. They sat down together, and chatted and worked.

Thereafter, attention in the form of smiling, chatting, and physical proximity was given only immediately after the emission of desired classroom behavior or some approximation of it in the desired direction. Undesirable behavior was consistently ignored. As a result of a month of this treatment, the frequency of bizarre spelling responses and other undesirable responses declined to a level close to zero per class session. At the conclusion of this study, the boy was working more efficiently, and was making adequate academic progress.

Case II

Subject S-2 was an 11-year-old boy, who, like S-1, had no apparent organic disorder and was also of normal intelligence. In initial class Sessions, S-2 emitted behavior considered undesirable in the classroom context with high frequency. He displayed temper tantrums (kicking, screaming, etc.), spoke baby-talk, and incessantly made irrelevant comments or posed irrelevant questions.

Several times a week, attendants dragged this boy down the hall to one of his classes as the boy screamed and buckled his knees. On several of these occasions, the boy threw himself on the floor in front of a classroom door. A crowd of staff members inevitably gathered around him. The group usually watched and commented as the boy sat or lay on the floor, kicking and screaming. Some members of the group hypothesized that such behavior seemed to appear after the boy was teased or frustrated in some way. However, the only observable in the situation was the consistent consequence of the behavior in terms of the formation of a group of staff members around the boy.

Observing one such situation which occurred before E's class, E asked the attendant to put the boy in the classroom at his desk and to leave the room. Then E closed the door. The boy sat at his desk, kicking and screaming; E proceeded to her desk and worked there, ignoring S-2. After two or three minutes, the boy, crying softly, looked up at E. Then E announced that she would be ready to work with him as soon as he indicated that he was ready to work. He continued to cry and scream with diminishing loudness for the next four or five minutes. Finally, he lifted his head and stated that he was ready. Immediately, E looked up at him, smiled, went to his desk, and said, "Good, now let's get to work." The boy worked quietly and cooperatively with E for the remainder of the class period.

The Handling of Tantrums, Irrelevant Verbal Behavior, and Baby-talk

Each time a tantrum occurred, E consistently ignored S-2. When tantrum behavior was terminated, E conversed with the boy, placed herself in his proximity, or initiated an activity which was appealing to him. After several weeks, class tantrums disappeared entirely. Because the consequence of tantrum behavior varied in other situations, no generalization to situations outside the classroom has been observed.

Furthermore the frequency of irrelevant verbal behavior and of baby-talk declined almost to the point of elimination following the procedure of withholding attention after the emission of such behavior. On the other hand, when S-2 worked quietly or emitted desirable classroom behavior, E addressed him cordially and permitted some verbal interchange for several seconds. When a lesson was being presented to the class at large and S-2 listened attentively, E reinforced him by asking him a question he could answer or by looking at him, smiling at him, etc. The reinforcement was delivered intermittently rather than continuously because: (a) reinforcing every desired response of one student was impossible since E's time was parcelled out among several students; and (b) intermittent reinforcement would probably be more effective than continuous reinforcement in terms of later resistance of the desired behavior to extinction. Like S-1, at the conclusion of the study this boy was working more efficiently in class and was making good progress. His speech was more generally characterized by relevancy and maturity.

Chapter 11

THE USE OF "EMOTIVE IMAGERY" IN THE TREATMENT OF CHILDREN'S PHOBIAS

ARNOLD A. LAZARUS
ARNOLD ABRAMOVITZ

SOME OF THE EARLIEST objective approaches to the removal of specific anxieties and fears in children were based on the fact that neurotic (learned, unadaptive) responses can be eliminated by the repeated and simultaneous evocation of stronger incompatible responses. An early and well-known example of this approach was the experiment of Jones (1924) in which a child's fear of rabbits was gradually eliminated by introducing a "pleasant stimulus" i.e., *food* (thus evoking the anxiety-inhibiting response of eating) in the presence of the rabbit. The general method of "gradual habituation" was advocated by Jersild and Homes (1935) as being superior to all others in the elimination of children's fears. This rationale was crystallized in Wolpe's (1958) formulation of the Reciprocal Inhibition Principle, which deserves the closest possible study:

> If a response antagonistic to anxiety can be made to occur in the presence of anxiety-evoking stimuli so that it is accompanied by a complete or partial suppression of the anxiety responses, the bond between these stimuli and the anxiety responses will be weakened.

A crucial issue in the application of this principle is the choice of a clinically suitable anxiety-inhibiting response. The most widely-used method has been that of "systematic desensitization" (Wolpe, 1961) which may be described as gradual habituation to the imagined stimulus through the anxiety-inhibiting response of *relaxation*. Lazarus (1960) reported several successful pediatric applications of this procedure, using both feeding and relaxation. It was subsequently found, however, that neither feeding nor relaxation was feasible in certain cases. Feeding has obvious disadvantages in routine therapy, while training in relaxation is often both time-consuming and difficult or impossible to achieve with certain children. The possibility of inducing anxiety-inhibiting *emotive* images, without specific training in relaxation, was then explored, and the results of our preliminary investigation form the subject of this paper.

Our use of the term "emotive imagery" requires clarification. In the present clinical context, it refers to those classes of imagery which are assumed to arouse feelings of self-assertion, pride, affection, mirth, and similar anxiety-inhibiting responses.

The technique which was finally evolved can be described in the following steps:

(a) As in the usual method of systematic desensitization, the range, intensity, and circumstances of the patient's fears are ascertained, and a graduated hierarchy is drawn up, from the most feared to the least feared situation.

(b) By sympathetic conversation and inquiry, the clinician establishes the nature of the child's hero-images—usually derived from radio, cinema, fiction, or his own imagination—and the wish-fulfillments and identifications which accompany them.

(c) The child is then asked to close his eyes and told to imagine a sequence of events which is close enough to his everyday life to be credible, but within which is woven a story concerning his favorite hero or *alter ego*.

(d) If this is done with reasonable skill and empathy, it is possible to arouse to the necessary pitch the child's affective reactions. (In some cases this may be recognized by small changes in facial expression, breathing, muscle tension, etc.)

(e) When the clinician judges that these emotions have been maximally aroused, he introduces, as a natural part of the narrative, the lowest item in the hierarchy. Immediately afterwards he says: "If you feel afraid (or unhappy, or uncomfortable) just raise your finger." If anxiety is indicated, the phobic stimulus is "withdrawn" from the narrative and the child's anxiety-inhibiting emotions are again aroused. The procedure is then repeated as in ordinary systematic desensitization, until the highest item in the hierarchy is tolerated without distress.

The use of this procedure is illustrated in the following cases:

Case I

Stanley M., aged 14, suffered from an intense fear of dogs, of 2½ to 3 years duration. He would take two buses on a roundabout route to school rather than risk exposure to dogs on a direct 300-yard walk. He was a rather dull (I.Q. 93), sluggish person, very large for his age, trying to be cooperative, but sadly unresponsive—especially to attempts at training in relaxation. In his desire to please, he would state that he had been perfectly relaxed even though he had betrayed himself by his intense fidgetiness. Training in relaxation was eventually abandoned, and an attempt was made to establish the nature of his aspirations and goals. By dint of much questioning and after following many false trails because of his inarticulateness, a topic was eventually tracked down that was absorbing enough to form the subject of his fantasies, namely racing motorcars. He had a burning ambition to own a certain Alfa Romeo sports car and race it at the Indianapolis "500" event. Emotive imagery was induced as follows: "Close your eyes. I want you to imagine, clearly and vividly, that your wish has come true. The Alfa Romeo is now in your possession. It is your car. It is standing in the street outside your block. You are looking at it now. Notice the beautiful, sleek lines. You decide to go for a drive with some friends of yours. You sit down at the wheel, and you feel a thrill of pride as you realize that you own this magnificent machine. You start up and listen to the wonderful roar of the exhaust. You let the clutch in and the car streaks off. . . . You are out in a clear open road now; the car is performing like a pedigree; the speedometer is climbing into the nineties; you have a wonderful feeling of being in perfect control; you look at the trees whizzing by and you see a little dog standing next to one of them—if you feel any anxiety, just raise your finger, etc." An item fairly high up on the hierarchy: "You stop at a café in a little town and dozens of people crowd around to look enviously at this magnificent car and its lucky owner; you swell with pride; and at this moment a large boxer comes up and sniffs at your heels—If you feel any anxiety, etc."

After three sessions using this method he reported a marked improvement in his reaction to dogs. He was given a few field assignments during the next two sessions, after which therapy was terminated. Twelve months later, reports both from the patient and his relatives indicated that there was no longer any trace of his former phobia.

Case II

A ten-year-old boy was referred for treatment because his excessive fear of the dark exposed him to ridicule from his 12-year-old brother and imposed severe restrictions on his parents' social activities. The lad became acutely anxious whenever his parents went visiting at night and even when they remained at home he refused to enter any darkened room unaccompanied. He insisted on sharing a room with his brother and made constant use of a night light next to his bed. He was especially afraid of remaining alone in the bathroom and only used it if a member of the household stayed there with him. On questioning, the child stated that he was not anxious during the day but that he invariably became tense and afraid towards sunset.

His fears seemed to have originated a year or so previously when he saw a frightening film, and shortly thereafter was warned by his maternal grandmother (who lived with the family) to keep away from all doors and windows at night as burglars and kidnappers were on the prowl.

A previous therapist had embarked on a program of counseling with the parents and play-therapy with the child. While some important areas of interpersonal friction were apparently ameliorated, the child's phobic responses remained unchanged. Training in "emotive imagery" eliminated his repertoire of fears in three sessions.

The initial interview (90 minutes) was devoted to psychometric testing and the development of rapport. The test revealed a superior level of intelligence (I.Q. 135) with definite evidence of anxiety and insecurity. He responded well to praise and encouragement throughout the test situation. Approximately 30 minutes were devoted to a general discussion of the child's interests and activities, which was also calculated to win his confidence. Towards the end of this interview, the child's passion for two radio serials, "Superman" and "Captain Silver" had emerged.

A week later, the child was seen again. In addition to his usual fears he had been troubled by nightmares. Also, a quarterly school report had commented on a deterioration in his schoolwork. Emotive imagery was then introduced. The child was asked to imagine that Superman and Captain Silver had joined forces and had appointed him their agent. After a brief discussion concerning the topography of his house he was given his first assignment. The therapist said, "Now I want you to close your eyes and imagine that you are sitting in the dining room with your mother and father. It is night time. Suddenly, you receive a signal on the wrist radio that Superman has given you. You quickly run into the lounge because your mission must be kept a secret. There is only a little light coming into the lounge from the passage. Now pretend that you are all alone in the lounge waiting for Superman and Captain Silver to visit you. Think about this very clearly. If the idea makes you feel afraid, lift up your right hand."

An ongoing scene was terminated as soon as any anxiety was indicated. When an image aroused anxiety, it would either be represented in a more challengingly assertive manner, or it would be altered slightly so as to prove less objectively threatening.

At the end of the third session, the child was able to picture himself alone in his bathroom with all the lights turned off, awaiting a communication from Superman.

Apart from ridding the child of his specific phobia, the effect of this treatment appeared to have diverse and positive implications on many facets of his personality. His schoolwork improved immeasurably and many former manifestations of insecurity were no longer apparent. A follow-up after eleven months revealed that he had maintained his gains and was, to quote his mother, "a completely different child."

Case III

An eight-year-old girl was referred for treatment because of persistent nocturnal enuresis and a fear of going to school. Her fear of the school situation was apparently engendered by a series of emotional upsets in class. In order to avoid going to school, the child resorted to a variety of devices including temper tantrums, alleged pains and illnesses, and on one occasion she was caught playing truant and intemperately upbraided by her father. Professional assistance was finally sought when it was found that her younger sister was evincing the same behavior.

When the routine psychological investigations had been completed, emotive imagery was introduced with the aid of an Enid Blyton character, Noddy, who provided a hierarchy of assertive challenges centered around the school situation. The essence of this procedure was to create imagined situations where Noddy played the role of a truant and responded fearfully to the school setting. The patient would then protect him, either by active reassurance or by "setting a good example."

Only four sessions were required to eliminate her school-going phobia. Her enuresis, which had received no specific therapeutic attention, was far less frequent and disappeared entirely within two months. The child has continued to improve despite some additional upsets at the hands of an unsympathetic teacher.

Discussion

The technique of "emotive imagery" has been applied to nine phobic children whose ages ranged from seven to fourteen years. Seven children recovered in a mean of only 3.3 sessions. The method failed with one child who refused to cooperate and later revealed widespread areas of disturbance which required broader therapeutic handling. The other failure was a phobic child with a history of encephalitis. He was unable to concentrate on the emotive images and could not enter into the spirit of the "game."

Of the seven patients who recovered, two had previously undergone treatment at the hands of different therapists. Two others had been treated by the same therapist (A.A.L.) using reassurance, relaxation and "environmental manipulation." In none of these four cases was there any appreciable remission of the phobic symptoms until the present methods were applied. In every instance where the method was used, improvement occurred contemporaneously with treatment.

Follow-up inquiries were usually conducted by means of home-visits, interviews and telephone conversations both with the child and his immediate associates. These revealed that in no case was there symptom substitution of any obvious kind and that in fact, favorable response generalization had occurred in some instances.

It has been suggested that these results may be due to the therapist's enthusiasm for the method. (Does this imply that other therapists are unenthusiastic about *their* methods?) Certainly, the nature of the procedure is such that it cannot be coldly and dispassionately applied. A warm rapport with the child and a close understanding of his wish-fulfillments and identifications are essential. But our claim is that although warmth and acceptance are necessary in any psychotherapeutic undertaking, they are usually not *sufficient*. Over and above such nonspecific anxiety-inhibiting factors, this technique, in common with other reciprocal inhibition methods, provides a clearly defined therapeutic tool which is claimed to have *specific* effects.

Encouraging as these preliminary experiences have been, it is not claimed that they are, as yet, anything more than suggestive evidence of the efficacy of the method. Until properly controlled studies are performed, no general inference can be drawn. It is evident, too, that our loose *ad hoc* term "emotive imagery," reflects a basic lack of theoretical systematization in the field of the emotions. In her review of experimental data on autonomic functions, Martin (1960) deplores the paucity of replicated studies, the unreliability of the measures used, and the lack of operational definitions of qualitatively labelled emotions. The varieties of emotion we have included under the blanket term "emotive imagery" and our simple conjecture of anxiety-inhibiting properties for all of them is an example of the *a priori* assumptions one is forced to make in view of the absence of firm empirical data and adequately formulated theory. It is hoped that our demonstration of the clinical value of these techniques will help to focus attention on an unaccountably neglected area of study, but one which lies at the core of experimental clinical psychology.

Summary

A Reciprocal Inhibition (Wolpe, 1958) technique for the treatment of children's phobias is presented which consists essentially of an adaptation of Wolpe's method of "systematic desensitization" (1961). Instead of inducing muscular relaxation as the anxiety-inhibiting response, certain emotion-arousing situations are presented to the child's imagination. The emotions induced are assumed, like relaxation, to have autonomic effects which are incompatible with anxiety. This technique, which the authors have provisionally labelled "emotive imagery" was applied to nine phobic children whose ages ranged from seven to fourteen years. Seven children recovered in a mean of 3.3 sessions and follow-up inquiries up to 12 months later revealed no relapses or symptom substitution. An outstanding feature of this pediatric technique is the extraordinary rapidity with which remission occurs.

REFERENCES

Jersild, A. T., and Holmes, F. B.: Methods of overcoming children's fears. *J Psychol*, 1:75-104, 1935.

Jones, M. C.: Elimination of children's fears. *J Exp Psychol*, 7:382-390, 1924.

Lazarus, A. A.: The elimination of children's phobias by deconditioning. In *Behavior Therapy and the Neuroses*. H. J. Eysenck (Ed.). Oxford, Pergamon Press, 1960.

Martin, I.: Somatic reactivity. In *Handbook of Abnormal Psychology*. H. J. Eysenck (Ed.). London, Pitman Medical Publishing Co. Ltd., 1960.

Wolpe, J.: *Psychotherapy by Reciprocal Inhibition*. Stanford, Stanford Univ. Press and Witwatersrand Univ. Press.

———: The systematic desensitization treatment of neuroses. *J Nerv Ment Dis*, 132:189-203, 1961.

Chapter 12

CLASSICAL AND OPERANT FACTORS IN THE TREATMENT OF A SCHOOL PHOBIA[1]

ARNOLD A. LAZARUS[2]
GERALD C. DAVISON
DAVID A. POLEFKA

ALTHOUGH THE FORMAL application of "learning theory" to clinical problems is widespread, the literature on this topic reflects a basic cleavage. Wolpe (1958) and Eysenck (1960) typify the use of the classical conditioning paradigm in the treatment of neurotic disorders, while Lindsley and Skinner (1954), King, Merrell, Lovinger, and Denny (1957), and Ferster (1961) exemplify the use of operant conditioning in the treatment of psychotic behavior. On the assumption that both "operants" and "respondents" enter into all therapeutic processes, the writers hypothesized that the deliberate and strategic use of both classical and operant conditioning procedures would have greater therapeutic effect than exclusive reliance on techniques derived from either procedure alone. The therapeutic utility of this rationale became obvious in the treatment of a severely disturbed (nonpsychotic) school-phobic child.

Strategy in "behavior therapy" consists essentially of introducing reinforcement contingencies that encourage the emergence of nondeviant response patterns. This may be achieved by pairing the reinforcer with a *stimulus* (as is the case in classical conditioning) and/or by making the reinforcer contingent upon a *response* (as is the case in operant conditioning). Apart from Patterson's (1965) successful application of predominantly operant techniques to a school-phobic child, the treatment of chil-

---

[1] Reprints may be obtained by writing to the second author at Stanford University.

[2] Now at the Witwatersrand University Medical School, Johannesburg, South Africa.

dren's phobias by conditioning methods has hitherto relied almost exclusively on the classical paradigm (Bentler, 1962; Jones, 1924; Lazarus, 1960; Lazarus and Abramovitz, 1962; Lazarus and Rachman, 1957; Wolpe, 1958). It could be argued, however, that some of the above-named investigators made inadvertent use of the operant rubric. In a case alluded to by Lazarus and Abramovitz (1962) for instance, a child with "widespread areas of disturbance" failed to benefit from counterconditioning therapy but required "broader therapeutic handling." The therapeutic mainstay in this instance actually amounted to persuading the parents to alter certain of their actions which were sustaining their child's deviant responses (i.e., an operant strategy). The reapplication of counterconditioning techniques then effected a rapid recovery. The present paper is an endeavor to illustrate how the deliberate (rather than inadvertent) use of these two theoretical models are crucial phases throughout treatment proved therapeutically expeditious.

Case Study

History of the Problem

When he was referred for therapy Paul, age 9, had been absent from school for three weeks. The summer vacation had ended six weeks previously, and on entering the fourth grade, Paul avoided the classroom situation. He was often found hiding in the cloakroom, and subsequently began spending less time at school each day. Thereafter, neither threats, bribes, nor punishments could induce him to reenter school.

Paul's history revealed a series of similar episodes. During his first day of kindergarten he succeeded in climbing over an extremely high wall and fled home. His first grade teacher considered him to be "disturbed." Serious difficulties regarding school attendance were first exhibited when Paul entered the second grade of a parochial school. It was alleged that the second grade teacher who, according to Paul, "looked like a witch," generally intimidated the children and was very free with physical punishment.[3] Paul retrospectively informed his parents that he felt as

---

[3] Vehement complaints from many parents finally led to the dismissal of this teacher.

though "the devil was in the classroom." At this stage he became progressively more reluctant to enter the school and finally refused entirely. A psychiatrist was consulted and is reported to have advised the parents to use coercion, whereupon Paul was literally dragged screaming to school by a truant officer. Paul was especially bitter about his experience with the psychiatrist. "All we did was talk and then the truant officer came." In the third grade, Paul was transferred to the neighborhood public school where he spent a trouble free year at the hands of an exceedingly kind teacher.

Family History

Paul was the fourth of eight children, the first boy in a devout, orthodox Roman Catholic family. His sisters were aged 14, 13, 11, 7, and 6 years, respectively; his two brothers were 8 and 2½ years old. The father was a moody, anxiously ambitious electronics engineer who had insight into the fact that his subjective occupational insecurities intruded into the home. A harsh disciplinarian—"I run a tight ship"—he impulsively meted out punishment for any act which deviated even slightly from his perfectionistic standards. He found it significant that Paul, of all the children, was particularly sensitive to his moods, and described himself as being "especially close to Paul" while commenting that "he rarely tells me things." In his desire to protect his family from everyday hazards he was inclined to emphasize extreme consequences: "Don't touch that fluorescent bulb, son; there's poison in it and it will kill you!"

The mother, although openly affectionate and less rigid and demanding than her husband, took pains to respond towards her eight children in an unbiased fashion. She stressed, however, that "Paul touches my nerve center," and stated that they frequently quarreled in the father's absence. She had always found Paul "less cuddlesome" than his siblings. When he was two years old, she would lock him out of the house, "so as to develop his independence." It is significant to note that this occurred immediately following the birth of his first brother. In general, she was inclined to be inconsistent when administering rewards and punishment. Psychometric testing suggested that Paul was uncertain whether a given response would meet with criticism and rejection or kind attention from his mother. It was nevertheless evident that Paul was eager to receive a greater share of his mother's highly-rationed time.

The lad himself was somewhat small and frail looking. Although reticent, essentially aloof and somewhat withdrawn, he was capable of unexpected vigor and self-assertion when he chose to participate in sporting activities. From the outset, the therapists noted his labile and expressive reactions to all stressful stimuli. The extent of his subjective discomfort was easily gauged by clearly discernible responses. As the magnitude of anxiety increased, there was a concomitant progression of overt signs—increased reticence, a postural stoop, a general constriction of movement, tearfilled eyes, mild trembling, pronounced blanching, culminating in sobbing and immobility. As will be shown below, these emotional indices were crucial in selecting appropriate therapeutic strategies.

A series of specific traumatic events commenced with his near-drowning when five years old. Towards the end of his third grade, he underwent a serious appendectomy with critical complications, which was followed by painful postoperative experiences in a doctor's consulting room. During one of these examinations, as Paul bitterly recounted, he had been left alone by his parents. Shortly after his recovery from surgery, he witnessed a drowning which upset him considerably. Following his entry into the fourth grade, the sudden death of a 12-year-old girl, who had been a close friend of his elder sister, profoundly affected the entire family. It is also noteworthy that Paul's father experienced personal stress in his work situation during the child's turbulent second grade, as well as immediately preceding fourth grade. Finally, Paul seemed to have been intimidated by a warning from his eldest sister that fourth grade school work was particularly difficult.

Therapeutic Procedure

After the initial interview, it was evident that Paul's school phobia was the most disruptive response pattern of a generally bewildered and intimidated child. Although subsequent interviews revealed the plethora of familial tensions, situational crises, and specific traumatic events outlined above, the initial therapeutic objective was to reinstate normal school attendance. Nevertheless it was clearly apparent that the home situation in general, and more particularly, specific examples of parental mishandling would ultimately require therapeutic intervention.

The application of numerous techniques in the consulting room (e.g., systematic desensitization[4]) was abandoned because of the child's inarticulateness and acquiescent response tendency. It was obvious that his verbal reports were aimed at eliciting approval rather than describing his true feelings. Desensitization *in vivo* was therefore employed as the principal therapeutic strategy.

The school was situated two and one-half blocks away from the home. The routine was for Paul to leave for school at 8:30 A.M. in order to arrive by 8:40. The first recess was from 10:00 10:30; lunch break from 12:00-1:00; and classes ended at 3:30 P.M. At the time when therapy was initiated, the boy was extremely surly and dejected in the mornings (as reported by the parents), refused breakfast, rarely dressed himself, and became noticeably more fearful toward 8:30. Parental attempts at reassurance, coaxing, or coercion elicited only sobbing and further withdrawal.

Accordingly, the boy was exposed to the following increasingly difficult steps along the main dimensions of his school phobia:
1. On a Sunday afternoon, accompanied by the therapists, he walked from his house to the school. The therapists were able to allay Paul's anxiety by means of distraction and humor, so that his initial exposure was relatively pleasant.

---

[4] Systematic desensitization entails the presentation of carefully graded situations, which are subjectively noxious, to the imagination of a deeply relaxed patient until the most personally distressing events no longer evoke any anxiety (see Wolpe, 1961).

2. On the next two days at 8:30 A.M., accompanied by one of the therapists, he walked from his house into the schoolyard. Again, Paul's feelings of anxiety were reduced by means of coaxing, encouragement, relaxation, and the use of "emotive imagery" (i.e., the deliberate picturing of subjectively pleasant images such as Christmas and a visit to Disneyland, while relating them to the school situation; see Lazarus and Abramovitz, 1962). Approximately fifteen minutes were spent roaming around the school grounds, after which Paul returned home.
3. After school was over for the day, the therapist was able to persuade the boy to enter the classroom and sit down at his desk. Part of the normal school routine was then playfully enacted.
4. On the following three mornings, the therapist accompanied the boy into the classroom with the other children. They chatted with the teacher, and left immediately after the opening exercises.
5. A week after beginning this program, Paul spent the entire morning in class. The therapist sat in the classroom and smiled approvingly at Paul whenever he interacted with his classmates or the teacher. After eating his lunch he participated in an active ball game, and returned to his house with the therapist at 12:30. (Since parent-teacher conferences were held during that entire week, afternoon classes were discontinued.)
6. Two days later when Paul and the therapist arrived at school, the boy lined up with the other children and allowed the therapist to wait for him inside the classroom. This was the first time that Paul had not insisted on having the therapist in constant view.
7. Thereafter, the therapist sat in the school library adjoining the classroom.
8. It was then agreed that the therapist would leave at 2:30 P.M. while Paul remained for the last hour of school.
9. On the following day, Paul remained alone at school from 1:45 P.M. until 2:45 P.M. (Earlier that day, the ther-

apist had unsuccessfully attempted to leave the boy alone from 10 until noon.)

10. Instead of fetching the boy at his home, the therapist arranged to meet him at the school gate at 8:30 A.M. Paul also agreed to remain alone at school from 10:45 A.M. until noon provided that the therapist return to eat lunch with him. At 1:45 P.M. the therapist left again with the promise that if the boy remained until school ended (3:30 P.M.) he would visit Paul that evening and play the guitar for him.
11. Occasional setbacks made it necessary to instruct the lad's mother not to allow the boy into the house during school hours. In addition, the teacher was asked to provide special jobs for the boy so as to increase his active participation and make school more attractive.
12. The family doctor was asked to prescribe a mild tranquilizer for the boy to take on awakening so as to reduce his anticipatory anxieties.
13. After meeting the boy in the mornings, the therapist gradually left him alone at school for progressively longer periods of time. After six days of this procedure, the therapist was able to leave at 10 A.M.
14. The boy was assured that the therapist would be in the faculty room until 10 A.M., if needed. Thus, he came to school knowing the therapist was present, but not actually seeing him.
15. With Paul's consent the therapist arrived at school shortly *after* the boy entered the classroom at 8:40 A.M.
16. School attendance independent of the therapist's presence was achieved by means of specific rewards (a comic book, and variously colored tokens which would eventually procure a baseball glove) contingent upon his entering school and remaining there alone. He was at liberty to telephone the therapist in the morning if he wanted him at school, in which event he would forfeit his rewards for that day.
17. Since the therapist's presence seemed to have at least as much reward value as the comic books and tokens, it was necessary to enlist the mother's cooperation to effect the

therapist's final withdrawal. The overall diminution of the boy's anxieties, together with general gains which had accrued to his home situation, made it therapeutically feasible for the mother to emphasize the fact that school attendance was compulsory, and that social agencies beyond the control of both therapists and parents would enforce this requirement eventually.
18. Approximately three weeks later, Paul had accumulated enough tokens to procure his baseball glove. He then agreed with his parents that rewards of this kind were no longer necessary.

Theoretical Implications

It should not be inferred that Paul's improvement followed a smooth monotonic progression. Numerous setbacks of varying degrees of severity occurred throughout the entire treatment program, which extended over 4½ months. These episodes were differently handled depending upon the therapist's assessment of the child's anxiety at that time, and his judgment of the degree to which the boy had mastered the preceding therapeutic steps.

It became apparent that the school phobia was comprised of two separate factors: (a) avoidance behavior motivated by intense fear of the school situation, and (b) avoidance behavior maintained by various secondary reinforcers, mainly attention from parents, siblings, and therapists. During the initial phases of therapy, the boy's high level of anxiety dictated the use of reciprocal inhibition methods (Wolpe, 1958). The therapists actively inhibited the boy's anxiety elicited by various aspects of the school setting (as in Step 2 above). The later stages of therapy were characterized by a decrease in Paul's overall anxiety without a concomitant decrease in avoidance behavior. After Step 15 the boy appeared to be minimally anxious. An operant strategy which made various rewards contingent on school attendance was therefore selected.

A Proposed Model

Although the division between classical and operant procedures became clearly discernible towards the terminal phases of treatment, many situations arose which necessitated the deliberate choice of one or other paradigm. A model was developed for determining when each was likely to prove maximally effective. On several occasions for instance, Paul left the classroom, entered the library and told the therapist, "I'm scared." At this point the choice of strategy became crucial. In strict operant terms, active attempts to reduce anxiety by means of attention and reassurance would reinforce classroom-leaving behavior. On the other hand, the classical paradigm would predict that to withhold immediate attention and make it contingent upon returning to the classroom would augment the child's anxiety and thus reinforce avoidance behavior. The critical factor in determining the appropriate procedure was the degree of anxiety as judged by the therapist.

An inappropriate use of the operant model could prove antitherapeutic. If the level of anxiety is very high, a premature re-exposure to the feared situation will probably lead to increased sensitivity. Moreover, if this heightened level of anxiety leads to another escape response, the resultant anxiety-reduction will strengthen the avoidance responses (classroom leaving behavior in this instance). It was also reasoned that when highly anxious, the boy would be unable to attend to the teacher, interact with his peers, or make any other responses which ordinarily reduced his anxiety.

An inappropriate use of the classical model would also impede therapeutic progress. The very acts of inducing relaxation, employing "emotive imagery," and giving reassurance may provide positive reinforcement for dependent behavior. The afore-mentioned difficulties in "phasing out" may be attributed to his possible side effect of *in vivo* desensitization. The gains which accrue when high levels of anxiety are thus decreased, however, temporarily out-weigh the disadvantages of increased dependency.

Discussion

It may be argued that a disproportionate amount of time and effort was expended in attaining the principal therapeutic objective, viz., normal school attendance. Urgent cases, however, who are neurotically incapacitated and unamenable to interview techniques, would seem to require therapeutic intervention beyond the confines of the consulting room. It should be emphasized that school phobia in a child is almost as pressing and disruptive a problem as occupational fears in an adult.

Since therapy *in vivo* makes heavy demands on the therapist's time, the senior author decided to enlist the assistance of two graduate students in clinical psychology (the co-authors). During the first exposure to school (see Step 1) Paul rapidly developed an attachment to one of the cotherapists (G.C.D.). As the application of reciprocal inhibition methods is conceivably facilitated by the nonspecific anxiety-inhibiting effects of a "good relationship" (Lazarus, 1961), this therapist carried out the first eight steps. Thereafter, the choice of therapist was partly determined by the academic and clinical commitments of the respective authors. Significantly, very little disturbance was occasioned by the constant change of therapists. There was often a distinct advantage in being able to alternate therapists; it was found, following a setback, that it was helpful to change therapists in order to offset the negative effects of being associated with sensitizing experiences.

The adjunctive use of a tranquilizer seemed to be of limited therapeutic value. Initially, it appeared to reduce the boy's anticipatory anxieties, but the absence of negative effects whenever it was forgotten, suggests that a placebo would have been as effective.

The therapists kept in close communication with the parents, who were encouraged to telephone whenever situational crises arose. As soon as normal school attendance had been more or less reinstated (Step 14), the therapists held a "family conference." In the main, the implications of the father's harsh and restrictive tendencies, along with the mother's inconsistent and ambivalent attitudes, were made clear to them. A long list of specific "do's" and "dont's" was drawn up and discussed. Apart from minor points of disagreement, the parents responded in an intelligent and receptive manner and subsequently implemented many of the recommendations.

According to the mother's reports, Paul's behavior also improved in areas outside of the school situation. She referred to his marked decrease in moodiness, his increased willingness to participate in household chores, more congenial relationships with his peers, and general gains in self-sufficiency.

Ten months after the termination of therapy, a follow-up inquiry revealed that Paul had not only maintained his gains, but had made further progress.

REFERENCES

Bentler, P. M.: An infant's phobia treated with reciprocal inhibition therapy. *J Child Psychol Psychiat*, 3:185-189, 1962.

Eysenck, H. J. (Ed.): *Behaviour Therapy and the Neuroses*. New York, Pergamon Press, 1960.

Ferster, C. B.: Positive reinforcement and behavioral deficits in autistic children. *Child Dev*, 32:437-456, 1961.

Jones, Mary C.: Elimination of children's fears. *J Exp Psychol*, 7:383-390, 1924.

King, G. F., Merrell, D., Lovinger, E., and Denny, M.: Operant motor behavior in acute schizophrenics. *J Pers*, 25:317-326, 1957.

Lazarus, A. A.: The elimination of children's phobias by deconditioning. In H. J. Eysenck (Ed.): *Behavior Therapy and the Neuroses*. New York, Pergamon Press, 1960.

———: Group therapy of phobic disorders by systematic desensitization. *J Abnorm Soc Psychol*, 63:504-510, 1961.

Lazarus, A. A., and Abramovitz, A.: The use of "emotive imagery" in the treatment of children's phobias. *J Ment Sci*, 108:191-195, 1962.

Lazarus, A. A., and Rachman, S.: The use of systematic desensitization in psychotherapy. *South Afr Med J*, 31:334-337, 1957.

Lindsley, O. R., and Skinner, B. F.: A method for the experimental analysis of the behavior of psychotic patients. *Am Psychol*, 9:419-420, 1954.

Patterson, G. R.: A learning theory approach to the treatment of the school phobic child. In L. Ullman and L. Krasner (Eds.): *Case Studies in Behavior Modification*. New York, Holt, Rinehart, & Winston, 1965.

Wolpe, J.: *Psychotherapy by Reciprocal Inhibition*. Stanford, Stanford Univ. Press, 1958.

———: The systematic desensitization treatment of neuroses. *J Nerv Ment Dis*, 132:189-203, 1961.

SECTION IV
CLASSROOM APPLICATION

Chapter 13

TOKEN REINFORCEMENT PROGRAMS IN SPECIAL CLASSES

SAUL AXELROD

A RECENT EXTENSION of the principles of operant conditioning includes the use of token reinforcement as a means of modifying behavior in the special education classroom. Token reinforcers are objects or symbols which in and of themselves probably have little or no reinforcing value (Birnbrauer, Wolf, Kidder, and Tague, 1965). However, they may be exchanged for a variety of objects or privileges which are reinforcing. For example, an individual might use his tokens to purchase several different kinds of candies, toys, or a trip to the zoo. As a result of this association with different types of reinforcement, the tokens should become generalized reinforcers which are independent of any particular state of deprivation or satiation which an individual is experiencing. The superiority of the token reinforcement system over other systems employing a particular primary reinforcer is considerable. For example, if food is used to reinforce a certain behavior, the effectiveness of the reinforcement procedure is greatly dependent upon the state of deprivation of the individual. Tokens, on the other hand, are not so limited, since they can be used to purchase several different types of reinforcers or can be saved until a later time when a particular state of deprivation does exist. In addition, several tokens can be accumulated and exchanged for some item that has more reinforcing value for an individual than a single piece of candy.

A significant advantage of token reinforcers over the use of grades in maintaining appropriate behavior in the classroom was reported by McKenzie, Clark, Wolf, Kothera, and Benson (1968). These investigators pointed out that grades have traditionally been the token reinforcement system of schools. However, the effectiveness of grades is often minimal since the amount of time between behavior and reinforcement is frequently between six and nine weeks. As a result, an association between responding and reinforcement is unlikely. In accordance with this notion, Clark, Lachowitz, and Wolf (1968) pointed out that a major benefit of a token program is that the token can be used as an immediate reinforcer of a response and thus can close the time lapse between the appropriate response and the backup reinforcer. For example, it would be difficult to provide a trip to the circus as an immediate reinforcer for completing a difficult reading assignment. However, it would be quite easy to administer a sufficient number of tokens for this trip immediately following the appropriate behavior.

Token reinforcement programs have generally been employed in classroom situations in which teacher attention has been ineffective in controlling the students' behavior (Kuypers, Becker, and O'Leary, 1968). The administration of a token is usually preceded by some type of approval (e.g., "good boy") so that teacher praise will eventually become a conditioned reinforcer. It is often intended (Kuypers *et al.*, 1968) that control over student behavior will be transferred from the tokens to the teacher through this conditioned reinforcement procedure.

Increasing Academic Performance

Mentally Retarded Populations

SEVERELY RETARDED CLASS. A study by Birnbrauer and Lawler (1964) appears to be the first published investigation of the use of a token reinforcement system in a special education classroom. Subjects for this experiment were 37 severely retarded children who were divided into classes of 6 to 13 pupils. Each teacher conducted his class without the help of teaching assistants. Of the 37 subjects, 14 had never attended school before, three had been dropped from school due to "incorrigibility," and four were "severe behavior problems." All had IQ's of 40 or less. The children were gradually introduced to a token reinforcement program using poker chips which could be exchanged for a variety of backup reinforcers. Chips were awarded for clearly defined behaviors. At the end of the school year, 33 of the 37 pupils hung up their coats upon entering the classroom, sat down quietly, and waited for their assignments. In addition, 11 worked without assistance on programed reading material which required 10 to 30 minutes to complete. It was found, however, that many of the children did not change their behavior outside the classroom.

PROGRAMED MATERIAL. Birnbrauer, Bijou, Wolf, and Kidder (1965) discussed a special education classroom in which a token reinforcement system was combined with programed instructional material (PI) to teach various school subjects (reading, writing, and arithmetic) and related practical skills (e.g., telling time). Subjects for the study were eight boys ranging in chronological age (CA) from 9 to 13 and in mental age (MA) from 5-5 to 7-3 (Peabody Picture Vocabulary Test: PPVT). Their clinical diagnoses included brain damage and familial retardation. A token reinforcement system was instituted after the discovery that the pupils would not work effectively for approval and knowledge of results. The student to teacher ratio was frequently one-to-one. The authors reported that within five months, seven of the eight pupils were "good students." It was claimed that the subjects studied longer, accomplished more work, and exhibited a minimal number of disruptive behaviors.

TOKENS VS TEACHER ATTENTION. The question of whether the reinforcement program or the greater attention paid to students' problems is responsible for producing increased student output is frequently raised. A study by Birnbrauer, Wolf, Kidder, and Tague (1965) shed some light on this matter. The purpose of this investigation was to determine the effectiveness of the reinforcers in maintaining appropriate behavior on the Sight Vocabulary Program by systematically withdrawing and reapplying the reinforcers. Of the 17 mentally retarded children who took part in this study, two were mongoloid, three were familial, nine were brain damaged, and three had no available diagnosis. IQ's ranged from 50 to 72 (PPVT). The study consisted of three conditions: The first (B) paired social approval with tokens; the second (NT) used teacher approval but no tokens; the third condition (B_2) was the same as the first. The study used one male certified teacher and three female assistants. The results indicated that five children showed no decrement in performance during NT. Six children made more errors during NT, but completed the same or a greater number of items and presented no greater number of behavior problems. Four children made more errors, did less work, and presented serious disciplinary problems during NT. After tokens were reinstated all subjects returned to the original level or better. It appeared, therefore, that the token reinforcement procedures rather than teacher attention accounted for the behavioral changes.

Bijou, Birnbrauer, Kidder, and Tague (1966) reported on three years of research in which a token reinforcement system was applied to teaching reading, writing, and arithmetic to retarded children. Subjects consisted of 27 boys and girls ranging in CA from 8-7 to 14-9. The average IQ (PPVT) for the group was 63. Eleven of the subjects were diagnosed as brain damaged, three as mongoloid, four as cultural-familial, and nine as uncertain or unknown. Although no mention was made of the number of teachers who were involved, the classroom situation was structured so that a newly admitted student would receive almost constant attention from a teacher. The authors implied that the results of this study were quite favorable, but failed to include objective data.

Other Populations

MULTIPLY HANDICAPPED TEENAGERS. Nolen, Kunzelman, and Haring (1967) performed a study which was directed toward improving the academic and social behavior of junior high age children with a variety of disorders. Subjects ranged in age from 12 to 16 years and in achievement levels from preschool to sixth grade. Etiologies included a variety of emotional and learning disorders, as well as mental retardation. The authors stressed, however, that their program centered on the diagnosis of skill problems rather than on physical or psychological deficits. Following the development of skill sequences and the determination of the students' functioning levels within these sequences, individual programs were devised. The teacher allotted points, which were exchangeable for reinforcers appropriate to teenagers, for each of a number of academic tasks. After 100 days, a median of 2.7 years gain in arithmetic and 2.05 years gain in reading was found. To test the effectiveness of the reinforcement, the experimenters administered rewards on a noncontingent basis for a period of time. This technique produced a significant decrease in appropriate academic behavior which was quickly resumed once reinforcement was reinstituted on a contingent basis. Follow-up studies of three students who were transferred from this classroom indicated that their performances were lower in the traditional classroom than in the experimental classroom. However, their productivity was still superior to other students' in their new class.

URBAN UNDERACHIEVERS. In accordance with current national problems, Wolf, Giles, and Hall (1968) conducted a program which was intended to improve the academic performance of low achieving children from an urban poverty area. Fifteen of the subjects for this study were from the sixth grade while the sixteenth was from the fifth grade. All subjects scored at least two years below their grade level on the reading portion of the *Stanford Achievement Test* (SAT). According to school records, IQ's ranged from 73 to 104. Classes, which were conducted by one teacher with two teaching assistants, were held after school hours and during summer months. In addition, students attended regular classes during school hours. A token reinforcement program which included a wide range of back-up reinforcers was instituted. The first of two experiments concerned two subjects and attempted to determine whether the rate of reading certain material was a function of the distribution of points. It was found that manipulation of the number of points earned by reading significantly affected the reading rate of both children. In one case, doubling the number of points the child could receive produced a significant level of response even though he had not responded at all under the original conditions. In the second experiment, subjects were given their choice of types of academic materials with which to work. However, the number of points which could be earned for completing various units was changed periodically. For example, at one time reading units were worth five points, while arithmetic and English units were worth two points. At another time, reading was worth eight points, arithmetic was worth two points, and English was worth one-half a point. The material a child chose varied according to the number of points that could be earned. At the end of the year the data indicated that the control group, which only attended regular classes, gained a median of .8 year on the SAT, while the experimental group showed a median gain of 1.5 years. These results were significant at the .01 level of confidence. In addition, subjective teacher remarks indicated that the children from the experimental group performed better while in the regular school classroom than they had previously.

DROPOUTS. A study by Clark and his colleagues (1968) also employed a population representative of contemporary problems. This investigation was directed toward improving the academic skills of school dropouts by means of a token reinforcement program. Subjects for the study were two groups of five girls matched according to differences between their number of years of formal education and their scores on the *California Achievement Test* (CAT). All the girls were between 16 and 21 years old. One group was termed the classroom group and received the token reinforcement program. The second group was designated the job group and received job placement. The classroom group subjects were given their choice of a variety of instructional materials. Points, which were exchangeable for money, were awarded on the basis of performance on these materials.

As the study progressed, the distribution of points was shifted to increase the probability of a student's working in an area in which she was deficient. For example, if a girl were deficient in arithmetic, more points would be awarded for appropriate arithmetic performance. One, and often two teachers were in the classroom. Four girls in the classroom group attended class for eight weeks and four days while the fifth attended 24 days. According to the CAT pretest and posttest scores, the classroom subjects gained a median of 1.3 years while the job group gained only .2 year.

LEARNING DISABLED. In order to improve the level of academic achievement in a learning disabilities class, McKenzie and his co-workers (1968) introduced a token reinforcement system. Subjects for this study were ten students ranging in age from 10 to 13 years. Although their ability levels did not indicate mental retardation, their achievement levels were retarded by at least two years in one or more academic areas. All were diagnosed as having minimal brain damage and emotional disturbance. Based on their academic performance, the children were reinforced with recess, special privileges, weekly grades, etc. Achievement under these conditions was judged to be less than optimal. A program conducted by a teacher and teacher aides was then instituted in which the amount of allowance a child would receive from his parents was determined by his weekly grades. Since the parents were already accustomed to giving their children allowances, a burden was not added to the parents' budgets. A significant increase in arithmetic and reading achievement was observed while using weekly allowances as back-up reinforcers. Due to the risk involved, no reversal of reinforcement conditions was attempted.

READING DISABLED. Haring and Hauck (1969) did a study concerned with improving the reading achievement level of four elementary school boys through a combination of PI material and token reinforcement. Subjects for this investigation were disabled in reading, but average or above in intelligence. According to the *Gates-McKillop Diagnostic Reading Tests,* reading development showed a lag of from one to five years. Several experimental conditions were employed. During condition A the material was presented without the answers. During the second condition (B), correct answers were provided following a response by the subject. Condition C included a counter which tallied the number of correct responses. This count was available both to the boys and the experimenters. Condition D provided continuous token reinforcement for correct responding, whereas condition E programed reinforcement on a variable ratio schedule (e.g., an average of every five correct responses was reinforced). A transfer from PI material to work lists, basal readers, and library books was involved in condition F. The teacher's role in this program was minimal since much of the material was automated. The study consisted of 91 sessions of 65 minutes each. The data showed that the later conditions produced higher rates of correct responding than conditions A and B. In addition, it was found that the boys gained from 1.5 to 4.0 years in reading achievement during the five months of the study, according to the *Sullivan Placement Test*. Transition to the more traditional situation in condition F was reported as successful, but definitive data were lacking.

EMOTIONALLY DISTURBED. Hewett, Taylor, and Artuso (1969) used an engineered classroom design with "emotionally disturbed" students. A total of 54 children were assigned to six classrooms with nine students in each. Each class had a teacher and a teacher aide. Children ranged in CA from 8-0 to 11-11 years with Full Scale WISC IQ scores between 85 and 113. Nearly all showed academic retardation. The experimental condition involved the use of checkmarks and back-up reinforcers for appropriate behavior. Any instructional approach which the teacher chose to follow except the use of tangible or token rewards was used in the control condition. Class 1 (E) stayed in the experimental condition for 32 weeks. Class 2 (C) stayed in the control condition for 32 weeks. Classes 3 and 4 (CE) and classes 5 and 6 (EC) were in the control condition for 16 weeks and the experimental condition for 16 weeks. The dependent variables were reading and arithmetic achievement measured by the CAT and task attention. A comparison of classes E and C indicated that the experimental condition produced superior task attention and arithmetic achievement but not reading achievement. The data of class C and Classes CE verified these findings. The data of classes EC indicated that removal of the experimental condition resulted in improved task attention and did not affect reading or arithmetic achievement levels. To account for these surprising observations, Hewett and his associates (1969) hypothesized that (a) the teachers became more effective secondary social reinforcers, and (b) the competence of group EC increased as a result of the experimental condition.

Reducing Disruptive Behaviors

Mentally Retarded Populations

HYPERACTIVITY. The purpose of a study by Patterson, Jones, Whittier, and Wright (1965) was to condition the attending behavior of a hyperactive child in a classroom situation. In addition, it was intended that the effect generalize to situations in which the conditioning apparatus was not being used. An experimental subject (ES) and a control subject (CS) were employed. ES was a brain injured, mentally retarded boy with a WISC IQ of 65. CS was a brain injured boy with a range in IQ scores from the eighties to the low nineties according to the PPVT and *Raven Matrices Test*. During conditioning trials ES wore an earphone into which a signal was passed for each ten seconds during which ES attended properly. Later a variable interval schedule was used. Each buzz indicated that a piece of candy or a penny was accumulated toward a total which was to be shared by the entire class. Following conditioning, the apparatus was removed and a four-week extinction period was begun. Differences between ES and CS were insignificant during baseline. However, after conditioning sessions were started, it was found that ES performed significantly more attending behaviors than did CS. These measurements were taken during the period prior to which ES would wear the conditioning apparatus for that day. During extinction, ES maintained a significantly higher rate of attending than did CS. Patterson therefore obtained generalization of the conditioning effect.

OBSCENE CONDUCT. Sulzbacher and Houser (1968) used a group contingency procedure to eliminate a disruptive behavior in a classroom. This design was constructed so that the rewards of each depended upon the behavior of the group as a whole. Subjects for this study were 14 educable mentally retarded children, seven of whom were boys. Ages ranged from 6-7 to 10-5. The problem behavior was the frequent occurrence of an obscene gesture. The children were informed that there would be a ten minute recess at the end of the day. However, each display or reference to the obscene gesture by any member of the class decreased recess time by one minute for the entire class. The program was designed so that one teacher could carry out the entire procedure without assistance. The frequency of undesirable behaviors decreased from a mean of 16 per day to 2.11 per day. After removal of the contingency, the behavior increased, but to a lower level than the baseline level.

MALADAPTIVE BEHAVIORS. Perline and Levinsky (1968) attempted to determine the effect of token reinforcement on the maladaptive behaviors of severely retarded children in a residential preschool setting. Subjects ranged in age from eight to ten years and in social quotient from 22 to 38. Five maladaptive behaviors were defined including aggression toward peers and throwing objects. Two experimental conditions were applied concurrently for ten days. All children were given tokens for lack of maladaptive behaviors and lost a token if they misbehaved. However, for half the children, each deviant behavior led to a time-out period consisting of 5 to 15 minutes during which the child was not allowed to move from a certain area. For the other half of the children, no additional contingencies were used. The data indicated that a decrease in maladaptive behaviors for each of the five categories occurred. However, there were no appreciable differences between using token reinforcement and token reinforcement with time-out.

Other Populations

HYPERACTIVITY. Patterson (1965) devised a token reinforcement program to control the disruptive behaviors of a child in a classroom setting. The subject was a nine-year-old boy in the second grade, who demonstrated hyperactive behavior and academic retardation. Neurological signs indicated minimal brain damage while IQ scores were in the borderline range. After observing the boy for several hours, it was decided that the greater part of his hyperactivity could be broken down into talking, pushing, and hitting. A small box with a flashlight bulb and an electric counter was then placed on the boy's desk. If he did not perform any disruptive behaviors for a period of time (which increased as trials progressed) the light flashed and the counter clicked. At the end of each session, all members of the class divided up the amount of candy or pennies corresponding to the number of points on the electric counter. This program required the presence of the teacher and an experimenter. The data indicated that 8.4 fewer disruptive responses per minute occurred during conditioning. This result was at the .01 level of significance. After the experiment was completed, the teacher reported that the boy was less disruptive and played more with other children.

EMOTIONALLY DISTURBED. An extension of the Patterson (1965) study was performed by Quay, Werry, McQueen, and Sprague (1966). Although an explicit description of the children was not given, it appears that the children were emotionally disturbed. Each student was given a box containing a light which could be flashed following attending behaviors of a fixed duration. The children were later given a piece of candy for each light flash. The program, which was conducted by one teacher and an experimenter, increased attending from 41 percent during baseline to 71 percent during the last 20 days of reinforcement. A return to baseline conditions was not attempted.

O'Leary and Becker (1967) attempted to devise a token reinforcement system which could be used by one teacher in an average size classroom. In addition, the authors were interested in the possibility of gradually withdrawing the tokens without an increase in deviant behavior by transferring control to teacher attention and grades. Subjects for this study were 17 nine-year-old children described as "emotionally disturbed." Kuhlmann-Anderson IQ scores ranged from 80 to 107. After the baseline period, the experimenter placed the following instructions on the blackboard: "In Seat, Face Front, Raise Hand. . . ." The children were told that they would receive points (which were determined by the experimenter) depending on how well they followed instructions. These points could be exchanged for a variety of backup reinforcers. The number of ratings made each day gradually decreased and the number of points required to obtain a prize gradually increased. By requiring more appropriate behavior to receive a reward and increasing the delay of reinforcement, it was hoped that transfer of control from tokens to teacher praise and attention would occur. During baseline, the daily mean of deviant behaviors varied between 66 and 91 percent. This decreased to a range of 3 to 32 percent during the token procedure. This result was significant at the .001 level. A return to baseline conditions during school sessions during the following fall was planned. However, extensive changes in the pupil population prevented this possibility. Anecdotal evidence, however, indicated that after the procedure was put into effect, the students behaved better during class sessions in which tokens were not used than they had previously.

OUT-OF-SEAT BEHAVIOR. A group contingency procedure was utilized by Gallagher, Sulzbacher, and Shores (1967) to reduce disruptive behaviors in a classroom. The subjects were five boys who were enrolled in an intermediate class for emotionally disturbed children. The boys ranged in age from 7-11 to 11-8. It was hypothesized that more deviant behaviors occurred when at least one member of the class was out of his seat. Hence, an attempt was made to eliminate out-of-seat behavior. The children were informed that they could have a 24 minute coke break at the end of the day if they did not leave their seats without permission. A chart was posted which displayed two-minute segments from 24 to 0. Each child's name was assigned a different color chalk. When a child left his seat without permission, the teacher marked off two minutes with the designated color from the entire class's coke time. The frequency of the boys' being out of their seats decreased from an average of 69.5 to 1.0 times per day. In addition, an overall decline in disruptive classroom behaviors was reported. Although the program used one master and three student teachers, it would appear that it could have been conducted by one teacher without assistance.

SOCIALLY MALADJUSTED. Kuypers, Becker, and O'Leary (1968) performed an experiment to reduce the number of disruptive behaviors in an adjustment class through the use of a token reinforcement program. Subjects for this study were six third grade and six fourth grade children who were described as socially maladjusted. Data were collected on only the six most disruptive children. They were given tokens (which could be used to purchase various items) for staying in their seats, facing front, and other attending behaviors. During baseline, deviant behavior occurred 54 percent of the time. This decreased to 27.8 percent during the token period and then increased to 41.5 percent when the tokens were removed. Generalization to other situations was minimal. The authors admitted that these results were less impressive than those obtained by O'Leary and Becker (1967). Kuypers attributed the limited success to the following: (a) the tokens were awarded on an absolute basis rather than for individual improvement, (b) the teacher was not trained in the use of operant conditioning techniques, and (c) the observers tended to be a disturbance to the class.

Criticisms

Although the studies reviewed above are almost unanimous in revealing the ability of token reinforcement to produce favorable changes in the special education classroom, the area has not been free of methodological and engineering difficulties. A frequent problem with many of the studies has been the failure of the experimenters to clearly demonstrate that contingent token reinforcement was responsible for the academic changes which occurred.

In an operant conditioning experiment, the researcher typically notes the frequency of the behavior of interest under normal or baseline conditions. He then applies some consequence to the behavior in an attempt to alter its rate of occurrence. If the rate changes in the predicted direction, the experimenter still cannot be certain that this change was due to the consequence which was applied to the behavior. It is possible that the alteration of the rate was due to the passage of time, maturation of the subjects, increased teacher effectiveness, or many other ongoing factors. To circumvent this difficulty, the experimenter will frequently return the subjects to the conditions which existed before the reinforcement techniques were applied. A return of the behavior to the original baserate lends credence to the idea that it was the contingent reinforcement or punishment which accounted for the behavioral change.

Nevertheless, many of the token studies have failed to include a reversal to baseline conditions (e.g., Birnbrauer and Lawler, 1964; Perline and Levinsky, 1968). It might be argued that the ability of operant principles to alter behavior has been demonstrated in a sufficient number of cases that a reversal phase is unnecessary, especially in a purely therapeutic situation. As Sidman (1960) noted however, "An investigator may, on the basis of experience, have great confidence in the adequacy of his methodology, but other experimenters cannot be expected to share his confidence without convincing evidence" (p. 75) (cited by O'Leary and Becker, 1967).

The manner in which many of the studies were conducted raises questions as to their usefulness in the special education classroom. One problem has been the use of a large number of personnel in order to execute the programs. Birnbrauer's (1965) study used three teachers in a classroom of eight boys, whereas the Patterson (1965) study required the presence of a teacher and an experimenter. Although it is desirable that such a personnel-teacher ratio exist ordinarily, it is unrealistic to expect this situation in many special education classrooms. A somewhat promising solution to this problem is given in the group contingency design used by Gallagher's group (1967) and by Sulzbacher and Houser (1968). These studies treated the entire class as a unit and thus simplified the administration of reinforcement and the bookkeeping procedures.

Another limitation of some of the above studies is that electronic equipment was required for their execution (e.g., Patterson, 1965; Patterson *et al.*, 1965). Although it could be argued that this equipment is not complex, it is doubtful that the necessary apparatus would be installed by many special education teachers without the assistance and encouragement of a researcher. The availability of the appropriate researcher is often limited.

Future Research

The Kuypers (1968) study stated that "a general goal of token systems is to transfer control of responding from token systems to other conditioned reinforcers such as teacher praise and grades" (p. 101). If this is an accepted aim of token reinforcement programs, future research must be conducted in this direction. The most frequent stated suggestion (e.g., Kuypers *et al.*, 1968) for achieving transfer from the token system to the more traditional classroom situation is to precede the delivery of tokens with praise. This arrangement is intended to eventually establish social events as conditioned reinforcers and to allow a teacher to maintain student behavior with social reinforcement alone.

Another proposal concerning the removal of tokens was given by O'Leary and Becker (1967). By requiring progressively more behavior to receive a prize and by increasingly delaying reinforcement, the authors claimed that a transfer from tokens to teacher praise could be achieved eventually.

Which, if either, of these proposals will be fruitful will be determined by future investigation. The question seems an important one, since it is unlikely that a token system would be applied indefinitely in any school setting.

In the present author's opinion, future token experiments should employ reinforcers already available in the classroom. Studies which are dependent on the introduction of candies and toys into the classroom can only be applied for a limited period of time because of the strain eventually placed on the school's or teacher's budget. Most special education teachers permit their students to have free play time, field trips, and games. Rather than permitting the students to engage in such activities independent of classroom performance, the privileges could be used as reinforcers in the token program. This approach has been successfully employed by Sulzbacher and Houser (1968) and offers the most economical and easily transferred system of behavior modification.

REFERENCES

Bijou, S. W., Birnbrauer, J. S., Kidder, J. D., and Tague, C. E.: Programmed instruction as an approach to the teaching of reading, writing, and arithmetic to retarded children. *Psychol Rec, 16*:505-522, 1966.

Birnbrauer, J. S., Bijou, S. W., Wolf, M. M., and Kidder, J. D.: Programmed instruction in the classroom. In L. P. Ullmann and L. Krasner (Eds.): *Case Studies in Behavior Modification.* New York, Holt, Rinehart & Winston, 1965, pp. 358-363.

Birnbrauer, J. S., and Lawler, J.: Token reinforcement for learning. *Ment Retard, 2*:275-279, 1964.

Birnbrauer, J. S., Wolf, M. M., Kidder, J. D., and Tague, C.: Classroom behavior of retarded pupils with token reinforcement. *J Exp Child Psychol, 2*:219-235, 1965.

Clark, M., Lachowitz, J., and Wolf, M.: A pilot basic education program for school dropouts incorporating a token reinforcement system. *Behav Res Ther, 6*:183-188, 1968.

Gallagher, P., Sulzbacher, S. I., and Shores, R. E.: A group contingency for classroom management of emotionally disturbed children. Paper read to Kansas Chapter, The Council for Exceptional Children, Wichita, March 1967.

Haring, N. G., and Hauck, M.: Improved learning conditions in the establishment of reading skills with disabled readers. *Except Child, 35*:341-352, 1969.

Hewett, F., Taylor, F., and Artuso, A.: The Santa Monica project: Evaluation of an engineered classroom design with emotionally disturbed children. *Except Child, 35*:523-529, 1969.

Kuypers, D. S., Becker, W. C., and O'Leary, K. D.: How to make a token system fail. *Except Child, 35*:101-109, 1968.

McKenzie, H. S., Clark M., Wolf, M. M., Kothera, R., and Benson, C.: Behavior modification of children with learning disabilities using grades as tokens and allowances as back up reinforcers. *Except Child, 34*:745-752, 1968.

Nolen, P., Kunzelmann, H. P., and Haring, N. G.: Behavioral modification in a junior high learning disabilities classroom. *Except Child, 34*:163-168, 1967.

O'Leary, K. D., and Becker, W. C.: Behavioral modification of an adjustment class. A token reinforcement program. *Except Child, 33*:637-642, 1967.

Patterson, G. R.: An application of conditioning techniques to the control of a hyperactive child. In L. P. Ullmann and L. Krasner (Eds.): *Case*

Studies in Behavior Modification. New York, Holt, Rinehart & Winston, 1965, pp. 370-375.

Patterson, G. R., Jones, R., Whittier, J., and Wright, M. A.: A behavior modification technique for the hyperactive child. *Behav Res Ther, 2:* 217-226, 1965.

Perline, I. H., and Levinsky, D.: Controlling behavior in the severely retarded. *Am J Ment Defic, 73:*74-78, 1968.

Quay, H. C., Werry, J. S., McQueen, M., and Sprague, R. L.: Remediation of the conduct problem child in the special class setting. *Except Child, 32:*509-515, 1966.

Sidman, M.: *Tactics of Scientific Research.* New York, Basic Books, 1960.

Sulzbacher, S. I., and Houser, J. E.: A tactic to eliminate disruptive behaviors in the classroom: Group contingent consequences. *Am J Ment Defic, 73:*88-90, 1968.

Wolf, M. M., Giles, D. K., and Hall, R. V.: Experiments with token reinforcement in a remedial classroom. *Behav Res Ther, 6:*51-64, 1968.

Chapter 14

BEHAVIOR MODIFICATION OF AN ADJUSTMENT CLASS: A TOKEN REINFORCEMENT PROGRAM

K. Daniel O'Leary
Wesley C. Becker

Praise, teacher attention, stars, and grades provide adequate incentive for most pupils to behave in a socially approved way. However, for some students—notably school dropouts, aggressive children, and some retarded children—these methods are relatively ineffective. Where the usual methods of social approval have failed, token reinforcement systems have proven effective (Birnbrauer, Bijou, Wolf, and Kidder, 1965; Birnbrauer and Lawler, 1964; Birnbrauer, Wolf, Kidder, and Tague, 1965; Quay, Werry, McQueen, and Sprague, 1966). Token reinforcers are tangible objects or symbols which attain reinforcing power by being exchanged for a variety of other objects such as candy and trinkets which are back-up reinforcers. Tokens acquire generalized reinforcing properties when they are paired with many different reinforcers. The generalized reinforcer is especially useful since it is effective regardless of the momentary condition of the organism.

For the children in this study, generalized reinforcers such as verbal responses ("That's right" or "Good!") and token reinforcers such as grades had not maintained appropriate behavior. In fact, their teacher noted that prior to the introduction of the token system, being called "bad" increased the children's inappropriate behavior. "They had the attitude that it was smart to be called bad. . . . When I tried to compliment them or tell them that they had done something well, they would look around the room and make faces at each other." It is a moot question whether the poor academic performance of these children was caused by their disruptive social behavior or vice versa. It was obvious, however, that the disruptive behaviors had to be eliminated before an academic program could proceed.

Although classroom token reinforcement programs have proved effective in modifying behavior, the pupil teacher ratio has usually been small. In the study of Birnbrauer, Wolf, et al. (1965), a classroom of 17 retarded pupils had four teachers in the classroom at all times. Quay (1966) had one teacher in a behavior modification classroom of five children. One purpose of this project was to devise a token reinforcement program which could be used by one teacher in an average classroom; a second purpose was to see if a token system could be withdrawn gradually without an increase in disruptive behavior by transferring control to teacher attention, praise, and grades, with less frequent exchange of back up reinforcers.

Subjects

The subjects for this study were 17 nine-year-old children described as emotionally disturbed. They had IQ scores (Kuhlmann-Anderson) ranging from 80 to 107. They had been placed in the adjustment class primarily because they exhibited undesirable classroom behaviors such as temper tantrums, crying, uncontrolled laughter, and fighting. The children were in the classroom throughout the day with the exception of some remedial speech and reading work. Although the token reinforcement system was in effect for the whole class, the study focused on the eight most disruptive children.

Method

The children's deviant behaviors were observed by two students in the classroom from 12:30 to 2:10 three days a week. A third student made reliability checks two days a week. Among the behaviors recorded as deviant were the following: pushing, answering without raising one's hand, chewing gum, eating, name calling, making disruptive noise, and talking. Each student observed four children in random order for 22 minutes each session. Observations were made on a 20 second observe/10 second record basis. Deviant behaviors were recorded on observation sheets. During the observations, the children had three structured activities: listening to records or stories, arithmetic, and group reading. During these activities, instruction was directed to the whole class, and the children were expected to be quiet and in their seats.

BASE PERIOD. The teacher was asked to handle the children as she normally did. To obtain data which reflected the frequency of deviant pupil behavior under usual classroom procedures, a base period was used. The observers were in the classroom for three weeks before any baseline data were recorded. At first the children walked up to the observers and tried to initiate conversation with them. As the observers consistently ignored the children, the children's approach behaviors diminished. Thus, it is likely that initial show-off behavior was reduced before baseline measures were obtained.

The average interobserver reliability for individual children during the four week base period, calculated on the basis of exact agreement for time interval and category of behavior, ranged from 75 to 100 percent agreement (Table 14-I). A perfect agreement was scored if both observers recorded the same behavior within a 20 second interval. The reliabilities were calculated by dividing the number of perfect agreements by the number of different responses observed. The percentage of each

TABLE 14-I

AVERAGE INTEROBSERVER RELIABILITIES DURING BASE AND TOKEN REINFORCEMENT PERIODS

Subject	Base Period		Token Reinforcement Period	
	Percentage of Perfect Agreement	Number of Reliability Checks	Percentage of Perfect Agreement	Number of Reliability Checks
1	85	3	88	9
2	82	2	94	9
3	92	3	96	9
4	100	1	93	5
5	77	3	87	9
6	75	4	87	9
7	80	4	80	8
8	75	3	88	8

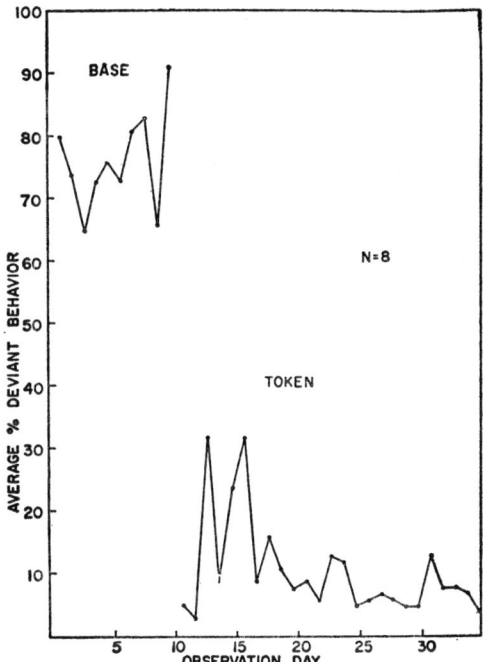

Figure 14-1. Average percentages of deviant behavior during the base and token periods.

child's deviant behavior for any one day was calculated by dividing the number of intervals in which one or more deviant behaviors occurred by the number of observed intervals for that day. As can be seen from Figure 14-1, there was a fairly stable base rate of deviant behavior with a slight increasing trend.

TOKEN REINFORCEMENT PERIOD. On the first day of the token period the experimenter placed the following instructions on the blackboard: In Seat, Face Front, Raise Hand, Working, Pay Attention, and Desk Clear. The experimenter then explained the token procedure to the children. The tokens were ratings placed in small booklets on each child's desk. The children were told that they would receive ratings from 1 to 10 and that the ratings would reflect the extent to which they followed the instructions. The points or ratings could be exchanged for a variety of backup reinforcers. The reinforcers consisted of small prizes ranging in value from 1 to 29 cents, such as candy, pennants, comics, perfume, and kites. The total cost of the reinforcers used during the two months was $80.76. All the pupils received reinforcers in the same manner during class, but individual preferences were considered by providing a variety of items, thus maximizing the probability that at least one of the items would be a reinforcer for a given child at a given time.

The experimenter repeated the instructions at the beginning of the token period each day for one week and rated the children to provide a norm for the teacher. It was the teacher, however, who placed the ratings in the children's booklets during the short pause at the end of a lesson period. The ratings reflected the extent to which the child exhibited the appropriate behaviors listed on the blackboard. Where possible, these ratings also reflected the accuracy of the child's arithmetic work.

The number of ratings made each day was gradually decreased from five to three, and the number of points required to obtain a prize gradually increased. For the first three days, the tokens were exchanged for reinforcers at the end of the token period. For the next four days, points were accumulated for two days and exchanged at the end of the token period on the second day. Then, for the next 15 days, a three day delay between token and reinforcers was used. Four day delays were employed for the remaining 25 school days. During the three and four day delay periods, tokens were exchanged for reinforcers at the end of the school day. By requiring more appropriate behavior to receive a prize and increasing the delay of reinforcement it was hoped that transfer of control from the token reinforcers to the more traditional methods of teacher praise and attention would occur.

After the first week, the teacher made the ratings and executed the token system without aid. Procedures were never discussed when the children were present.

The children also received group points based on total class behavior, and these points could be exchanged for popsicles at the end of each week. The group points ranged from 1 to 10 and reflected the extent to which the children were quiet during the time the ratings were placed in the booklets. The number of group ratings made each day were gradually decreased from five to three as were the individual ratings. However, since the children were usually very quiet, the number of points required to obtain a popsicle was not increased. The points were accumulated on a thermometer chart on the blackboard, and the children received popsicles on seven of the eight possible occasions.

At first the teacher was reluctant to accept the token procedure because of the time the ratings might take. However, the ratings took at most three minutes. As the teacher noted, "The class is very quiet and usually I give them a story to read from the board while I give the ratings. One model student acts as the teacher and he calls on the students who are well-behaved to read. . . . This is one of the better parts of the day. It gave me a chance to go around and say something to each child as I gave him his rating. . . ."

The rating procedure was especially effective because the teacher reinforced each child for approximations to the desired final response. Instead of demanding perfection from the start, the teacher reinforced evidence of progress.

In addition to the token procedure, the teacher was instructed to make comments, when appropriate, such as: "Pat, I like the way you are working. That will help your rating." "I am glad to see everyone turned around in their seats. That will help all of you get the prize you want." "Good, Gerald. I like the way you raised your hand to ask a question."

A technique used by the teacher to extinguish the deviant behavior of one child was to ignore him, while at the same time reinforcing the appropriate behavior of another child. This enabled the teacher to refrain from using social censure and to rely almost solely on positive reinforcement techniques, as she had been instructed.

The investigators also were prepared to use time out from positive reinforcement (Wolf, Risley, and Mees, 1964) to deal with those behaviors which were especially disruptive. The time out procedure involves isolating the child for deviant behavior for a specified period of time. This procedure was not used, however, since the frequency of disruptive behavior was very low at the end of the year.

The average interobserver reliability for individual children during the token period ranged from 80 to 96 percent. As indicated in Table 14-I, the reliabilities were recorded separately for the base and token periods because reliabilities were higher during the token period when the frequency of deviant behavior was low.

Results

As can be seen from Figure 14-1, the average percentage of deviant behavior at the end of the year was very low. The daily mean of deviant behavior during the token procedure ranged from 3 to 32 percent, while the daily mean of deviant behavior during the base period ranged from 66 to 91 percent. The average of deviant behavior for all children during the base period was 76 percent as contrasted with 10 percent during the token procedure. As can be seen from the F ratio (Table 14-II) the change from the base period to the token period was highly significant ($p < .001$). Using an omega squared, it was estimated that the treatment accounted for 96 percent of the variance of the observed deviant behavior.

An examination of the individual records (Fig. 14-2) shows the small degree of individual variation and differences in deviant behavior from the base to the token period. Although subjects 2 and 7 exhibited more deviant behavior than others during the token period, the percentage of deviant behavior was obviously less than during the base period. The percentage of de-

TABLE 14-II

ANALYSIS OF VARIANCE ON DEVIANT BEHAVIOR SCORES (N = 8)

Source	df	MS	F
Between subjects	7	72.86	
Within subjects	8	2203.00	
Treatment	1	17424.00	609.87*
Residual	7	28.57	

* $p < .001$.

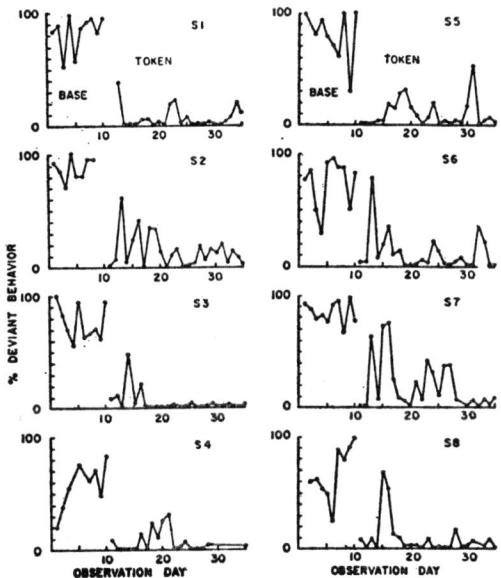

Figure 14-2. Percentages of deviant behavior for individual children during base and token periods.

viant behavior declined for all pupils from the base to the token period.

Discussion

At least two variables in addition to the token procedure and social reinforcement possibly contributed to the change in the children's behavior. First, during the baseline and token phases of this demonstration, the teacher was enrolled in a psychology class which emphasized operant and social learning principles. The influence of this class cannot be assessed, although the dramatic and abrupt change from the base to the token phase of the demonstration makes it seem highly implausible that the psychology class was the major variable accounting for the change. However, in a replication of this study now being planned, the teacher will receive only a short introduction to the basic principles and subsequent instruction by the experimenter throughout the procedure.

Secondly, the reduction in deviant behavior enabled the teacher to spend more time giving children individual attention during the token phase of the experiment. She had time to correct and return the children's work promptly, thus giving them immediate feedback. She was also able to use teaching materials not previously used. Some children who had not completed a paper for two years repeatedly received perfect scores. The immediate feedback and new materials probably contributed to the maintenance of appropriate behavior.

An experiment within the Skinnerian paradigm involves the establishment of a stable base rate of behavior; next, environmental contingencies are applied and the maladaptive behavior is reduced. The contingencies are then withdrawn and there is a return to base conditions. Finally, the environmental contingencies are again instituted and the maladaptive behavior decreased. This procedure of operant decrease, increase, and finally decrease of maladaptive behavior in association with specific environmental conditions demonstrates the degree of stimulus control obtained by the technique.

A return to base conditions early in the treatment period of this study was not carried out because of a concern that the enthusiasm and cooperation generated by the program throughout the school system might be severely reduced. There is little doubt that a return to base conditions following three or four weeks of the token procedure would have resulted in an increase in disruptive behavior. When a reversal was used by Birnbrauer, Wolf, *et al.* (1965), a number of children showed a decline in the amount of studying and an increase in disruptive behavior. As an alternative, it was planned to return gradually to baseline conditions during the following fall, but radical changes in pupil population prevented this reversal.

Without a reversal or a return to baseline conditions it cannot be stated that the token system and not other factors, such as the changes that ordinarily occur during the school year, accounted for the observed reduction of deviant behavior. To demonstrate clearly the crucial significance of the token procedure itself, a systematic replication with different children and a different teacher is planned. As Sidman (1960) noted, "An investigator may, on the basis of experience, have great confidence in the adequacy of his methodology, but other experimenters cannot be expected to share his confidence without convincing evidence" (p. 75).

Two interesting implications of this study are the effects of delay of reinforcement and generalization. The use of tokens provides a procedure which is intermediate between immediate and delayed tangible reinforcement. In Birnbrauer, Wolf, et al.'s (1965) class of severely retarded children this delay was extended from a few seconds to over an hour. Some educable children studied for many days for check marks only and, presumably, the knowledge that they were approaching a goal. All the children in the present study worked for four days without receiving a back up reinforcer. In addition, more than one child made the comment toward the end of school that next year they would be old enough to behave and work well without the prizes.

Anecdotal records indicate that after the token procedure was put into effect, the children behaved better during the morning session, music, and library periods. These reports suggest that a transfer to normal classroom control using social reinforcement and grades would not be very difficult. Also, the gang behavior of frowning upon "doing well" disappeared. Some children even helped enforce the token system by going to the blackboard just before class began and reading the instructions to the class.

REFERENCES

Birnbrauer, J. S., Bijou, S. W., Wolf, M. M., and Kidder, J. D.: Programmed instruction in the classroom. In L. P. Ullman and L. Krasner (Eds.): *Case Studies in Behavior Modification*. New York, Holt, Rinehart and Winston, 1965, pp. 358-363.

Birnbrauer, J. S., and Lawler, Julia: Token reinforcement for learning. *Ment Retard*, 2:275-279, 1964.

Birnbrauer, J. S., Wolf, M. M., Kidder, J. D., and Tague, Cecilia E.: Classroom behavior of retarded pupils with token reinforcement. *J Exp Child Psychol*, 2:219-235, 1965.

Quay, H. C., Werry, J. S., McQueen, Marjorie, and Sprague, R. L.: Remediation of the conduct problem child in the special class setting. *Except Child*, 32:509-515, 1966.

Sidman, M.: *Tactics of Scientific Research*. New York, Basic Books, 1960.

Wolf, M. M., Risley, T. R., and Mees, H. L.: Application of operant conditioning procedures to the behavioral problems of an autistic child. *Behav Res Ther*, 1:305-312, 1964.

Chapter 15

THE EFFECTS OF LOUD AND SOFT REPRIMANDS ON THE BEHAVIOR OF DISRUPTIVE STUDENTS

K. Daniel O'Leary
Kenneth F. Kaufman
Ruth E. Kass
Ronald S. Drabman

A NUMBER OF STUDIES demonstrate that teacher attention in the form of praise can reduce disruptive classroom behavior (Becker, Madsen, Arnold, and Thomas, 1967; Hall, Lund, and Jackson, 1968; Madsen, Becker, and Thomas, 1968; Walker and Buckley, 1968). In these studies, praising appropriate behavior was usually concomitant with ignoring disruptive behavior. In addition, shaping appropriate behavior or reinforcing successive approximations to some desired terminal behavior was stressed. Despite the generally positive results obtained when a teacher used these procedures, a closer examination of the studies reveals that (a) they were not always effective (Hall *et al.*, 1968), (b) the teacher did not actually ignore all disruptive behavior (Madsen *et al.*, 1968), and (c) in one class of disruptive children, praising appropriate behavior and ignoring disruptive behavior resulted in classroom pandemonium (O'Leary, Becker, Evans, and Saudargas, 1969).

One might argue that where praising appropriate behavior and ignoring disruptive behavior prove ineffectual, the teacher is not appropriately shaping the children's behavior. Although such an argument is theoretically rational, it is of little solace to a teacher who unsuccessfully attempts to reinforce approximations to desired terminal behaviors. Furthermore, the supposition that the teacher is not appropriately shaping ignores the power of peers to reinforce disruptive behavior. Disregard of disruptive behavior is based on two premises—that it will extinguish if it is not reinforced and that praising appropriate behavior which is incompatible with disruptive behavior will reduce the frequency of the latter. However, even when a teacher ignores disruptive behavior, other children may reinforce it by giggling and smiling. These peer reactions may occur only occasionally, but they may make the disruptive behavior highly resistant to extinction. Thus, the teacher may ask what she can do when praise and ignoring are not effective. The present studies were designed to assess one alternative to ignoring disruptive behavior: reprimanding the child in a soft manner so that other children in the classroom could not hear the reprimand.

The effectiveness of punishment in suppressing behavior of animals has been amply documented (Solomon, 1964). Similarly, the effectiveness of punishment with children in experimental settings has been repeatedly demonstrated (Parke and Walters, 1967). However, experimental manipulations of punishment or reprimands with disruptive children have not often been investigated in applied settings. One attempt to manipulate teacher reprimands was made by O'Leary and Becker (1968) who varied aspects of teacher attention and found that soft reprimands were effective in reducing disruptive behavior of a class of first grade children during a rest period. Since soft reprimands seemed to have no adverse side effects in the study and since ignoring disruptive behavior is not always effective, further analyses of the effects of soft reprimands seemed promising.

Soft reprimands offer several interesting advantages over loud ones. First of all, a soft reprimand does not single out the child so that his disruptive behavior is made noticeable to others. Second, a soft reprimand is presumably different from the reprimands that disruptive children ordinarily receive at home or in school, and, consequently, it should minimize the possibility of triggering conditioned emotional reactions to reprimands. Third, teachers consider soft reprimands a viable alternative to the usual methods of dealing with disruptive behavior. Two experiments are presented here which assessed the effects of soft reprimands.

Experiment I

Two children in a second grade class were selected for observation because of their high rates of disruptive behavior. During a baseline condition, the frequency of disruptive behaviors and teacher reprimands was assessed. Almost all reprimands were loud, i.e., many children in the class could hear them. During the second phase of the study, the teacher was asked to voice her reprimands so that they would be audible only to the child to whom they were directed. The third phase of the study constituted a return to the teacher's former loud reprimand. Finally, during the fourth condition, the teacher was requested to again use soft reprimands.

SUBJECTS. Child D was described as nervous and restless. He bit his nails, drummed his fingers on his desk, and stuttered. He was often out of his seat talking and bothering other children. D avoided any challenging work. He was quick to argue and was known to get into trouble in the neighborhood.

Child S was described as uncooperative and silly. He paid little attention to his work, and he would often giggle and say things out loud. His teacher said that he enjoyed having other children laugh at him and that he acted in this manner to gain attention.

OBSERVATION. Before base period data were collected, college undergraduates were trained over a three-week period to observe in the classroom. During this time, the observers obtained reliabilities of child observations exceeding 70 percent agreement. There were two undergraduate observers. One observed daily, and the other observed less frequently, serving as a reliability checker. The observers were instructed to neither talk nor make any differential responses in order to minimize their effect on the children's behavior.

Each child was observed for 20 minutes a day during the arithmetic lesson. Observations were made on a 20-second observe, 10-second record basis: The observer would watch the child for 20 seconds and then record in 10 seconds the disruptive behaviors which had occurred during that 20-second period. The disruptive behaviors were categorized according to nine classes modified from the O'Leary and Becker study (1967). The nine classes of disruptive behavior and their associated general definitions are:

1. *Out-of-chair:* Movement of the child from his chair when not permitted or requested by teacher. No part of the child's body is to be touching the chair.
2. *Modified out-of-chair:* Movement of the child from his chair with some part of the body still touching the chair (exclude sitting on feet).
3. *Touching others' property:* Child comes into contact with another's property without permission to do so. Includes grabbing, rearranging, destroying the property of another, and touching the desk of another.
4. *Vocalization:* Any unpermitted audible behavior emanating from the mouth.
5. *Playing:* Child uses his hands to play with his own or community property so that such behavior is incompatible with learning.
6. *Orienting:* The turning or orienting response is not rated unless the child is seated and the turn must be more than 90 degrees, using the desk as a reference point.
7. *Noise:* Child creating any audible noise other than vocalization without permission.
8. *Aggression:* Child makes movement toward another person to come into contact with him (exclude brushing against another).
9. *Time off task:* Child does not do assigned work for entire 20-second interval. For example, child does not write or read when so assigned.

The dependent measure, mean frequency of disruptive behavior, was calculated by dividing the total number of disruptive behaviors by the number of intervals observed. A mean frequency measure was obtained rather than frequency of disruptive behavior per day since the length of observations varied due to unavoidable circumstances such as assemblies. Nonetheless, only three of the 27 observations for child D lasted less than 20 minutes and only four of the 28 observations for child S were less than 20 minutes. Observations of less than ten minutes were not included.

RELIABILITY. The reliabilities of child observations were calculated according to the following procedure. A perfect agreement was scored if both observers recorded the same disruptive behavior within a 20-second interval. The reliabilities were then calculated by dividing the number of perfect agreements by the number of different disruptive behaviors observed providing a measure of percent agreement. There were three reliability checks during the base period (Loud I) and one during the first soft period for child D. There were two reliability checks during the base period and one reliability check during the first soft period for child S. The four reliability checks for child D yielded the following results: 81, 72, 64, and 92 percent agreement; the three for child S resulted in: 88, 93, and 84 percent agreement.

The reliability of the observations of the teacher's loud and soft reprimands to the target children was also checked. On two different days these observations were taken simultaneously with the observation of the target children. One reliability check was made during the base period and one check was made during the first soft period. A perfect agreement was scored if both observers agreed that the reprimand was loud or soft and if both observers scored the reprimand in the same 20-second interval. The consequent reliabilities were 100 percent and 75 percent during the base period and first soft period respectively.

Procedures

BASE PERIOD (LOUD I). During the base period the teacher was asked to handle the children as she normally would. Since few, if any, soft reprimands occurred during the base period, this period was considered a loud reprimand phase.

SOFT REPRIMANDS I. During this phase the following instructions were given to the teacher:

1. Make reprimands soft all day, i.e., speak so that only the child being reprimanded can hear you.

2. Approximately one-half hour before the observers come into your room, concentrate on using soft reprimands so that the observers' entrance does not signal a change in teacher behavior.
3. While the observers are in the room, use only soft reprimands with the target children.
4. Do not increase the frequency of reprimands. Reprimand as frequently as you have always done and vary only the intensity.
5. Use soft reprimands with all the children, not just the target children.

LOUD REPRIMANDS II. During this phase the teacher was asked to return to loud reprimands, and the five instructions above for the soft period were repeated with a substitution of loud reprimands for soft ones.

SOFT REPRIMANDS II. During this final period, the teacher was asked to return to the soft reprimand procedures.

Results

CHILD D. Child D displayed a marked reaction to soft reprimands. The mean frequency of disruptive behavior during the four conditions was: Loud I, 1.1; Soft I, 0.8; Loud II, 1.3; Soft II, 0.9. A reversal of effects was evident. When the loud reprimands were reinstated disruptive behavior increased while disruptive behavior declined during the second soft period (Fig. 15-1). In addition, in order to more closely examine the effects of the two types of reprimands, there was an assessment of the frequency of disruptive behaviors in the two 20-second intervals after a reprimand, when another reprimand had not occurred in one of the two intervals. The results revealed that the average number of disruptive behaviors in these two intervals during the four conditions was: Loud I, 2.8; Soft I, 1.2; Loud II, 2.6; and Soft II, 1.6.

CHILD S. Child S also displayed a marked reaction to soft reprimands. The mean frequency of his disruptive behavior during the four conditions was: Loud I, 1.4; Soft I, 0.6; Loud II, 1.1; Soft II, 0.5. Again a reversal of effects was evident when the

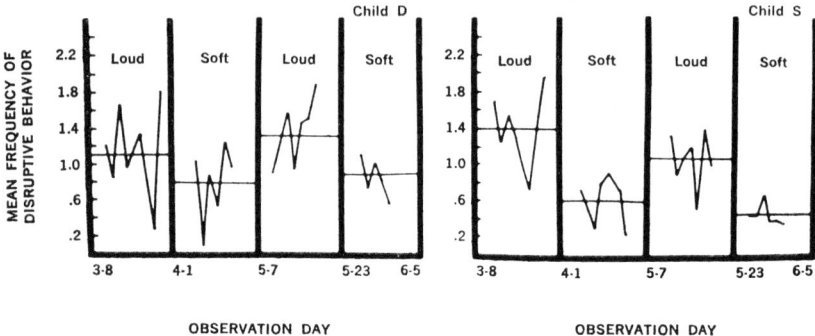

Figure 15-1. Disruptive behavior of children D and S in Class A.

loud reprimands were reinstated. The average number of disruptive behaviors in the two 20-second intervals just after a reprimand was made was as follows during the four conditions: Loud I, 2.9; Soft I, 1.5; Loud II, 2.1; Soft II, 0.9.

TEACHER. Although teacher A was asked to hold constant the incidence of her reprimands across conditions, the mean frequency of her reprimands to child D during the four conditions was: Loud I, 7; Soft I, 5; Loud II, 12; Soft II, 6. Similarly, she also had difficulty in holding constant her reprimands to child S across conditions as the following data show: Loud I, 6; Soft I, 4; Loud II, 8; Soft II, 3. Thus, there is some possibility that the increase in disruptive behavior during the second loud phase was a consequence of increased attention to the behavior per se, rather than a consequence of the kind of attention given, whether loud or soft. As the disruptive behavior increased, teacher A felt it impossible to use the same number of reprimands that she had used during the soft period.

Because the frequency of loud reprimands was greater than the frequency of soft reprimands, one could not conclude from Experiment I that the loudness or softness of the reprimands was the key factor in reducing disruptive behavior. It was clear, however, that if a teacher used soft reprimands, she could use fewer reprimands and obtain better behavior than if she used loud reprimands.

Experiment II

Experiment II was conducted to assess the effects of loud and soft reprimands with the frequency held constant and to test whether all the children's disruptive behavior decreased when the teacher used soft reprimands. Experiment II is divided into three parts. Part I followed the same ABAB paradigm described in Experiment I (Loud, Soft, Loud, Soft), but Parts II and III involved variations which will be described later.

Part I

SUBJECTS. Class B, Grade 2: Child Z was a large boy who said that he wanted to be a bully when he grew up. He was the only child in the class who deliberately hurt other children. He constantly called out answers without raising his hand and his work habits were poor. Child V was extremely talkative. He loved to be with other children and he was always bursting with something to say. He was also mischievous, but never intentionally hurt anyone. His work habits were poor and his papers were never completed.

Class C, Grade 3: Child E was an extremely nervous child. When she directed all her energy to her studies she could perform well. However, she was very undependable and rarely did her work. She was in and out of her seat and talked endlessly. Child W was a disruptive child whose reaction to most situations was to punch, kick, throw things, and to shove others out of his way. He did little work and devoted his time to such activities as chewing his pencils and punching holes in his papers.

OBSERVATION. The observational procedures described earlier in Experiment I were identical to those used in Experiment II. Each target child was observed during a structured academic lesson for 20 minutes each day on a 20-second observe, 10-second record basis. The nine classes of disruptive behavior were the same as those in Experiment I with some definitional extensions and a slight change in the definition of aggression. The dependent measure was calculated in the same manner as described in Experiment I.

To minimize the possibility of distance as the key factor in reprimanding the children, the target children in both classes were moved near the front of the room so that the teacher could administer soft reprimands without walking a great distance. This seating arrangement made it easier for the teacher to reprimand the target children either loudly or softly and decreased the possibility of the teacher's serving as a cue for appropriate behavior by her walking to the child.

The occurrence of loud and soft reprimands was recorded throughout the study by a teacher-observer. As mentioned previously, the teachers were asked to hold the frequency of reprimands constant both to the target children and to the class throughout the study. The teacher was also asked to hold other behaviors as constant as possible so that behaviors such as praise, "eyeing down" a child, and reprimands to the class as a whole would not confound the results. A graduate student observed almost daily and gave the teachers feedback to ensure adherence to these requirements.

In addition to observations on target children, daily observations of disruptive behavior were taken on all the other children by a sampling procedure for one hour each day. Each nontarget child was observed consecutively for two minutes. The observer watched the children in a predetermined order each day, looking for the disruptive behaviors that had been observed in the target children.

RELIABILITY. The reliabilities of child observations for both

TABLE 15-I

THE AVERAGE OF THE MEAN LEVELS OF DISRUPTIVE BEHAVIOR DURING THE LAST FIVE DAYS OF EACH CONDITION FOR THE TARGET CHILDREN

Subjects	Condition			
	Loud I ($\bar{x}=1.3$)	Soft I ($\bar{x}=0.9$)	Loud II ($\bar{x}=1.2$)	Soft II ($\bar{x}=0.5$)
Child Z	1.0	0.9	1.3	0.8
Child V	1.7	1.4	1.3	0.6
Child E	0.9	0.6	1.1	0.4
Child W	1.6	0.8	0.9	0.3

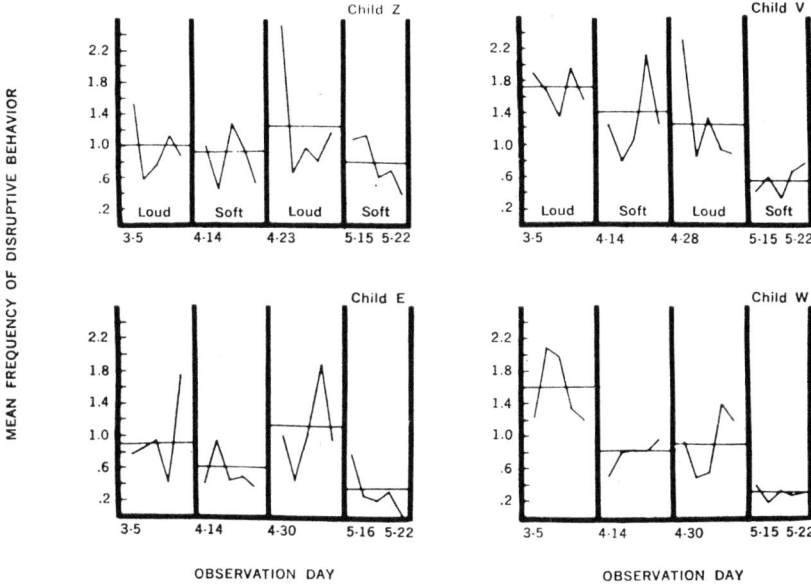

Figure 15-2. Disruptive behavior of children Z and V in Class B and children E and W in Class C.

the target children and the class samples were calculated according to the procedures discussed in Experiment I. There were three reliability checks during the base period for both target children and the class sample. The average reliability for the target children was 84 percent and for the class sample was 79 percent. Nine additional reliability checks of the observations averaged 79 percent for the target children and 82 percent for the class sample.

The reliability of the observations during the base period of loud and soft reprimands used by Teacher B was 79 percent and 80 percent respectively. The reliability of the observation of loud and soft reprimands used by Teacher C was 82 percent and 72 percent respectively.

RESULTS. Because there were definite decreasing trends of disruptive behavior during both soft conditions for three of the four target children, the average of the mean levels of disruptive behavior during the last five days of each condition for the target children are reported in Table 15-I. There were changes in children's behavior associated with changes in teacher behavior (see Fig. 15-2). There was a decrease in the children's disruptive behavior in the soft reprimand phase and then an increase in the disruptive behavior of three of the four children during the reinstatement of loud reprimands. Finally, the second soft period was marked by a decrease in disruptive behavior. Although the disruptive behavior of child V did not increase during the reinstitution of loud reprimands, a reduction of disruptive behavior was associated with each introduction of soft reprimands—particularly during the second soft phase. Consequently, soft reprimands seemed to influence the reduction of disruptive behavior of each of the four children. A mean reduction of 0.4 and 0.7 disruptive behaviors was associated with each introduction of soft reprimands for these children.

In order to demonstrate that the reduction of disruptive behavior was not a function of changes in frequency or reprimands, the frequencies of loud and soft reprimands are provided in Table 15-II. Although there was some slight reduction of reprimands for individual children during the soft reprimand

TABLE 15-II

AVERAGE FREQUENCY OF LOUD AND SOFT REPRIMANDS PER DAY

Condition	Type of Reprimand to Child Z		Condition	Type of Reprimand to Child V	
	Loud	Soft		Loud	Soft
Loud I	3.8	2.0	Loud	6.8	2.2
Soft I	0.6	2.6	Soft	0.5	6.7
Loud II	3.0	1.7	Loud	3.5	1.0
Soft II	0.1	2.6	Soft	0.1	3.6
Condition	Reprimand to Child E		Condition	Reprimand to Child W	
	Loud	Soft		Loud	Soft
Loud I	3.5	0.6	Loud	3.3	0.7
Soft I	0.4	5.0	Soft	0.4	2.3
Loud II	5.7	0.9	Loud	5.3	0.3
Soft II	0.2	3.4	Soft	0.1	4.6

phases, the teachers were able to hold the frequency of reprimands relatively constant across days and conditions, despite an obvious change in the children's behavior. The mean total reprimands, loud and soft, during the four conditions were as follows: Loud I, 5.7; Soft I, 4.6; Loud II, 5.3; Soft II, 3.7. Also of particular significance was the constancy of praise comments across conditions. There was an average of less than one praise comment per day given to each child in each of the four conditions. It can be inferred from these data that soft reprimands can be influential in modifying classroom behavior of particularly disruptive children.

The data from the class samples taken during the last five days of each condition did not show that soft reprimands reduced disruptive behavior for the whole class. Because of the variability within conditions and the lack of any clear relationship between type of reprimands and level of disruptive behavior, those data are not presented here. However, the changes in the behavior of the target children are evident when one considers that the mean frequency of disruptive behavior for the class sample B was .9 throughout the experiment and .8 during the second soft condition. The mean frequency of disruptive behavior for the class sample C was .6 throughout the experiment and .5 during the second soft condition. Thus one should note that the disruptive behavior of the four target children during the second soft period was less than the level of disruptive behavior for the class.

Part II

Two target children and a class sample were observed in the class of a third-grade teacher. A baseline (Loud I) of disruptive behavior was obtained in this class during a structured academic lesson using the procedures described in Experiment I. In the second phase of the study (Soft I) the teacher was asked to use soft reprimands, just as the other teachers had done. Because of the infrequency of her reprimands in the second phase, the teacher was asked to double her use of soft reprimands in phase three (Soft II-Double). During phase four (Loud II), she was asked to maintain her more frequent use of reprimands but to make them loud. Both child and teacher observations were made in accord with the procedures described in Part I of Experiment II.

SUBJECTS. Child B was reported to be a happy extrovert who was a compulsive talker. Child R was described by his teacher as a clown with a very short attention span.

RELIABILITY. The reliability of child observations was obtained for the target children on seven occasions, and the reliability of the class sample on five occasions. The resultant average reliabilities were 87 percent and 87 percent, respectively.

The reliability of the observations of teacher behavior was checked on two occasions during the base period and once during the first soft period. The average reliability of the observations of loud and soft reprimands was 82 percent and 72 percent, respectively.

RESULTS. Child B's disruptive behavior declined from 1.6 during the last five days of baseline (loud reprimands) to 1.3 during the last five days of soft reprimands. In contrast, child R's disruptive behavior increased from 1.5 in the last five days of baseline to 1.9 during the last five days of soft reprimands (see Fig. 15-3). With the instructions to increase the use of soft reprimands during phase three (Soft II-Double), child B's disruptive behavior showed a slight drop to 1.1 while child R's increased slightly to 2.0. The return to loud reprimands was asso-

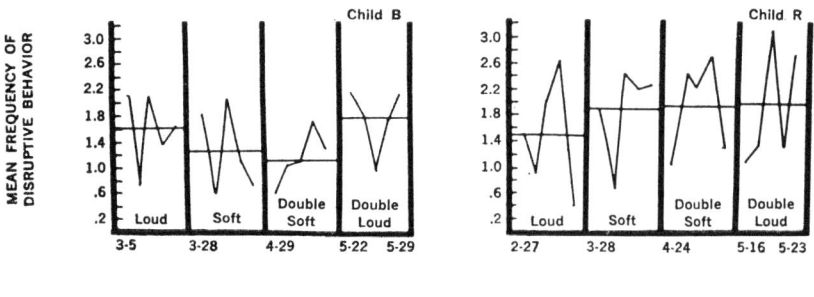

Figure 15-3. Disruptive behavior of children B and R in Class D.

TABLE 15-III

AVERAGE FREQUENCY OF LOUD AND SOFT REPRIMANDS PER DAY

Condition	Type of Reprimand to Child B		Condition	Type of Reprimand to Child R	
	Loud	Soft		Loud	Soft
Loud I	2.0	0.4	Loud	1.5	0.2
Soft I	0.5	1.0	Soft	0.2	0.0
Soft II (Double)	1.8	1.1	Double soft	0.0	0.8
Loud II	3.1	2.3	Loud	2.5	0.0
Condition	Reprimand to Child D		Condition	Reprimand to Child J	
	Loud	Soft		Loud	Soft
Loud	4.5	1.3	Loud	1.3	0.2
Soft	0.2	3.2	Soft	0.0	2.2

ciated with an increase to 1.8 for child B and almost no change for child R.

The increase in child R's disruptive behavior from the loud to the first soft condition cannot be attributed to the soft reprimands. In fact, the change appeared to be due to a decrease in both loud and soft reprimands. Even with the instructions to double the use of soft reprimands, the teacher observations reported in Table 15-III indicate that the frequency of total reprimands during the double soft phase was less than during baseline. However, since child R's disruptive behavior did not increase with the return to loud reprimands, the experimental control over R's behavior was minimal or nonexistent. On the other hand, child B's disruptive behavior appeared to lessen with the use of soft reprimands.

Again, the data from the class sample did not show that soft reprimands reduced disruptive behavior for the whole class. Those data will not be presented here in detail. The mean frequency of disruptive behavior for the class sample throughout the experiment was .62.

Discussion. The failure to decrease child R's disruptive behavior by soft reprimands may have been due to his very deficient academic repertoire. He was so far behind his classmates that group instruction was almost meaningless for him. It is also possible that the teacher felt frustrated because of increases in child R's disruptive behavior when she used soft reprimands; teacher D found them particularly difficult to use. She stated, "It was difficult for me to give soft reprimands as I feared they were a sign of weakness. The walking and whispering necessary to administer soft reprimands to the disruptive child were especially strenuous for me. As the day wore on, I found that my patience became exhausted and my natural tendency to shout like a general took over." Also of particular note was an observer's comment that when verbal reprimands were administered, whether in a loud or soft phase, they were rarely if ever soft in intensity. In summary, teacher D's data showed that soft reprimands did reduce disruptive behavior in one child. Because of lack of evidence for any consistent use of soft reprimands to the second child, nothing can be said conclusively about its use with him.

Part III

In a third grade class of a fourth teacher, two target children and a class sample were observed during a structured academic activity. A baseline of disruptive behavior was obtained in the class with procedures identical to those of Experiment I. In the second phase of the study, the teacher was asked to use soft reprimands, just as the other teachers had done. Because of some unexpected results following this second phase, the general nature of the study was then changed and those results will not be presented here. Both child and teacher observations were made according to the procedures described in Part I of Experiment II.

SUBJECTS. Child D was a very intelligent boy (135 IQ) who scored in the seventh grade range on the reading part of the Metropolitan Achievement Test but he was only slightly above grade level in mathematics. His relations with his peers were very antagonistic.

Child J was occasionally considered disruptive by his teacher. However, he did not perform assigned tasks and would often pretend to be working while he actually was not.

RELIABILITY. The reliability of child observations was obtained for the target children on fifteen occasions, and the reliability of the class sample was obtained on three occasions. The resultant average reliabilities were 88 percent for the observations of the target children and 91 percent for the observations of the class sample.

The reliability of the observations of teacher behavior was checked on two occasions during the base period and once during the soft period. The average reliability of the observations of loud and soft reprimands on these three occasions was 78 percent and 79 percent respectively.

RESULTS. Child D's disruptive behavior increased from .9 during the last five days of baseline (loud reprimands) to 1.0 during the last five days of soft reprimands. Child J's disruptive behavior increased from .4 to .8 from baseline to the soft reprimand period (see Fig. 15-4). There was no change in the class sample from baseline to the soft reprimand period. The mean frequency of disruptive behavior for the class sample during the loud and soft phase was .6 and .5 respectively.

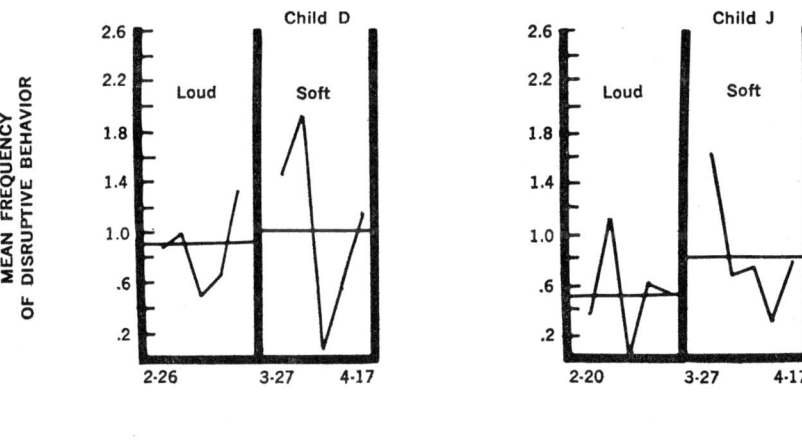

Figure 15-4. Disruptive behavior of children D and J in Class E.

As can be seen in Table 15-III teacher E's behavior with child D and child J did appear to have been influenced by the experimental instructions.

DISCUSSION. The reasons that soft reprimands failed to decrease disruptive behavior in this class are not clear. Several factors may have been important. First of all, teacher E was always very skeptical about the possibility that soft reprimands could influence disruptive behavior whereas the other teachers were willing to acknowledge the probability of their influence. Second, it is possible that the children learned to control the teacher's behavior since a soft reprimand had to be made while the teacher was close to the child. That is, a child might realize that he could draw the teacher to his side each time he misbehaved during the soft reprimand period. In addition, this teacher tolerated more disruptive behavior than the other teachers, and her class was much less structured. Probably most important, she wished to investigate the effectiveness of various types of instructional programs rather than soft reprimands.

Conclusions

These two experiments demonstrated that when teachers used soft reprimands, they were effective in modifying behavior in seven of nine disruptive children. Because of a failure to document the proper use of soft reprimands by one teacher (D) to one child, it is impossible to assess the effectiveness on that child. Of particular significance was the finding that soft reprimands seemed to be associated with an increase in disruptive behavior of one—and possibly two—target children in one teacher's class although the soft reprimands did not influence the level of disruptive behavior for the class as a whole. The results of Experiments I and II lead to the conclusion that with particularly disruptive children a teacher can generally use fewer soft reprimands than loud ones and obtain less disruptive behavior than when loud reprimands are used.

The authors wish to make clear that they do not recommend soft reprimands as an alternative to praise. An ideal combination would probably be frequent praise, some soft reprimands, and very occasional loud reprimands. Furthermore, it is always necessary to realize that classroom management procedures such as praise and types of reprimanding are no substitute for a good academic program. In the class where soft reprimands were ineffective for both target children, a type of individualized instruction was later introduced, and the disruptive behavior of both the target children and the class sample declined.

Because soft reprimands are delivered by a teacher when she is close to a child, it is possible that a soft reprimand differs from a loud one in dimensions other than audibility to many children. Although observations of teachers in this study did not reveal that teachers made their soft reprimands in a less harsh, firm, or intense manner than their loud reprimands, it might be possible for a teacher to utilize soft reprimands in such a manner. If the latter were true, soft reprimands might require less teacher effort than loud reprimands. Ultimately soft reprimands might prove more reinforcing for the teacher both because of the relatively small expenditure of effort and the generally positive and sometimes dramatic changes in the children's behavior. The inherent nature of the soft reprimand makes its use impossible at all times, particularly when a teacher has to remain at the blackboard or with a small group in one part of the room. As one teacher mentioned, "I had to do more moving around, but there appeared to be less restlessness in the class."

In sum, it is the authors' opinion that soft reprimands can be a useful method of dealing with disruptive children in a classroom. Combined with praise, soft reprimands might be very helpful in reducing disruptive behavior. In contrast, it appears that loud reprimands lead one into a vicious cycle of more and more reprimands resulting in even more disruptive behavior.

REFERENCES

Becker, W. C., Madsen, C. H., Jr., Arnold, C., and Thomas, D. R.: The contingent use of teacher attention and praise in reducing classroom behavior problems. *J Spec Educ*, 1:287-307, 1967.

Hall, R. V., Lund, D., and Jackson, D.: Effects of teacher attention on study behavior. *J Appl Behav Anal*, 1:1-12, 1968.

Madsen, C. H., Becker, W. C., and Thomas, D. R.: Rules, praise, and ignoring: Elements of elementary classroom control. *J Appl Behav Anal, 1:* 139-150, 1968.

O'Leary, K. D., and Becker, W. C.: Behavior modification of an adjustment class: A token reinforcement program. *Except Child, 33:*637-642, 1967.

———: The effects of a teacher's reprimands on children's behavior. *J School Psychol, 7:*8-11, 1968.

O'Leary, K. D., Becker, W. C., Evans, M. B., and Saudargas, R. A.: A token reinforcement program in a public school: A replication and systematic analysis. *J Appl Behav Anal, 2:*3-13, 1969.

Parke, R. D., and Walters, R. H.: Some factors influencing the efficacy of punishment training for inducing response inhibition. *Monogr Soc Res Child Dev, 32:*(1, Serial No. 109) 00, 1967.

Solomon, R. L.: Punishment. *Am Psychol, 19:* 239-253, 1964.

Walker, H. M., and Buckley, N. K.: The use of positive reinforcement in conditioning attending behavior. *J Appl Behav Anal, 1:*245-250, 1968.

Chapter 16

THE SANTA MONICA PROJECT: EVALUATION OF AN ENGINEERED CLASSROOM DESIGN WITH EMOTIONALLY DISTURBED CHILDREN

FRANK M. HEWETT
FRANK D. TAYLOR
ALFRED A. ARTUSO

APPLICATION OF BEHAVIOR modification methodology in educational programs for children with emotional disturbance has provided evidence that systematic manipulation of stimuli and consequences in the classroom often result in significant behavioral and academic improvement (Patterson and Ebner, 1965; Quay, Werry, McQueen, and Sprague, 1966; Whelan, 1966; Nolen, Kunzelmann and Haring, 1967). The teacher approaches the disturbed child as a behavior and learning problem rather than an "ill" or "impaired," and while demands which the child cannot handle emotionally or which call for competencies he lacks are not arbitrarily made, appropriate and reasonable behavioral and academic goals are established. In general, selection of these goals is based on a desire to aid the child in changing maladaptive behavior to adaptive behavior. At best, these concepts of "maladaptive" and "adaptive" provide only the broadest of guidelines for selection of specific behavioral goals. In this sense the powerful methodology of the behavior modification approach is not matched by concern with goals in learning. Teachers are provided with an efficient means of taking emotionally disturbed children someplace, but are not substantially aided in the selection of where to go.

It is this lack of balanced emphasis on goals and methods that may preclude the acceptance of behavior modification in the field of education, particularly in the public school, and thereby may greatly limit its usefulness. An interesting parallel to this state of affairs can be drawn with reference to psychoanalytic theory and psychodynamic psychology. These approaches have had an important influence on special education for the emotionally disturbed over the past several decades, but their preoccupation with therapeutic goals to the almost complete exclusion of concern with educational methodology has restricted their acceptance and effectiveness in public school programs for these children.

Engineered Classroom Design

The engineered classroom design attempts to approach education of the emotionally disturbed with a balanced emphasis on goals and methods. The disturbed child is viewed as a socialization failure and assessed in terms of his developmental learning deficiencies. These deficiencies are determined with reference to a developmental sequence of educational goals (Hewett, 1968) which postulates that in order for the child to learn successfully he must pay *attention,* make a *response, order* his behavior, accurately and thoroughly engage in multisensory *exploratory* behavior, gain *social* approval, and require *mastery* of self care and cognitive skills. Finally he must function on a self motivated bases with *achievement* in learning providing its own reward.

The room arrangement, teacher-pupil ratio, schedule, and operations of the engineered classroom support attainment of these goals, and manipulation of stimuli and consequences in the program is done in accord with the behavior modification methodology. The room is divided into three major centers: (a) the mastery and achievement center including the students' desks and two study booths where academic assignments are given; (b) the exploratory-social center where science, art, and communication activities take place; and (c) the attention-response-order center which provides simple direction following tasks. There are nine students, a teacher, and an aide in each classroom. The four hour class day is divided into two hours of reading, written language, and arithmetic; one hour of exploratory activities; and a total of one hour of physical education and recesses. Each child carries a Work Record Card with him throughout the day, and earns a possible ten checkmarks every 15 minutes. Checkmarks are given for starting and working on tasks and for behavior related to the levels on the developmental sequence which are most critical for each individual child. Completed Work Record Cards may be exchanged weekly for tangible rewards in Phase I of the program, for time to pursue self-selected activities in Phase II, and for daily graphing of total checkmarks earned in Phase III. The Santa Monica Project as reported here utilized only the Phase I approach. Throughout the day, a given child may be assigned tasks relating to any level on the developmental sequence in an effort to keep him learning and earning checkmarks as a successful student. A complete description of the program and the planned interventions directed toward assuring students success has been reported elsewhere (Hewett, 1966, 1967, 1968a, 1968b).

The Santa Monica Project was undertaken by the authors to assess the effectiveness of the engineered classroom design in maintaining student attention to tasks and in improving academic achievement level. It was done in the Santa Monica Unified School District, Santa Monica, California, during 1966-1967. Santa Monica is a coastal community near the city of Los Angeles with a broad range of socioeconomic levels similar in proportion to the greater Los Angeles county area.

Subjects

Fifty-four children with learning and behavior problems, the majority of which were considered "emotionally disturbed," were assigned to six project classrooms with nine students in each. These children ranged in age from 8-0 to 11-11 years and ranged in Full Scale IQ score from 85 to 113 as determined by the Wechsler Intelligence Scale for Children. Academically the children were functioning in reading from 0 to 6.2 grade levels and in arithmetic fundamentals from 0 to 5.2 grade levels, as measured by the California Achievement Test (elementary level). With the exception of five children, all students were two or more years below their expected grade level in reading and all but seven were two or more years below in arithmetic fundamentals.

TABLE 16-I

MEAN VALUES FOR IQ, AGE, AND ACHIEVEMENT LEVEL FOR THE SIX PROJECT CLASSROOMS

Class	Mean IQ	Mean Age	Mean Total Reading Grade Equivalent	Mean Total Arithmetic Grade Equivalent
1	93	10-4	3.0	3.9
2	95	10-6	2.0	3.4
3	92	10-8	2.5	3.0
4	96	10-1	3.2	3.3
5	98	9-9	3.0	3.4
6	93	10-4	2.3	3.0

In the assignment of individual children to project classrooms, an attempt was made to arrive at comparable class groupings with respect to IQ, age, and reading and arithmetic achievement. Since so few girls were located, control could not be exerted over the variable of sex. Table 16-I reports the mean values for IQ, age, and achievement level in each of the six project classrooms.

Teachers

Six female elementary school teachers were selected from teaching applicants to the Santa Monica District prior to the 1966-1967 school year. None had taught previously in the district, one had never taught before, and the teaching experience of the others ranged from three to eight years. Only one teacher had worked before with emotionally disturbed children. Their final selection was made by the Santa Monica School District personnel office on the basis of strong qualifications and an expression of willingness to participate in the project. Six female teacher aides (without prior teaching experience) were also selected from a group of housewives and graduate students who applied.

A two-week training program was conducted prior to the beginning of the school year to acquaint all of the teachers and aides with the goals and methods of the engineered classroom design. This training program included lectures, group discussions, and demonstrations conducted by the authors. Following this training program each teacher and aide was randomly assigned to a project classroom which had previously been designated as either experimental or control.

Procedure

The experimental condition of the project involved rigid adherence to the engineered classroom design and systematic reliance on the giving of checkmarks. The control condition of the project consisted of any approach the teacher chose to follow, including aspects of the engineered design except use of tangible or token rewards. Conventional grading, verbal praise, complimentary written comments on completed assignments, and awarding privileges for good work were all acceptable. To facilitate assessment of the effect of introducing and withdrawing the experimental and control condition, the project classes were assigned as shown in Table 16-II.

Class E maintained the experimental condition for the entire project year while Class C maintained the control condition during that time. Classes CE began as control, but abruptly introduced the experimental condition at midyear. The reverse was true for Classes EC which started as experimental and then abruptly shifted to control at the project's midpoint.

As has been stated, the independent variable in the project was rigid adherence to the engineered design and use of the checkmark system. The dependent variables also were briefly mentioned—student task attention and academic functioning level in reading and arithmetic.

TABLE 16-II

ASSIGNMENT OF PROJECT CLASSES TO EXPERIMENTAL AND CONTROL CONDITIONS

Class	Fall Semester	Spring Semester
1 (E)	Experimental	Experimental
2 (C)	Control	Control
3 and 4 (CE)	Control	Experimental
5 and 6 (EC)	Experimental	Control

Two observers sat in front of each project classroom for 2½ hours daily during the 34-week project period. These observers were undergraduate college students recruited and trained for this assignment. Each observer held a stopwatch and was assigned four or five children to observe regularly. The children were observed for five minute segments throughout the observation period in random order so that at least five separate samples of task attention were obtained on each student each day. Observers recorded the number of seconds the student's eyes (or in some cases his head and body) were appropriately oriented toward an assigned task. Specific criteria for crediting a student for "task attention" were established. The project observers were trained by two graduate students who had reached a 90 percent or better agreement between themselves for task attention measurement. Each observer was then paired with one of the graduate students until reliability was established at a level of 90 percent or better. Every two weeks the graduate students rotated through the classrooms rechecking reliability and at no point in the project was agreement found to be below the 85 percent level. Daily individual task attention percentages were obtained on each child; these percentages were totalled for all the children in a class, and a weekly task attention percentage mean was obtained for each project class.

All students were retested twice with parallel forms of the California Achievement Test used in the initial screening—once at midyear and once at the close of the project.

The six project classrooms were visited each week by the authors and the project coordinator. Weekly meetings were held with the teachers, at which time problems with individual students were taken up with the project coordinator. In general he continually referred to the engineered design and its resources for handling problems presented by experimental teachers. With the control teachers he made similar suggestions (without reference to the giving of tangible or token rewards) but usually offered several alternatives. Separate meetings of the project staff and the parents of children enrolled in each class were held near the start of the project. The class program was presented and questions brought up by the parents were discussed at this time. There was no other systematic attempt to meet or work with the parents during the project.

On the first Monday morning of the spring semester the teachers in Classes CE introduced the engineered design to their students. At the same time, the teachers in Classes EC announced that checkmarks would not be used any more. These teachers had altered the room arrangement and were free to conduct the program from that point on any way they wished but without the previous reward system. Class E continued as a year long experimental class and Class C continued using the control condition for the remainder of the year.

Results

The results of the Santa Monica Project evaluation will be discussed in reference to three main questions:

1. What was the effect on task attention and achievement level of introducing the experimental condition to emotionally disturbed children who had previously been in a regular class?
2. What was the effect on task attention and achievement level of introducing the experimental condition to emotionally disturbed children who had previously been in a small, individualized class under the control condition?
3. What was the effect on task attention and achievement level

TABLE 16-III

MEAN TASK ATTENTION PERCENTAGES FOR ALL CLASSES, AVERAGED FOR 4 WEEKS INTERVALS DURING FALL AND SPRING SEMESTERS

Class	Fall Semester				Spring Semester			
	1 Weeks 2-5	2 Weeks 6-9	3 Weeks 10-13	4 Weeks 14-17	5 Weeks 2-5	6 Weeks 6-9	7 Weeks 10-13	8 Weeks 14-17
E	82.3	87.6	94.2	93.8	92.0	93.9	94.8	94.0
C	90.7	84.5	81.1	89.0	86.7	86.3	86.7	84.4
EC	85.5	85.8	87.7	86.6	85.6	90.0	91.8	91.3
CE	76.2	78.0	84.3	81.6	84.5	91.0	92.0	90.5

of abruptly withdrawing the experimental condition from a class of emotionally disturbed children who had become accustomed to it over a semester?

Table 16-III presents the mean task attention percentages for all project classrooms, averaged for four-week intervals during the fall and spring semesters. The mean task attention percentages are based on five daily five minute observations made on each child in a given class; in most cases at least 100 such observations were made on every child during each four week interval. Figure 16-1 shows these four week interval mean task attention percentages.

Table 16-IV reports the achievement data obtained during initial screening, at the midyear point, and at the end of the project year.

In the discussion which follows a difference reported as "significant" represents the .05 level of confidence or better. Specific reference to the statistical method used to evaluate project data (analysis of variance, covariance, and t test) will not be made nor will the complete data from the evaluation be presented. However, this has been reported elsewhere (Hewett, Taylor, and Artuso, 1967).

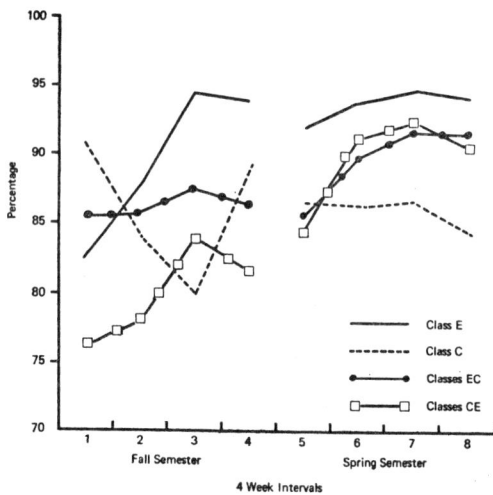

Figure 16-1. Mean task attention of Class E, Class C, Classes EC and Classes CE averaged for 4-week intervals during the fall and spring semesters.

TABLE 16-IV

MEAN RAW SCORES AND GRADE EQUIVALENTS IN
READING AND ARITHEMETIC FOR ALL PROJECT CLASSES

Test	Initial Screening			Midyear				End of Year			
	E	C	EC	CE	E	C	EC	CE	E	C	EC	CE
CAT Total	31.4 (3.2)[a]	23.1 (2.8)	28.1 (3.1)	24.8 (2.9)	33.1 (3.3)	34.4 (3.4)	32.9 (3.3)	33.4 (3.3)	38.0 (3.6)	30.6 (3.2)	35.9 (3.5)	37.8 (3.6)
Reading												
CAT Arithmetic Fundamentals	15.1 (3.9)	10.5 (3.4)	10.7 (3.4)	11.1 (3.5)	20.7 (4.6)	13.9 (3.8)	15.2 (3.9)	13.5 (3.8)	24.9 (5.0)	11.7 (3.6)	19.8 (4.5)	19.7 (4.5)

[a] Figures in parentheses represent grade equivalents.

Classes E and C provide information with reference to question one cited earlier. While Class C enjoyed a significant task attention advantage over Class E during interval 1 in Figure 16-1, this disappeared in interval 2. Beginning with interval 3 Class E maintained superiority in task attention for the remainder of the project year.

Achievement data in Table 16-IV reveal no significant difference in reading between the classes, but a significant difference in arithmetic fundamentals in favor of Class E is seen. Class E showed a 1.2 year gain while Class C gained only 0.4 year during the project. The experimental condition, then, was related to significantly higher task attention among students coming from regular classes from interval 3 on, and was also related to a significant gain in arithmetic over the year.

Question 2 may be considered by comparing Class C and Classes CE. During the fall semester, all three classes utilized the control condition. At midyear Classes CE shifted to the experimental condition, thus providing evidence regarding the effect of this condition on children already enrolled in a small class group. Class C maintained a significantly higher task attention percentage during intervals 1, 3, and 4 during the control phase over Classes CE. But by interval 5 when Classes CE introduced the experimental condition there was no such difference, and during intervals 6, 7, and 8 these classes attained a significantly higher task attention level than Class C. While no significant differences emerged in reading, Classes CE made a significant gain over Class C in arithmetic fundamentals during the spring semester when they utilized the experimental condition. Therefore both task attention and arithmetic gains were related to the introduction of the experimental condition.

In relation to question 3, Class E and Classes EC provided information. All three classes utilized the experimental condition during the fall semester but at midyear Classes EC eliminated rigid adherence to the experimental condition and use of checkmarks and tangible rewards. Evidence was then obtained regarding the effect of abrupt withdrawal of the experimental condition on a small class that had become accustomed to it. Except for intervals 1 and 2, Class E achieved a significantly higher task attention level during the fall semester than Classes EC when all were using the experimental condition. This continued during intervals 5 and 6 but ceased to exist during the last half of the spring semester. During these intervals Classes EC attained their highest task attention level, indicating with respect to task attention that removal of the experimental condition had a facilitating effect. There were no significant differences in reading or arithmetic between Class E and Classes EC either semester. Class E and Classes EC made their gain in arithmetic consistently over the entire year. In summary, removal of the experimental condition resulted in improved task attention in Classes EC but did not affect achievement levels in reading or arithmetic.

Discussion and Conclusions

The major findings of the Santa Monica project can be summarized as follows: task attention of students was significantly facilitated by the experimental condition when that condition was introduced to emotionally disturbed children following placement in either a regular or control condition class. Task attention was also facilitated by removal of the experimental condition from classes which had become accustomed to it over a one semester period. Reading achievement was not significantly affected by either the experimental or control condition but gains in arithmetic fundamentals were significantly correlated with the presence of the experimental condition.

The facilitating effect of the experimental condition on student task attention is seen as related to the emphasis in the engineered design on building *attention, response,* and *order* behaviors. The planned routine of the classroom, the provision for systematic acknowledgment of functioning level by means of the checkmark system, and continual reassignment to tasks promoting success undoubtedly contributed to students' becoming more willing, efficient, and consistent in paying attention. The teacher in Class C, which enjoyed a significant task attention advantage over Class E during interval 1, was concerned with maintaining her students at a high task attention level since she, as did all the other teachers, knew this was being measured by the observers. Without the checkmark system she had to use considerable verbalization and social reinforcement in controlling student behavior. While this technique made her initially more effective in orienting them toward assigned tasks, its effectiveness quickly diminished following the first four weeks. This may be related to the questionable responsiveness of emotionally disturbed children to social reinforcement, which has been reported by Levin and Simmons (1962) and Quay and Hunt (1965). The more objective and neutral checkmark system, while admittedly providing reinforcement on a more primitive level, may be better suited for initiating contact with disturbed students and starting them toward success in school.

The correlation between arithmetic improvement and presence of the experimental condition is also probably a reflection of the emphasis on attention, response, and order behavior present in classes utilizing this condition. The building of these basic learning competencies may more directly and immediately apply to arithmetic than to language arts subjects such as reading.

Perhaps the most interesting and somewhat surprising finding was that Classes EC actually improved in task attention following removal of the experimental condition. This change was apparently not just due to time in a special class alone since Class E and Class C showed no such improvement during the second half of the year. Another hypothesis to explain Classes EC improvement under the control condition might center on a novelty effect; any major innovation, even the taking away of something supposedly desirable such as tangible rewards, might be expected to bring about an initial change in student behavior. This hypothesis is rejected because of the long period of time covered in the evaluation. A novelty effect might exert influence over the first several weeks but it is doubtful it would be maintained over a 17 week period. A more logical explanation is to view the improvement of Classes EC in task attention under the control condition as resulting from (a) the increased effectiveness of the teachers in these classes to function as secondary social reinforcers due to their semester long association with a success oriented approach using a primary reward system, and (b) the investment made in building competencies at the attention, response, and order levels during the experimental condition which readied the students for participation in a teacher centered, more traditional educational program utilizing exploratory, social, and mastery tasks and rewards.

Certainly evidence was provided that the use of tangible rewards on a temporary basis does not doom children to dependence on them. On the contrary, it appears such rewards may be extremely useful in launching children with behavior and learning problems into successful learning in school.

The engineered classroom design as evaluated in the Santa Monica Project appears basically a launching approach. Its provision for increasing the teacher's effectiveness as a social reinforcer through systematic association with student success and primary rewards and for building fundamental learning competencies often forgotten about in education past the primary grades may greatly aid the disturbed child in taking the first step toward achieving success in school.

REFERENCES

Hewett, F.: The Tulare experimental class for educationally handicapped children. *Calif Educ*, 3:6-8, 1966.

———: Educational engineering with emotionally disturbed children. *Except Child*, 33:459-467, 1967.

———: An engineered classroom design for emotionally disturbed children. In J. Hellmuth (Ed.): *Educational Therapy*. Seattle, Special Child Publications, 1968(a), vol. 2.

———: *The Emotionally Disturbed Child in the Classroom: A Developmental Strategy for Educating Children With Maladaptive Behavior.* Boston, Allyn and Bacon, 1968(b).

Hewett, F., Taylor, F., and Artuso, A.: *The Santa Monica Project: Demonstration and evaluation of an engineered classroom design for emotionally disturbed children in the public school, phase 1: Elementary level.* Final Report. Project No. 62893, Demonstration Grant No. OEG-4-7-062893-0377, Office of Education, Bureau of Research, US Department of Health, Education and Welfare, 1967.

Levin, G., and Simmons, J.: Response to praise by emotionally disturbed boys. *Psychol Rep*, 11:10, 1962.

Nolen, P., Kunzelmann, H., and Haring, N.: Behavioral modification in a junior high learning disabilities classroom. *Except Child*, 34:163-169, 1967.

Patterson, G., and Ebner, M.: Application of learning principles to the treatment of deviant children. Paper presented at the meeting of the American Psychological Association, Chicago, September 1965.

Quay, H., and Hunt, W.: Psychopathy, neuroticism and verbal conditioning: A replication and extension. *J Consult Psychol, 29:*283, 1965.

Quay, H., Werry, J. S., McQueen, M., and Sprague, R. L.: Remediation of the conduct problem child in the special class setting. *Except Child, 32:*509-515, 1966.

Whelan, R. J.: The relevance of behavior modification procedures for teachers of emotionally disturbed children. In P. Knoblock (Ed.): *Intervention Approaches in Educating Emotionally Disturbed Children.* Syracuse, Syracuse University Press, 1966.

Chapter 17

BEHAVIOR MODIFICATION OF CHILDREN WITH LEARNING DISABILITIES USING GRADES AS TOKENS AND ALLOWANCES AS BACK UP REINFORCERS

Hugh S. McKenzie
Marilyn Clark
Montrose M. Wolf
Richard Kothera
Cedric Benson

A NUMBER OF INVESTIGATIONS have indicated that behavior modification techniques can be highly effective in the beneficial change of social and academic behaviors of both normal and exceptional children. Recent research has applied these techniques to bright, preschool children (Bushell, Wrobel, and McCloskey, 1967); to school dropouts (Clark, Lackowicz, and Wolf, in press); to emotionally disturbed children (O'Leary and Becker, 1967); and to low achieving culturally deprived children (Wolf, Giles, and Hall, in press). More extensive reviews of this growing body of experimental literature may be found in Anderson (1967) and Whelan (1966). The approach that these investigations have taken has been to employ token reinforcers such as colored chips or point cards to improve and maintain improvement of social and/or academic behaviors. Items such as candy, gum, toys, and money have served as back-up reinforcers to these tokens, since tokens are exchanged for them.

The problems which can be created, even by an effective token reinforcement system, may be numerous. Not only can token systems be costly in terms of teacher time, but they also may involve an additional burden to already strained school budgets. The administration of tokens such as colored chips and the overseeing of the exchange of tokens for back up reinforcers such as toys may be an unfamiliar role for teachers. Also, parents may be given no function in a token system, although it is recognized that parents can play an integral part in an effective program for children with special needs (Cruickshank, 1967).

These considerations mean that a token system must make a contribution to the amelioration of the children's learning difficulties which is significantly greater than that possible with less costly procedures. As O'Leary and Becker (1967) have indicated, the rationale usually offered for employing token systems is that other incentives available to the school, such as teacher attention and grades, have not been effective, since the children involved still exhibit a high frequency of asocial and nonacademic behaviors.

The primary goal of the present research was to assess whether a pay for grades token reinforcement system could increase academic behavior to levels higher than those achieveable with the usually available school incentives. Another aim was to reduce the problems often associated with token systems. By employing grades as tokens, the teacher was not subjected to an unfamiliar role. With weekly allowances as back-up reinforcers for grades, parents were able to administer the exchange aspect of the system and were consequently involved in the program. Because parents managed the exchange of tokens for back up reinforcers, and because corrections and some form of grades are an integral part of almost any instructional program, the teacher spent little extra time in the execution of this system. Since the parents of the children of the present study were accustomed to giving their children allowances, neither parents nor school assumed added costs.

Method

SUBJECTS. The subjects were ten students in a learning disabilities class which was held in Skyline Elementary School, Roeland School District #92, Shawnee Mission, Kansas, during the 1966-1967 school year. This class was one of several special classes operated by the Northeast Johnson County Cooperative Program in Special Education, Johnson County, Kansas.

These ten students, eight boys and two girls, ranged in age from ten to 13 years and were selected for a learning disabilities class on the basis that although their ability levels were above the educable mentally retarded range, their achievement levels were retarded by at least two years in one or more academic areas. All students had received medical and/or psychological evaluations which had suggested minimal brain damage with accompanying emotional disturbance. Case histories reported all students to be highly distractible and prone to engage in disruptive behaviors.

Data are reported on eight of the ten students, as data were incomplete on two students who returned to regular classes after the first week of the pay for weekly grades period.

TEACHER. Prior to teaching the Skyline special class, the teacher had had five years of full time teaching and five years of teacher substitute work in grades K-8. She had obtained her M.Ed. in Special Education from the University of Kansas, with the major part of the academic work for this degree involving courses in behavior modification and operant psychology. Her master's thesis dealt with a basic education program for school dropouts employing a token reinforcement system (Clark, Lackowicz, and Wolf, in press).

Volunteers from a women's service organization also participated in the program as teacher aides. These aides served mainly to correct and grade the children's academic work.

CLASSROOM. The Skyline special classroom is similar to self contained classrooms found in many elementary schools. With the exception of desk shields extending about twenty inches above and on three sides of a desk's writing surface, no effort was made to reduce stimuli in the room to a bare minimum, as is sometimes recommended (Cruickshank, 1967). Decorative curtains served as window drapes; different colors surfaced walls, floor, and ceiling; books, teaching materials, and art supplies were always in full view. Walls served as display areas for the children's art work and construction projects. The room often had a festive air as the children decorated it for the various seasons.

INSTRUCTIONAL MATERIAL AND PROGRAMING. The commercially available academic materials used were those which might be found in any elementary classroom. Where possible, the children worked on programed instructional materials (e.g., the SRA reading series). Otherwise, children did workbook assignments (e.g., Ginn's arithmetic workbooks). Such materials were used because they require overt responses.

Prior to the beginning of school and during the first two days of school, the teacher tested the children with the Durrell Analysis of Reading Difficulty and the SRA Achievement Tests. On the basis of these measures, children were placed at academic levels in each of the five instructional areas of the class: reading, arithmetic, spelling, penmanship, and English composition and grammar.

Children were given weekly assignments in each of these five instructional areas, with one assignment sheet for each area. Assignment sheets listed the materials to be worked on each day and the total number of responses assigned, and provided space for the child to record his starting and finishing time and for the teacher (or aide) to record daily the number of responses completed, the number correct, and the child's grade. In each academic area, children were required to complete all previous assignments before going on to new work. If any work was not completed by the week's end, it was assigned for the following week as a new assignment.

OBSERVATIONS AND RECORDING PROCEDURES. Children were observed by a research assistant through the one-way mirror of a room adjacant to the classroom. A sound system was arranged so that the assistant could hear what occurred.

Observation time covered the first three hours of every morning: the reading and arithmetic periods, together with a short break between these periods in which the children had physical education or recess. Attending was defined as direct orientation toward work materials, i.e., a child was scored as attending if he was sitting at his desk with materials open and before him, and eyes directed toward these materials. Any contact with teacher or aide (raising hand for teacher help or discussion of assignment) was likewise scored as attending. In group work, a child was scored as attending if he was oriented toward work materials, to a reciting fellow student, or to the teacher, or if he himself was responding orally to a lesson. All behaviors other than those specified above were scored as nonattending.

An attending score was obtained for each child once every three minutes. From 90 to 120 seconds were required to observe and score the entire class. The remaining 60 to 90 seconds of the three minute period were used to note teacher and aide behaviors and prepare for the next group of observations.

The reading period lasted about 80 minutes and the arithmetic 60, so that approximately 26 and 20 measures of attending to reading and arithmetic, respectively, could be made on each child on each school day. A child would at times finish an assignment early, resulting in fewer observations of that child for that assignment period. The observer stopped recording the behavior of a child when he had turned his materials in to the teacher or aide and these materials had been certified as complete.

Although the observer was aware of the general orientation of the investigation, he was informed neither of the details of the pay for grades procedure, nor of when it was put into effect.

BASELINE PEROID. Incentives available in the school were employed as described below.

1. *Recess.* The children earned recess by the successful completion of all of their assignments for the given assignment week up to the point of a given recess period. Children were required to work through recess if their work was not complete.
2. *Free Time Activities.* When a child had completed all of his assigned work before a given academic period had ended, he was free to go to a free time table to draw, paint, or construct, or he could read a book of his choice at his seat. Free time activities were not available to children until all work was complete.
3. *Special Privileges.* School errands were run by those children who were working hard and well, or who had shown recent improvement in the quality of their work. Line leaders and monitors were chosen on the same basis.
4. *Group versus Individual Lunch.* Children who had all of

their work complete by lunchtime earned the privilege of eating in the school cafeteria with the rest of the school. Those whose work was incomplete ate at their desks, in silence.

5. *Teacher Attention.* The attention of the teacher was contingent upon appropriate working behaviors of the children. For example, the teacher would say to a hard working child, "Good for you, you're working well, and that's the way you'll become smart in arithmetic and return to regular class sooner." Inappropriate behavior was either ignored or, if disruptive, was punished.

6. *Weekly Grades.* Every week children were given grades to take home to their parents. The parents signed the grade sheets, which the children then returned to the teacher. Both daily and weekly grades were included on these grade sheets. *A* grades indicated that a child had finished his work with 90 percent correct, *B* indicated 80 to 90 percent, *C* indicated 79 percent and below, and *Incomplete* indicated that a child had failed to finish his assigned work.

The teacher conducted group parent conferences once a month at the school, during which time the parents were instructed to praise grades of *A* and *B* and to compliment children for their hard work. Grades of *C* were acceptable, while brief expressions of sorrow were to be paired with grades of *Incomplete* (e.g., "That's too bad you didn't finish all your work in reading this week"), and children were to be encouraged to finish all work for the next week.

Discussions about academic behaviors and their reinforcers were undertaken by the teacher with individual children as well as with the entire group. These discussions were kept brief and never were held when a child was emotionally upset. Through these discussions it was hoped that the children would gain a further awareness of how they could succeed academically and what rewards would accompany such achievement.

To be maximally effective, reinforcers must be consistently applied. In this case, academic behaviors were consistently reinforced, while nonacademic behaviors were extinguished (not reinforced) or punished (resulting in the removal of some reinforcer). To ensure consistency, both the observer and the first author observed the teacher (and aides, where appropriate) and made at least one report a day to the teacher concerning her application of behavior modification techniques. For example, a tally sheet was kept of the number of times the teacher attended to academic behaviors during the school day and of the number of times she incorrectly attended to inappropriate, nonacademic behaviors. By daily discussion of this tally sheet, the teacher was able to increase her frequency of attending to good behaviors and could virtually ignore the unacceptable ones.

The teacher was likewise informed if a child had earned but not been awarded the opportunity to run a school errand, and if a child should not have been allowed recess because of incomplete work. With this information feedback, the teacher appeared to increase her behavior modification skills.

PAY FOR WEEKLY GRADES PERIOD. All procedures employed during the baseline period were continued in identical fashion during the pay period. However, the weekly grades of the baseline period now acquired an additional back up reinforcer: the payment of a weekly allowance to children by their parents on the basis of the children's grades for all subject areas. All the children had received some allowance previous to this period, but the amount received had not depended on their weekly grades. Children were paid for the average weekly grade of each subject area.

At a parent teacher conference toward the end of the baseline period, parents were instructed in the pay for grades procedures. As an example, parents were told that a child might be paid ten cents for *A's*, five cents for *B's*, and one cent for *C's*, while *Incompletes* would lead to a subtraction of the *A* amount, or minus ten cents. The parents determined the precise amounts on the basis of how much money their child was accustomed to having and the cost of the items he would be expected to purchase from his earnings. Amounts actually paid by parents for the weekly grades ranged from the values in the above example up to five times each grade amount in the example. Thus, with the five areas of the special class, plus physical education and music which the children took with the other children in the school, children's maximum earnings varied from $.70 to $3.50. With *Incompletes* being subtracted from earned allowance, it was possible for a child to owe his parents money. Toward this eventuality, parents were told to allow such an indebted child to perform some household chores over the weekend to square his debt. No money beyond the debt was to be earned, however. One indebted child, during the early part of the pay period, settled the debt by cleaning the garage.

Parents were asked to sit down with their child each Friday afternoon when the child brought home his weekly grades, calculate with the child the amount earned, and then pay him this amount. This was to be made an important weekly event. Parents were also asked to see that a large portion of the allowance be immediately consumed, and that the child be expected to pay with his earnings for all items he valued highly. Such things as movies, sweets, models, dolls, horseback riding, the purchase and care of pets, makeup, and inexpensive clothes were to be the children's financial responsibility. The children were not allowed to earn other money about the home, and any added money which came as presents or which was earned outside the home was to be banked. Such procedures helped to maintain the child's need and desire for money at high levels so that money would continue to serve as an effective reinforcer for academic behavior.

Parents informed their children of the pay procedure on the day before the start of the week which would lead to the first payment for weekly grades. Parents also told their children what items the child would be expected to purchase with his earned allowance.

The pay procedure was continued for the remainder of the year for all children, including children who returned to regular classes. Regular classroom teachers were instructed to give these children grades of D and F, as well as higher grades, when their work was at these levels. A grade of D substracted the B amount from a child's allowance, while a grade of F subtracted the A

amount. When a child had successfully made the transition to regular class and had performed well for an extended period of time, the length of grade periods was increased, e.g., from once a week to once every two weeks, with appropriate increases in amounts paid for grades. In this way it was hoped to strengthen the child's academic behavior further and to prepare him for the longer grading periods he would encounter in his future schooling.

Results

A marked increase in attending to reading occurred in the pay period compared with the baseline period (see Fig. 17-1). Overall medians increased from 68 percent in the baseline period to 86 percent in the pay period.

It is necessary to be certain that the increases in the pay period cannot be attributed to progressive, though perhaps gradual, increases during the baseline period, since the consequences employed during the baseline period may have been increasing attending. Since the most powerful test for such trends was desired, an analysis of variance, rather than a nonparametric test, was performed on the baseline data, yielding an F ratio of less than one (see Table 17-I) which allows the retention of the hypothesis that the baseline procedures had no tendency to increase attending to reading. By computing eta square, it was estimated that trends accounted for only 6 percent of the variance of the baseline period.

The increase in attending to reading from the baseline period

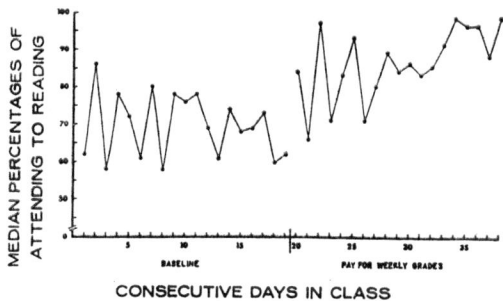

Figure 17-1. Patterns of medians in attending to reading.

TABLE 17-I

ANALYSIS OF VARIANCE FOR BASELINE TRENDS
OF PERCENTAGES OF ATTENDING TO READING

Source	SS	df	MS	F
Between subjects	32345.368	7		
Within subjects	36351.684	144		
Trends	4337.302	18	240.96	<1
Residual	32014.382	126	254.08	

to the pay period was significant (see Table 17-II); $p < .005$, one tailed Wilcoxon Matched Pairs Signed Ranks Test (Siegel, 1956). The data for each student conformed very closely to the pattern of medians shown in Figure 17-1. Thus, it can be inferred that the token reinforcement system led to substantial gains in attending to reading for all students.

Similar results were obtained in arithmetic (see Fig. 17-2). Overall medians increased from 70 percent in the baseline period to 86 percent in the pay period. The analysis of variance for trends during the arithmetic baseline period also yielded an insignficant F ratio (see Table 17-III; $F = 1.154, p > .25$). Through eta square, it was estimated that only 8 percent of the baseline arithmetic variance could be accounted for by trends.

Attending to arithmetic also showed significant increases for the pay period over the baseline period (see Table 17-IV; $p <$

TABLE 17-II

SUBJECTS' MEDIAN PERCENTAGES OF ATTENDING TO READING

Subjects	Baseline	Pay	Increase
S1	71	89	18
S2	82	95	13
S3	23	77	54
S4	83	93	10
S5	72	83	11
S6	72	79	7
S7	75	83	8
S8	62	75	13

Note: Wilcoxon $T = 0$; $p < .005$ (one tailed test).

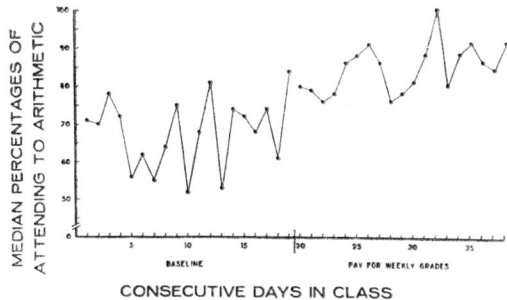

Figure 17-2. Patterns of medians in attending to arithmetic.

.005, one tailed Wilcoxon Test). Six subjects' graphs showed the same general form as the median graph in Figure 17-2. Thus, it can be inferred that the token system led to substantial gains in attending to arithmetic for these six subjects. The remaining two subjects (Subjects 2 and 7) showed gradual but steady increases in attending to arithmetic for the last ten days of the baseline period. Consequently, it cannot be concluded that the increases in attending to arithmetic shown by these two subjects for the pay period over the baseline period can be attributed solely to the pay for weekly grades procedure.

Percentages of attending were determined in the following way: if a total of 20 observations were made on a child in arithmetic, and if, of these, ten were scored as attending, the child's percentage of attending to arithmetic on that day was 10/20 × 100 or 50 percent. Reliability checks were made between the first

TABLE 17-III

ANALYSIS OF VARIANCE FOR BASELINE TRENDS OF PERCENTAGES OF ATTENDING TO ARITHMETIC

Source	SS	df	MS	F
Between subjects	36957.158	7		
Within subjects	51337.684	144		
Trends	7265.842	18	403.678	1.154*
Residual	44071.842	126	349.776	

* $p > .25$.

TABLE 17-IV

SUBJECTS' MEDIAN PERCENTAGES OF ATTENDING TO ARITHMETIC

Subjects	Baseline	Pay	Increase
S1	67	88	21
S2	89	94	5
S3	36	79	43
S4	80	94	14
S5	83	88	5
S6	63	76	13
S7	64	81	17
S8	53	68	15

Note: Wilcoxon $T = 0$; $p < .005$ (one tailed test).

author and the observer on four occasions, two for reading and two for arithmetic. Reliability coefficients, estimated by the Pearson product moment formula and calculated across subjects with day and academic area held constant, were .91 and .95 for reading and .88 and .90 for arithmetic.

The attending data were obtained during October, November, and part of December, 1966. The month of September was used to refine the observational techniques and to ensure that instructional procedures and materials were adequate to meet each child's needs.

Although the observations were stopped after Christmas vacation, the number of *Incompletes* (with the exception of Subject 8) and the percentages of correct responses indicated that subjects maintained for the remainder of the school year the level of academic behavior attained during the pay period. Students' earnings varied from week to week and ranged from 30 to 85 percent of maximum possible earnings.

As the working efficiency of the students increased, larger assignments were given. At the end of the school year, all ten students were working successfully one to four levels above their starting levels in all academic areas. Six of the ten students were returned full time to regular classes to one grade higher than the ones they had been in during the previous school year. For two of these six, grading periods were extended to four weeks and for one, to two weeks, while the other three remained on the one week period since they were returned to regular classes with only two months of the school year left. In spite of the fact that regular classroom teachers were instructed to give grades of D and F when appropriate, half of the returned students consistently earned B averages and half earned C averages. At the close of the school year, all six of the returned students were again promoted, this time by their regular classroom teachers.

Discussion

The present study demonstrated that a token reinforcement system with grades as tokens and allowances as back-up reinforcers can significantly increase levels of academic behavior beyond those maintained by the systematic application of other reinforcers available to a school.

All students, with the exception of Subject 8, maintained these increased levels of academic behavior. This subject, with the pay still in effect, would alternate several weeks of complete work and high grades with several weeks of incomplete work. His parents reported that they had never reached agreement on the proper administration of the pay procedures and were, consequently, very inconsistent in its application. The subject was originally required to purchase his weekly movie and a construction model, yet his parents said that they gave him these rewards even when his earnings were insufficient to purchase them. One parent, on several occasions, had claimed all of his earnings as payment for misdemeanors committed at home. In the spring of the year he acquired a high level of social and academic behavior which was maintained for the remainder of the school year. This change in his behavior was coincidental with the death of one of his parents.

Grades have long been the token reinforcement system of schools. But as a reinforcer's effectiveness is directly proportional to its immediacy of presentation (Bijou and Baer, 1961), an apparent weakness of this grade system has been that grade reports are presented to children every six to nine weeks, a long delay of reinforcement for a child of elementary school age.

Teachers must correct children's work to ensure learning, and it is but a small step from corrections to grades. Although the teacher of the present study had volunteer aides to assist in the grading, the teacher felt that she could carry out the daily grading and weekly reports, and actually did for the many days that aides were absent.

No test was made to test the effect of the allowance back-up reinforcer in the maintenance of high levels of academic behavior for the remainder of the school year. This effect could have been tested by paying the children their allowances independently of their weekly grades. If attending to academic materials had decreased significantly with this change, evidence would have been provided for a maintaining effect for this back-up reinforcer. The risk of returning students to their less efficient levels of the baseline period overruled the possible gains in scientific information, and this analysis was not made.

Conclusion

The token reinforcement system used in the present study increased levels of academic behavior with highly distractible and disruptive children. Several additional advantages are inherent in this token system. First, teachers need not spend valuable time in overseeing the exchange of tokens for back-up reinforcers. Parents can manage this task at home. Secondly, parents are frequently able to bear the cost of the allowance back-up reinforcer, as many parents provide allowances for their children anyway. For parents unable to bear this cost, it seems likely that a service organization could be found which would contribute funds which parents could then pay to their children on the basis of weekly grades. Finally, the present system can open, as it did in this case, an effective channel of communication and cooperation between parents and teachers of children with special educational needs.

REFERENCES

Anderson, R. C.: Educational psychology. In P. R. Farnsworth (Ed.): *Annual Review of Psychology*. Palo Alto, California, Annual Reviews, 1967. pp. 129-164, vol. 18.

Bijou, S. W., and Baer, D. M.: *Child Development*. New York, Appleton-Century-Crofts, 1961, vol. 1.

Bushell, D., Wrobel, P. A., and McCloskey, M. L.: Some effects of norma-

tive reinforcement on classroom study behavior. Unpublished manuscript, Webster College, 1967.
Clark, M., Lackowicz, J., and Wolf, M.: A pilot basic education program for school dropouts incorporating a token reinforcement system. *Behav Res Ther,* 6(2):in press, 1968.
Cruickshank, W. M.: *The Brain-Injured Child in Home, School, and Community.* Syracuse, New York, Syracuse University Press, 1967.
O'Leary, K. D., and Becker, W. C.: Behavior modification of an adjustment class: a token reinforcement system. *Except Child,* 33:637-642, 1967.
Siegel, S.: *Nonparametric Statistics.* New York, McGraw-Hill, 1956.
Whelan, R. J.: The relevance of behavior modification procedures for teachers of emotionally disturbed children. In P. Knoblock (Ed.): *Intervention Approaches in Educating Emotionally Disturbed Children.* Syracuse, New York, Syracuse University Press, 1966, pp. 35-78.
Wolf, M. M., Giles, D. K., and Hall, V. R.: Experiments with token reinforcement in a remedial classroom. *Behav Res Ther,* 6:51-64, 1968.

Chapter 18

A BEHAVIOR MODIFICATION CLASSROOM FOR HEAD START CHILDREN WITH PROBLEM BEHAVIORS

K. Eileen Allen
Keith D. Turner
Paulette M. Everett

HEAD START PROGRAMS across the country represent a diversity of educational models. Klein (1969) described a number of these: the traditional nursery school approach exemplified by the Bank Street program, the Deutsch-type programs based on sequential programing with heavy emphasis on listening, the autotelic-discovery approach espoused by Nimnicht and the Far West Laboratory, the cognitively oriented programs modeled after Weickart's work at Ypsilanti, and the "pressure-cooker" approach of Engelmann and Becker, to name a few. These programs have demonstrated, in varying degrees, their effectiveness in ameliorating the accumulated deficits of young poverty children.

But what about the children with severe behavior disorders who seem to profit little or not at all from a head start program? Although they are relatively few in number, perhaps only one or two in a head start class (about the same ratio as in middle-class nursery schools), they do exist, regardless of the educational model upon which the class is based. These children exact a heavy toll of teachers' time and energy, often to the detriment of the other children.

The Demonstration Project

It is imperative that effective programs be created for these children. One possible approach is described in this paper. The project, entitled the Demonstration Head Start Classroom (Haring, Hayden, and Nolen, 1969), has three major goals: (a) to furnish remedial services for children with marked behavioral excesses or deficits; (b) to provide a training program for the teachers of these children; and (c) to conduct research in behavior modification procedures through analyses of teacher-child interactions.

Twelve of 15 children are enrolled in the class at one time with individual enrollment periods varying from three weeks to six months. The children are referred by head start teachers in consultation with a head start interdisciplinary team. Some of the reasons given for referral include severely disruptive, excessively withdrawn, lacking in communication skills, hyperactive, incontinent, schizoid, echolalic, and brain damaged.

The ideal program for each child study contains four phases:
1. Observation of the child and his teachers and the accumulation of baseline data in the home classroom prior to the child's entry in the demonstration class.
2. Enrollment in the demonstration class for a period of time adequate to ameliorate the child's problems.
3. Involvement of home classroom teachers in an in-service training program.
4. Return of the child to his home classroom with collection of followup data and guidance for the teacher.

Behavior Modification Procedures

The overall philosophy of the demonstration class is based on the application of behavior modification techniques derived from principles of reinforcement. An abundant literature attests to the effectiveness of such procedures in dealing with the aberrant behaviors of preschool children. A few examples include: regressive crawling (Harris, Johnston, Kelley, and Wolf, 1964), hyperactivity (Allen, Henke, Harris, Baer, and Reynolds, 1967), operant crying (Hart, Allen, Buell, Harris, and Wolf, 1964), and mutilative self-scratching (Allen and Harris, 1966).

A single unifying theme is apparent in each of these experimental analyses: The common, everyday social behaviors or responses of preschool teachers are powerful determinants of child behavior. Therefore, the child behaviors that teachers respond to will increase while the child behaviors that teachers fail to respond to will decrease. If a teacher wishes to eliminate the isolate tendencies of an excessively shy child (Allen, Hart, Buell, Harris, and Wolf, 1964), she withholds her smiles, nods, conversation, suggestions, and presentation of materials as long as the child isolates himself from the group. But the moment the isolate child moves toward a peer or a peer group activity, the teacher immediately directs attention to him, reinforcing (providing consequences for) his first approximations to social behavior. By controlling the timing of responses, that is, holding responses contingent on the child's emission of appropriate rather than maladaptive behaviors, preschool teachers have demonstrated that beneficial behavior changes can be effected (Harris, Wolf, and Baer, 1964).

Individualized Programing

In accordance with the principles of systematic application of behavior modification procedures, the demonstration class emphasizes an individualized program for each child within the context of a typical preschool program. The daily schedule, though flexible, has a basic structure which enables children to acquire skills in self-management. Such skills are, or should be, one of the major educational goals of a well-designed preschool program. However, the program is also organized to promote each child's acquisition of social, verbal, preacademic, and motor skills. To this end, a variety of quiet, sedentary activities are balanced by vigorous play activities; child-initiated activites are balanced by teacher-structured and teacher-directed activities. Regardless of the activity in progress, the teachers are continually on the alert to reinforce target behaviors peculiar to each child's individual needs.

During outdoor play, for example, when the overall emphasis is on free play and vigorous large motor activities, a dozen different programs may be in effect: for one child, the teachers may be reinforcing appropriate peer contacts; for another, constructive use of materials; for a third child, more creative use of the equipment. Several different verbal development programs may be in progress: reinforcement of one child for more audible verbal output, of another for simply joining two words, of a third for asking for instead of grabbing. Span of attention, sharing, concept development, visual and auditory discriminations—all of these skills and many more, a teacher can teach (reinforce) in the context of a free play situation if she has carefully specified in advance the target learning or behaviors for each child.

Part of the daily program is devoted to a more formal, preacademic work time when the children sit at tables in small groups. The tasks consist of activities designed to extend attention span, increase perceptual-motor skills, refine visual and auditory discrimination skills, and develop basic concepts of size, shape, color, equivalence, seriation, and spatial relationships. Again, the program is individualized and is based on the skill levels of each child at the time of his entry into the class. Materials used are those found in every preschool classroom: puzzles, pegboards, matching cards, color cubes, formboards, and a variety of teacher-made materials. The materials are carefully sequenced, however, so that each child acquires specific learning in gradual increments. Correct responses and error rates over time are recorded by the teacher on each task for each child (Nolen, Hulten, and Kunzelmann, 1968). These data provide the teachers with a basis for preparing individual lesson kits so that maximum success comes to each child as he acquires the basic school performance skills.

Natural Contingencies

The natural reinforcers in the environment are also carefully monitored by the teachers. For example, receiving a snack is contingent on completion by each child of his preacademic tasks. However, for a new child or an excessively active child, material may be so programmed that he is required to attend to academic tasks for as little as three minutes at first (30 seconds has been a beginning requirement in some cases). The time depends entirely on the individual child's behavior. The crucial factor is that the teacher set the first approximation in accordance with the target behavior.

Another example of the monitoring of the natural reinforcers in the preschool environment is the opportunity to go out of doors. Going outside to play is always contingent on the child's putting away blocks, housekeeping materials, or whatever else the child was playing with at the time. Thus, in the demonstration class, all activities and teacher attention are devoted to molding appropriate behaviors, and nothing is expended on attending to maladaptive responses. Three adults effectively manage and provide a sound educational program for 12 to 15 children who only a short time before were causes for grave concern in their home classrooms. To illustrate individual behavior modification programs, two case studies are presented.

Case Study I

Townsend was 4½ years old when he was transferred to the demonstration class. Collection of data (according to the system described by Bijou, Peterson, Harris, Allen, and Johnston, 1969) continued after his transfer to the demonstration class, where the teachers were instructed during the baseline period to replicate as nearly as possible the homeroom teachers' methods of handling Townsend: rechanneling his disruptive activities, comforting him during outbursts, and physically restraining him when he attacked other children. Maladaptive behaviors continued at a high rate during baseline conditions.

Tantrum Behavior

On Townsend's eleventh day in the demonstration classroom a first step in behavior modification was initiated. All tantrums, regardless of duration or intensity, were to be ignored, that is, put on extinction. Absolute disregard of the tantrum, no matter how severe it might become, had to be thoroughly understood by the teachers inasmuch as there are data (Hawkins, Peterson, Schweid, and Bijou, 1966) which indicate that when tantrums are put on extinction, extremes of tantrumming may temporarily ensue. Townsend's data were no exception to the classic extinction curve. His first tantrum under the nonattending contingency lasted 27 minutes (average duration of previous tantrums had been 5 minutes), becoming progressively more severe up to the 20-minute point. When it became obvious that the tantrum was going to be lengthy, the other children were taken to the playground by a teacher and a volunteer while the second teacher stationed herself immediately outside the classroom door. When Townsend quieted down, the teacher opened the door to ask in a matter-of-fact voice if he was ready to go to the playground. Before the teacher had a chance to speak, Townsend recommenced his tantrum. The teacher stepped back outside to wait for another period of calm. Twice more Townsend quieted down, only to begin anew at the sight of the teacher. Each time, however, the episodes were shorter (6, 3, and 1 minutes, respectively).

On the second day of tantrum intervention there was one tantrum of fifteen minutes with two two-minute follow-up tantrums when the teacher attempted to reenter the room. On the third day there was one mild four-minute tantrum. No further tantrums occurred in the demonstration class nor was there a recurrence when Townsend returned to his regular head start class.

Disruptive Behaviors

Modification of generally aggressive and disruptive behaviors such as hitting and kicking children, spitting, and running off with other children's toys was instituted on the sixteenth session. On the first day of modification the teachers were instructed to give their undivided attention to the child who had been assaulted, while keeping their backs to Townsend. Nine episodes of aggressive behavior were tallied on this day. During the next eleven sessions, there was a marked decrease (an average of three per session). During the twelfth session, there was an upswing to seven episodes, then a gradual decrease until finally, no more grossly aggressive and disruptive acts occurred. A zero rate was recorded for the remainder of the sessions.

Bus Program

Another behavior modification project with Townsend involved the use of consumable reinforcers. Townsend had been banned from the head start bus for failing to sit in a seat with the seat belt fastened, attempting to open the doors while the bus was in motion, playing with the instrument panel, and throwing himself upon the bus driver while the latter was driving. Staying buckled in the seat was the target behavior.

On the first day of the program Townsend's seat belt was fastened, and the teacher immediately put a peanut in Townsend's mouth commenting, "Good, you are sitting quietly, all buckled up snug in your seat belt." She then quickly dispensed peanuts to every child on the bus with approving comments about their good bus riding habits. Rounds of peanut dispensing and approving comments were continued at 30 to 90 second intervals throughout the fifteen minute bus ride. The peanuts were dispensed at longer intervals for the next four days. On the following three days the peanuts were saved until the children got off the bus.

On the ninth day, Townsend rode the bus without a rewarding adult other than the bus driver who had been instructed to praise the children for their good bus riding behavior as he let them off the bus and to ignore Townsend if he had not stayed buckled. When the teacher and social worker, waiting at the bus stop, heard the bus driver praise Townsend, they voiced approval and gave him a small sucker as they accompanied him to his house. Gradually all consumable reinforcement was eliminated and only occasional social reinforcement, in the form of praise for Townsend's independent bus riding was used.

Shaping Play Skills

Establishing appropriate behaviors incompatible with his maladaptive behaviors was the area on which his teachers concentrated the greatest time, energy, and planning in Townsend's program. Data from the home classroom indicated that he had few play skills and also, that he had a low rate of interaction with other children. It seemed futile to attempt to build cooperative play with children until Townsend had acquired some play skills. Therefore, the teachers began a step-by-step program of teaching play with each of the materials considered important in a preschool program. For example, a teacher helped Townsend duplicate what at first were simple block models. If he

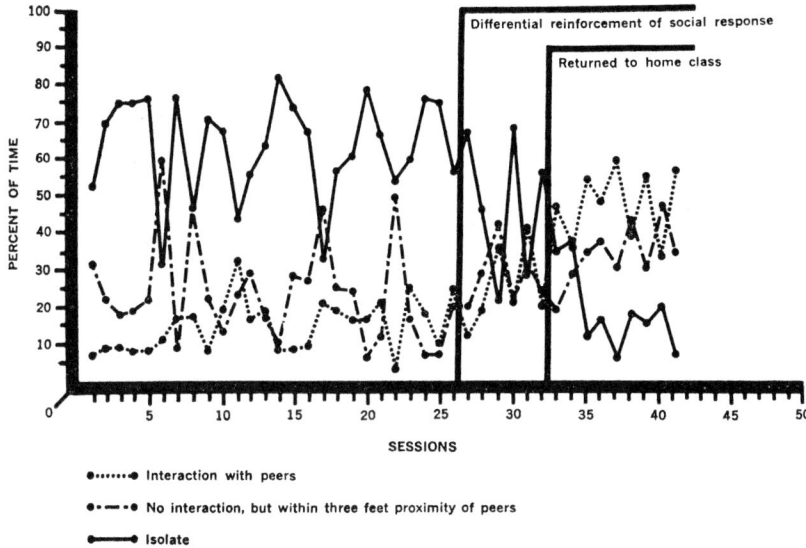

Figure 18-1. Case Study I—Townsend: Social behavior with peers.

refused to participate in a play lesson he forfeited the attention of all adults in the classroom. The moment he returned to the play materials, the attention of the teacher was again forthcoming. He was also reinforced for all divergent or unique uses of materials and equipment as long as the divergence was within the broad limits acceptable to preschool teachers.

Between sessions 6 and 26 Townsend acquired a functional repertoire of play skills with a variety of materials and equipment. It was decided, therefore, to change reinforcement contingencies: Adult social reinforcement would be available only when Townsend engaged in constructive use of play materials and interacted appropriately with another child. The change in contingencies appeared to have a positive effect. Between sessions 26 and 32 (Fig. 18-1) there was a steady increase in the rate of cooperative play.

Return to Home Classroom

Analysis of the data at this point indicated that it was an appropriate time to return Townsend to his home classroom.

Townsend's original teachers had had three days of in-service training in the demonstration classroom and had worked with the staff person who had been assigned to Townsend's home classroom. The staff person provided coaching on sessions 33 to 36 (Fig. 18-1), at which point the data indicated that Townsend's teachers were able to continue the contingency management procedures on their own. Not only were there no incidents of disruptive behaviors, but Townsend's social skills continued to hold at a high stable rate as measured by the amount of cooperative play (Fig. 18-1, sessions 37-41). Several postchecks were made throughout the remainder of the school year. These indicated that Townsend continued to function in an acceptable manner.

Case Study II

Doreen was 4¾ years old when she entered the demonstration class. The reasons for referral were many: immaturity, incessant crying, frequent physical attacks on other children, excessive dependency on adults, severe deficits in large motor skills, little interaction with peers, and speech that was either echolalic or unintelligible mumbling. Data taken for six sessions in the home classroom prior to her transfer to the demonstration class confirmed referral reports.

Shaping Motor Skills

Where does one begin with a child displaying so maladaptive and deficient a repertoire? As with Townsend it was reasoned that a child needs play skills to participate even minimally in the preschool program. However, in Doreen's case, basic motor skills had to be developed first. Therefore, a program was planned beginning with very simple skills such as walking a low, wide board and progressing to more complex activities like climbing on the outdoor equipment, riding the wheel toys, and pumping on the swings. A teacher's hand and other forms of physical contact were forthcoming only when Doreen was making an effort to engage in a motor task. At all other times the teachers disengaged her hands and turned away when she clung to them or to their clothing. Within five weeks Doreen was using all the outdoor equipment competently and independently. One data photography sequence shows her going up and over a 6-foot climber without assistance. Concurrently, the teachers ignored totally her repeated attacks on children. They gave their attention to the child who had been attacked, inserting themselves between Doreen and the other child, with their backs to Doreen. Attacks on children became infrequent, occurring only once or twice a week.

Differential Reinforcement of Verbal Behavior

Doreen's verbal behavior continued to be of a low order. The verbal data were broken down into categories: (a) appropriate verbalizations as specifically defined, e.g., intelligible words relevant to the situation, and (b) inappropriate verbalizations or vocalizations as specifically defined. The latter included her whimpering cries, echolalic or parroted responses, and unintelligible monologues. The baseline data taken in the classroom indicated that the teachers tended to respond more to her inappropriate verbalizations than they did to her appropriate ones (Fig. 18-2, sessions 1-6). When Doreen entered the demonstration class, the teachers were instructed to attend as frequently as possible to her appropriate verbalizations and to attend as infrequently as possible to her inappropriate ones. As can be seen in Figure 18-2, the teachers rarely succeeded in totally ignoring the inappropriate verbalizations. Nevertheless they did, for the most part, give a proportionately greater share of their attention to the appropriate responses. Under this regimen, appropriate verbalizations began an irregular increase with inappropriate verbalizations slowly declining at an irregular rate; the latter eventually constituted a relatively small percentage of the child's total verbal output (Fig. 18-2, sessions 34-39). Six days of data taken after Doreen's return to the home classroom indicated that appropriate verbalizations continued to dominate her verbal output and, further, that her teachers were responding in an appropriately differential fashion.

No specific program to increase Doreen's social interaction with peers was instituted though the question was posed: Will amelioration of the major behavior disorders be accompanied

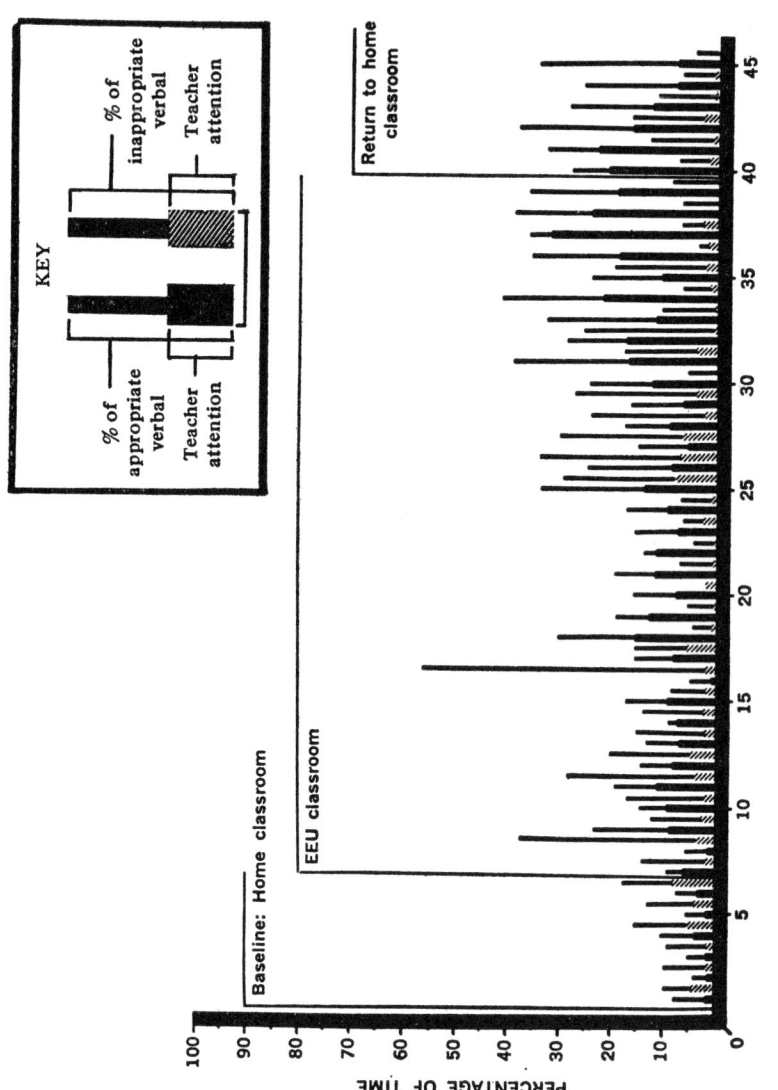

Figure 18-2. Case Study II—Doreen: Proportion of appropriate to inappropriate verbal behavior; ratio of adult social reinforcement for each category.

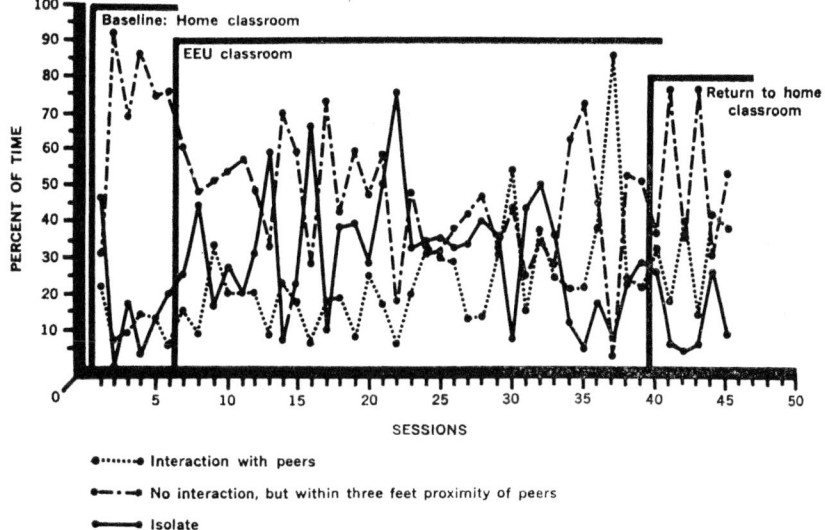

Figure 18-3. Case Study II—Doreen: Social behavior with peers.

by improved social interaction with peers? The data indicate that cooperative interaction with peers did increase from an average of 10 percent of each session during baseline in the home classroom to an average of 26 percent (Fig. 18-3) in the demonstration class. It seems probable that as assault behaviors decreased, verbalizations became less bizarre and improved motor skills enabled her to use the play equipment, Doreen became a more desirable play companion, thus making peer as well as adult social reinforcement available to her.

Conclusions

These behavior modification projects have been described in detail in order to illustrate the application of reinforcement principles by preschool teachers in a field setting. The principles and techniques as they relate to these specific case studies follow:
1. Preschool teachers can readily employ reinforcement procedures to produce desired changes in children's behavior. To do so effectively, a teacher must assess children objectively, select specific target behaviors, keep continuous records, and

use these records as a basis for program planning and continuous assessment.
2. Modification of only one or two of a child's behaviors at a time is essential to a successful program. A teacher's responses may become scattered and unsystematic if too many contingencies must be kept in mind for each child.
3. Every adult involved in a child's environment is potentially a powerful social reinforcer. Thus, every adult who interacts with children in the preschool situation must carefully monitor his responses to each child. When strict monitoring is not exercised, progress will be slower and more irregular.
4. The preschool environment abounds in natural reinforcers —play materials, snack time, outdoor play, special games and activities. Preschool teachers must make these reinforcers work for the child by making them available contingent on responses which will enhance the child's progress.
5. Though the extinction process (withholding reinforcement) is a highly effective means of freeing a child of his maladaptive response it does not automatically provide an alternate set of appropriate behaviors. Therefore, it is critical that teachers give their attention to desired behaviors so that the child may acquire a functional response repertoire.
6. Reinforcement of successive approximations to the target behaviors (shaping) is essential to achieve successful behavior modification. Reinstatement of Townsend as a bus rider is one example of shaping procedures.
7. A careful step-by-step reduction in the amount of reinforcement (learning the schedule) is necessary if a response is to be self-maintained. The bus riding sequence is again cited as an example.
8. Elimination of maladaptive behaviors simultaneous with shaping of appropriate behaviors often correlates with other favorable changes in the child's behavioral repertoire. The concurrent changes in improved cooperative play patterns in the second case study demonstrate this effect, an ef-

fect which has been noted previously (Allen, Henke, Harris, Baer, and Reynolds, 1967).

It would appear from this demonstration project, as well as from many other experimental analyses of behavior, that the teacher's differentiated responsiveness is the crucial variable in determining what and how the young child learns. No educational model, no preschool curriculum alone can insure optimum progress for a child. The deciding factor is the teacher's behavior and appropriate reinforcement techniques. Successful behavior modification depends on correct teacher-child interaction.

REFERENCES

Allen, K. E., Hart, B. M., Buell, J. S., Harris, F. R., and Wolf, M. M.: Effects of social reinforcement on isolate behavior of a nursery school child. *Child Dev*, 35:511-518, 1964.

Allen, K. E., and Harris, F. R.: Elimination of a child's excessive scratching by training the mother in reinforcement procedures. *Behav Res Ther*, 1:305-312, 1966.

Allen, K. E., Henke, L. B., Harris, F. R., Baer, D. M., and Reynolds, N. F.: The control of hyperactivity by social reinforcement of attending behavior in a preschool child. *J Educ Psychol*, 58:231-237, 1967.

Bijou, S. W., Peterson, R. F., Harris, F. R., Allen, K. E., and Johnston, M. S.: Methodology for experimental studies of young children in natural settings. *Psychol Rec*, 19:177-210, 1969.

Haring, N. G., Hayden, A. H., and Nolen, P. A.: Accelerating appropriate behaviors of children in a Head Start program. *Except Child*, 35:773-784, 1969.

Haring, N. G., Hayden, A. H., and Allen, K. E.: *Building Social Skills in the Preschool Child*. 16mm color film. Experimental Education Unit, Child Development and Mental Retardation Center, University of Washington, 1968.

Harris, F. R., Johnston, M. K., Kelley, C. S., and Wolf, M. M.: Effects of positive social reinforcement on regressed crawling in a preschool child. *J Educ Psychol*, 55:35-41, 1964.

Harris, F. R., Wolf, M. M., and Baer, D. M.: Effects of adult social reinforcement on child behavior. *Young Child*, 1:8-17, 1964.

Hart, B. M., Allen, K. E., Buell, J. S., Harris, F. R., and Wolf, M. M.: Effects of social reinforcement on operant crying. *J Exp Child Psychol*, 1:145-153, 1964.

Hawkins, R. P., Peterson, R. F., Schweid, E., and Bijou, S. W.: Behavior therapy in the home: Amelioration of problem parent-child relations with the parent in a therapeutic role. *J Exp Child Psychol,* 4:99-107, 1966.

Klein, J. W.: Innovative approaches in project Head Start. Paper presented at the Council for Exceptional Children, Special Conference on Early Childhood Education, New Orleans, December 1969.

Nolen, P. A., Hulten, W. J., and Kunzelmann, H. P.: Data diagnosis and programing. In John I. Arena (Ed.): *Successful Programing: Many Points of View.* Boston, Fifth Annual International Conference of the Association for Children with Learning Disabilities, 1968, pp. 409-418.

Chapter 19

EFFECTS OF TEACHER ATTENTION AND A TOKEN REINFORCEMENT SYSTEM IN A JUNIOR HIGH SCHOOL SPECIAL EDUCATION CLASS

MARCIA BRODEN
R. VANCE HALL
ANN DUNLAP
ROBERT CLARK

A SERIES OF STUDIES carried out in nursery schools (Harris, Wolf, and Baer, 1964), special education classes (Hall and Broden, 1967; Zimmerman and Zimmerman, 1962), and regular public schools (Hall, Lund, and Jackson, 1968; Hall, Panyan, Rabon, and Broden, 1968; Thomas, Becker, and Armstrong, 1968) have demonstrated that contingent teacher attention could be effective in increasing appropriate classroom behavior.

Similarly, token reinforcement systems backed up by food, field trips, toys, money, and grades were demonstrated to be effective in increasing academic behaviors of pupils in special education programs including classrooms for the retarded (Birnbrauer, Wolf, Kidder, and Tague, 1965), remedial classrooms for poverty area elementary age children (Wolf, Giles, and Hall, 1968), and for elementary special education pupils (McKenzie, Clark, Wolf, Kothera, and Benson, 1968; O'Leary and Becker, 1967).

With the exception of the study by Hall, Panyan, Rabon, and Broden (1968), however, these studies were carried out by experienced teachers and dealt with preschool and elementary age children. Those using token reinforcement systems used reinforcers primarily extrinsic to the classroom, and most often there was more than one teacher available to conduct the class and carry out the experimental procedures.

In contrast, the present study was carried out in a public junior high school special education classroom by a first year teacher without prior teaching experience. When systematic teacher attention to appropriate behavior proved to be limited in its effect, a token reinforcement system backed by reinforcers available to most junior high school teachers was used to reduce extremely disruptive behavior and to increase appropriate study behavior.

Subjects and Setting

The subjects were thirteen seventh and eighth grade students, eight boys and five girls, in a special education class in Bonner Springs Junior High School, Bonner Springs, Kansas. All students were several years behind in at least one major academic area and had other problems, including severe reading deficits, almost incoherent speech, emotional instability, and acts of delinquency. Some specific problem behaviors involved cursing the teacher; refusing to obey teacher requests or to do assignments; throwing pencils, pens, or paper; fighting; chasing each other about the room; and eating a variety of snacks.

The inappropriate behaviors described had persisted through the first four months of school although the teacher had used generally accepted methods for maintaining classroom control, including some praise for appropriate behavior and reprimands or a trip to the counselor or principal's office for misconduct.

The class met for five periods of the eight period day. The entire class was present for the first, fifth, and eighth periods. Only the seven seventh graders were present for the second and sixth periods, and only the six eighth graders were present during the third and seventh periods.

OBSERVATIONS. The system used was essentially that developed by Broden (1968) for recording classroom study behavior. Daily observations were made by an observer equipped with a recording sheet and stopwatch. Data were recorded on the recording sheet at five-second intervals. At the five-second mark the behavior of the first pupil was recorded, at the ten-second mark the behavior of a second pupil was recorded, at the fifteen-second mark that of the third student, and so on until every student had been observed once; then the sequence was begun again. Thus the behavior of a different pupil was recorded every five seconds on a consecutive rotation basis.

As is shown in Figure 19-1, the recording sheet was divided into triple rows of squares with a different pupil's name entered at the top of each column of three vertical squares. The middle row of squares was used to record whether or not the pupil was studying. An "S" (for study) was recorded if the pupil were attending to or oriented toward the appropriate book when he had been assigned reading to do, if he were attending to the teacher or another pupil who was speaking during class discussions, if he were writing spelling words during spelling period, or if he were otherwise engaged in a teacher assigned task. All other behaviors were designated as "N" except for the specific nonstudy behavior "out of seat" which was recorded as "O."

The top row of squares was used to record verbalizations by the teacher to a subject or to the class. A "T" designated teacher verbalization directed to an individual pupil during that five-second interval.

The bottom row of squares was used to record pupil verbalizations. A "V" designated verbalizations recognized by the teacher.

Observations lasted from 30 to 40 minutes during any given period.

Computing the percentage of the total five-second intervals in which "S" had been recorded revealed the class study rate. It was also possible to compute individual study rates by dividing the number of "S" intervals for the pupil by the total number of intervals that the individual pupil was observed and multiplying

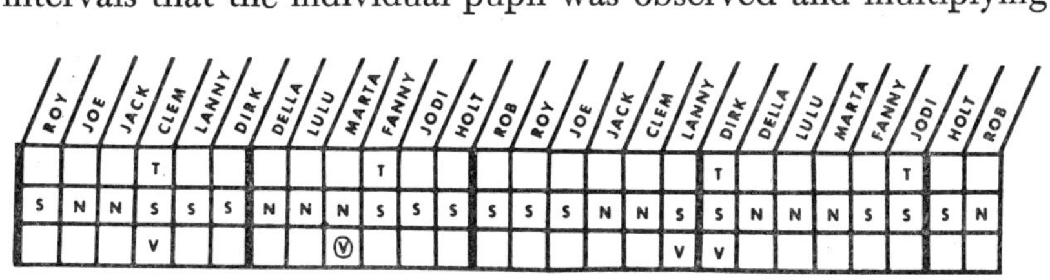

Row 1 T = Teacher verbalization directed to pupil
Row 2 S = Study behavior, N = Nonstudy behavior
Row 3 V = Appropriate pupil verbalization, v = Inappropriate verbalization

Figure 19-1. Observer recording sheet and symbol key.

the result by 100. Thus both class and individual study rates could be obtained.

Reliability checks were made periodically throughout the study. A second observer made independent, simultaneous observations. This record was compared with that of the primary observer, interval by interval. The percentage of agreement was then computed. Observer agreement for this study ranged from 83 to 98 percent.

Experiment I

Initially, daily observations were begun during the fifth period when all thirteen pupils were present. Assigned study tasks included reading, writing, and participation in class discussions.

During the first (baseline) seven days of observation the teacher was asked to conduct class in her usual manner and to ignore the observer. Care was taken not to mention possible experimental procedures. Pupils were told someone would be coming in at various times to assist the teacher. All contact between the observer and teacher or pupils was avoided during class sessions.

Figure 19-2 presents the data for the seven baseline sessions. The broken horizontal line indicates that the mean rate of study behavior was 29 percent. During baseline sessions the teacher was observed giving attention to both study and nonstudy behaviors.

Prior to the eighth day of observation a conference was held with the teacher. She was shown the baseline study data and was asked to begin giving attention to study behavior only and to ignore all nonstudying. During the next 11 days the teacher went to pupils who were studying and commented on their good study behavior and work, called only on pupils who raised their hands, and complimented the entire group when all were studying quietly.

As can be seen in the Social Reinforcement$_1$ phase of Figure 19-2, this procedure resulted in an increase in study behavior to a mean rate of 57 percent. Although an improvement over baseline rates, there were still frequent outbursts of inappropriate verbalizations, out of seat, and other disruptive behaviors. Therefore a new contingency for appropriate study was introduced.

During the next eighteen sessions a kitchen timer was placed on

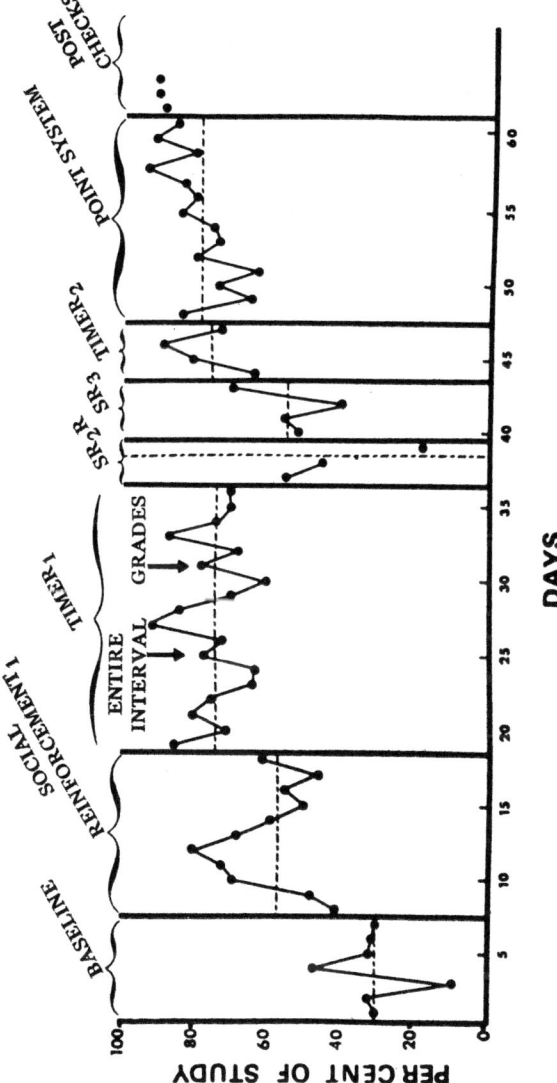

Figure 19-2. A record of fifth period study behavior during Baseline₁, Social Reinforcement₁, Timer₁, Social Reinforcement₂ (SR₂), Reversal (R), Social Reinforcement₃ (SR₃), Timer₂, Point System, and Postcheck conditions.

the teacher's desk and set to go off at random intervals averaging eight minutes. Pupils who were in their seats and quiet when the timer sounded were given a mark on a card taped to their desk tops. Each mark earned allowed them to leave one minute earlier for lunch. Teacher attention for study was continued during this phase.

As can be seen in the Timer$_1$ phase of Figure 19-2, an immediate increase in study behavior resulted. Beginning in the 25th session ("Quiet Entire Interval" in Fig. 19-2) pupils were required to be quiet during the entire interval between timer rings in order to receive a mark. Beginning in the 31st session marks (grades) were continued as before, but a grade of E (excellent) was also given if the pupil had been engaging in study behavior. These conditions seemed to have little additional effect on study level.

The mean study rate for the entire Timer$_1$ phase was 74 percent, and according to the subjective judgments of the teacher and observer there was noticeably less disruptive behavior.

In order to see if the reinforcement procedures were the primary factors in increasing study, a brief return to prior conditions was made. For two days the timer early dismissal contingency was removed and only social reinforcement for study was given. This resulted in a drop in study behavior to 55 percent the first day and to 45 percent the second (Social Reinforcement$_2$). The following day (session 39) social reinforcement for study was also withdrawn. The teacher attended only to nonstudy behavior and ignored study behavior. This complete reversal of procedures resulted in a breakdown of study behavior and almost complete disruption of the class. As can be seen in Figure 19-2 (R-Reversal) the study level during this one day reversal was only 18 percent.

During the next phase (Social Reinforcement$_3$) the teacher again attended to study behavior and ignored nonstudy. The level rose to 55 percent. During the next four days the timer and marks for early lunch dismissal plus grades for study were reinstituted. Under these conditions (Timer$_2$) the mean study level was 76 percent.

Beginning in session 48, the timer condition was discontinued and pupils were put on a token point system described in Experiment II. The data presented in the Point System phase of Figure 19-2 indicate that the higher study levels established with the timer were not only maintained but also slightly increased under the token point system. In fact, the mean study level rose to 90 percent.

Postchecks taken over the next month and a half after conclusion of daily monitoring indicated that the higher study levels were maintained through the remainder of the school year despite the fact the teacher was not informed prior to observation time when these checks would occur.

Experiment II

After a few days of higher study levels achieved by the procedures described above, the teacher and principal concurred in their judgment that pupil behavior during the fifth period was indeed under much better control. However, they reported that the higher study rates had not transferred to the other five daily class periods. Therefore, an attempt to increase study during these periods also was made.

First, observations were made in order to determine the actual level of study during these five other periods. Nineteen 30-minute observations were made on ten different days. Although the mean number of observations was a little less than two per day, the number on any one day ranged from 1 to all 5 (the number monitored on days 7 and 8). As can be seen in Figure 19-3 the mean levels of study for the ten days of observation ranged from 33 to 47 percent. The mean baseline level as indicated by the dotted horizontal line was 39 percent.

Following baseline a token reinforcement system was instituted. A point system using a combination of available privileges and punishments was selected. (These periods were not followed by lunch and therefore earlier dismissal for lunch could not be utilized as it had been for period five.)

Each pupil was given a copy of the point system values similar to that shown in Table 19-I.

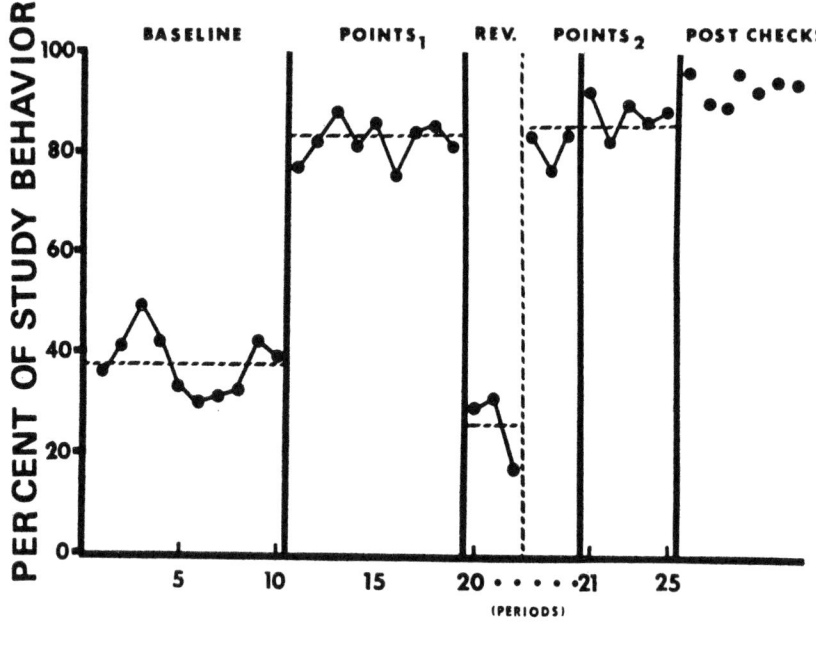

Figure 19-3. A record of study behavior during the entire day, under Baseline, Points, Reversal (Rev.), Points$_2$ and Post Check conditions. Post Checks were taken periodically during the six weeks of school after termination of regular observations.

The "Earn Points" section was comprised of items suggested by the teacher, principal, and observer as desirable pupil behaviors. Earn Points were assigned so that a pupil could accumulate about 20 points per class period by engaging in reasonably appropriate behavior such as remaining in his seat and being quiet. (Pupils were given the option of when and for what they would spend the points earned.)

The "Spend Points" section was comprised of activities and privileges which included those suggested by the pupils when they were asked, "What would you like to do if you had one free period?" Other Spend Point items were recommended by the teacher, principal, and the observer as probable reinforcers which could be administered within existing school policy. Spend Points were assigned so that behaviors thought to be highly desired were more costly than less desired ones.

The "Minus Points" section was comprised of undesirable pupil behaviors. Minus Points were assigned values so that the most disruptive behaviors cost the most. Pupils who accumulated twen-

TABLE 19-I

POINT SYSTEM

Earn Points:
- 5 in seat
- 5 quiet
- 5 doing assignment
- 2 extra credit (after regular assignment is complete)
- 3 an "A" on an assigned task
- 2 a "B" on an assigned task
- 1 a "C" on an assigned task
- 0 a "D" on an assigned task

Minus Points:
- 15 out of seat without permission
- 1 talking out of turn: hand is not raised, teacher hasn't called on you
- 20 out of the room without permission
- 5 incomplete assignment (per period)
- 3 namecalling, swearing
- 20 throwing, hitting
- 20 arguing with the teacher
- 20 teacher must tell you more than once to stop

Spend Points:
- 50 five minute pass to the rest room
- 50 permission to go five minutes early to lunch
- 10 permission to get out of your seat for one minute
- 50 permission to move your desk for one period
- 100 permission to move your desk for one day
- 300 permission to move your desk permanently
- 20 pass to get a drink of water
- 10 permission to talk to another person for five minutes
- 50 Friday snack
- 400 field trip
- 20 nonacademic activities approved by the teacher such as knitting, puzzles, games, records

To Earn Off Minus Points:
- 1 stay after school (per minute)
- 1 five earned positive points (earns off one minus point)

---

* teacher assigned academic task
* the teacher determines the task and the point value

ty or more minus points were required to stay after school for 1½ hours on Thursday afternoon, which was the schoolwide detention period. Minus points could also be bought off by Earn Points at a ratio of five earned points to one minus point.

The teacher kept account of points during the period on a form at her desk which listed all pupils and had columns for posting point totals earned, spent, or lost. Point totals were posted on the chalkboard at the end of each period and pupils could see how many Earn Points and how many Minus Points each had acquired.

The results of instituting the point system were immediate and dramatic. As can be seen in the Points$_1$ phase of Figure 19-3, the mean class study rate rose to 83 percent on the first day. Study was maintained at high levels throughout the Points$_1$ phase of the experiment.

This increase in study level was recorded even though three pupils argued that it was childish, stated that they would refuse to cooperate, would quit school, and would complain to the principal and counselor. These remarks were largely ignored and the second day, two of the three showed increased study rates. Over the next four days the third objector, Rob, became extremely disruptive. He cursed the teacher, erased the board, tore up assignments, left the room, fought with other pupils, and said he wouldn't work and that no one could make him do it. When he was told to go to his seat or to the office he refused. Under the point system he soon accumulated 512 minus points and nineteen positive points. By the fourth day other class members were spending increasing time watching Rob and laughing at his antics. Wolf, Risley, and Mees (1964) had demonstrated that isolation procedures could be used effectively to reduce tantrum behaviors in a preschool child. Since much of Rob's behavior resembled tantrums, these procedures were explained to both the teacher and the principal and a modified version of isolation was decided upon. It was agreed that if Rob refused to obey the teacher's direction to be quiet or sit down he would be sent immediately to the office. Unlike other times he had been sent there, he was not to be allowed back into the classroom until he had stated that he would be quiet and stay in his seat.

During the first period of the fifth day Rob refused to obey a teacher direction to be quiet and was sent directly to the principal's office. To reduce the chance that office procedures would reinforce him, the principal had an area screened off so that the student could not see who entered the office or what they were doing. He was not given work to do. He remained there until the end of the school day. The next day when he arrived at school he requested that he be returned to class and stated that he would stay in his seat and be quiet. When he returned to class his talking and out of seat behaviors decreased and his study behaviors increased. From that point on Rob presented no particular problem and obeyed the teacher. Though he refused to study for a time, he did begin to read a library book, then began to do individual work, and finally began to participate in group discussions. He began accumulating earn points and working off the minus points. He freely spent points, seldom accumulating enough for a field trip. By the end of school, however, he was able to participate in a field trip and an auction which was held to use up surplus earn points.

After nine days of increased study under the point system a reversal procedure was instituted. The experimenters agreed to allow reinstitution of the point system immediately if class behavior deteriorated to former levels and the teacher seemed to be losing control. It was thought that the effect of reversal might be observable over a three or four day period.

Reversal conditions were begun during first period of day 20. The pupils were told that the point system was no longer in effect and the teacher discontinued giving attention for appropriate study although she provided verbal reprimands for nonstudy behaviors.

The data for day 20 are shown on a period by period basis in Figure 19-3 (Reversal). Study dropped to 29 percent in the first period. Second period it was 31 percent and third period it dropped to 16 percent. Because of the extremely chaotic situation and the prior agreement to discontinue reversal if control was lost, the point system was put back into effect during the fourth period. As can be seen in Figure 19-3 this resulted in a dramatic return to high study rates in the final three class periods of the day.

Period by period observations during the next five days showed that the mean study rate was above 80 percent.

Observations taken intermittently beginning two weeks later showed that over the next 1½ months of the remainder of the school year, high study rates were being maintained under the point system (see Postchecks, Figs. 19-2 and 3).

The high Postcheck rate (90 percent) was maintained even though the system was changed so that Minus Points were subtracted from earned points on a one to one basis in the interest of simplifying the record keeping system.

The data indicated that in addition to study behavior, inappropriate talking and the number of times pupils were out of their seats were affected by the experimental procedures. During baseline, inappropriate verbalizations were recorded in 84 percent of the observed intervals. Under $Points_1$ conditions inappropriate talking dropped to 10 percent. It rose to 44 percent during Reversal. It dropped to 5 percent when the point system was reinstated and was at 7 percent during the Postcheck period.

Pupils were out of their seats an average of 70 seconds per period during baseline. When the point system was instituted the mean rate was ten seconds per period. In the brief and chaotic three period Reversal phase the time out of seats rose to mean rate of 215 seconds per period. Out of seats time returned to ten seconds per period during the $Points_2$ and Postcheck phases. These data indicated that control of these specific inappropriate behaviors as well as increases in study had been achieved.

Individual Data

Since a record was kept of which student was being observed during each five-second interval it was possible to compute individual study rates for each experimental condition by dividing the number of study intervals by the total number of intervals that particular individual was observed and multiplying by 100.

An analysis of the data revealed that there was considerable individual variation in study rates and in the effects of the various experimental conditions on individuals. During the fifth period baseline phase, for example, study levels ranged from 11 to 62 percent. Although teacher attention was effective in increasing study for all pupils, it was much more effective for some than for others. For instance, one girl's study level increased from 14 to 64 percent while one boy's study increased only from 12 to 18 percent. Similarly, though the $Timer_1$ condition backed by early dismissal for lunch resulted in further increases in study for all other pupils, it resulted in an actual decrease in study level for one.

Reversal effects varied from pupil to pupil also. During the reversal phase all showed decreased study levels, although study for six students remained at levels substantially higher than baseline rates while almost no study was recorded for the three pupils who had the lowest baseline study rates.

An analysis of the data for the point system also showed variations in study levels. Marked increases in study levels over baseline were achieved for all pupils under the points system. All pupils showed a marked decrease in study during the brief reversal phase when the point system was withdrawn. In the $Points_2$ and Postcheck phases data indicated that even though the three pupils who had the lowest baseline study levels were still studying less than their classmates, all three were above the 70 percent level, higher than the highest study rate recorded for any pupil during baseline.

Discussion

This study showed that systematic reinforcement procedures using contingencies available in most junior high school classrooms could be used by a beginning teacher to gain control of an extremely disruptive junior high school special education class. Systematic teacher attention increased study levels but was limited in its effect. For most pupils classroom privileges, including such activities as early dismissal to lunch, getting a drink, sharpening a pencil, and talking to another pupil for five minutes, were more powerful than teacher attention alone for motivating desired behavior. Reversal procedures demonstrated the functional relationship between the reinforcement contingencies and the increases in appropriate behaviors.

The data also revealed that the effectiveness of a given procedure varied from pupil to pupil. In the case of one pupil it was necessary to institute a time out procedure to gain participation in the point system. Once participation was gained increases in study were dramatic.

In discussing the point system it should be mentioned that there was no rationale for the number of points assigned for particular activities or for the selection of the activities other than a seemingly suitable balance between the behaviors required to earn points and the reinforcing value of the activities and privileges for which they could be spent. Another teacher would doubtless have to adjust the system to fit his particular classroom group and the resources available to him.

Evaluating the point system in terms of value and convenience to the teacher is necessarily subjective but relevant to a discussion of the overall worth of the system. In her evaluation the teacher stated that the system was helpful for it gave both the student and the teacher "a black and white list of what is allowed in the classroom." She also stated that it was easier for her to be fair, since the clearly stated penalties and rewards stopped arguments over the teacher's handling of misconduct. She also reported that pupils did a great deal more classwork and made better grades. At times she had difficulty keeping up with the amount of extra credit work since pupils would choose extra work over any other activities if they were working for a highly prized privilege. She reported further that most pupils indicated they liked the order the system helped provide.

According to the teacher the system could be improved by establishing a simpler system for computing point totals. She felt it was important to post the totals every hour so pupils would have more immediate feedback on their status, but daily instead of hourly computations would reduce the amount of teacher time needed to figure points. She also suggested that the pupils should be more involved in establishing the point system. Such involvement might reduce the initial resistance to the system. She reported that allowing the class to take part in modifying the system when problems arose had helped them accept it.

It is understood by the authors that the procedures used to bring about classroom control in this study are not new or startling. Good teachers have used teacher attention and access to privileges to motivate appropriate pupil behavior for many years. The results reported here are of interest, however, for they demonstrate a means by which a teacher who had not managed to do so was helped to organize the environmental consequences available to her and bring about desired classroom behavior. In essence the point system acted as a convenient means for the teacher and the pupils to link desired study behavior with participation in desired activities.

It is conceded that a point system may not be necessary or appropriate in many junior high school classrooms. It may, however, be a valuable aid to teachers who have difficulty in maintaining classroom control over children with highly deviant and disruptive behaviors.

REFERENCES

Birnbrauer, J. S., Wolf, M. M., Kidder, J. D., and Tague, E.: Classroom behavior of retarded pupils with token reinforcement. *J Exp Child Psychol,* 2:219-235, 1965.

Broden, M.: Notes on recording. Observer's Manual for Juniper Gardens Children's Project, Unpublished manuscript, Bureau of Child Research, 1968.

Hall, R. V., and Broden, M.: Behavior changes in brain-injured children through social reinforcement. *J Exp Child Psychol,* 5:463-479, 1967.

Hall, R. V., Lund, D., and Jackson, D.: Effects of teacher attention on study behavior. *J Appl Behav Anal,* 1:1-12, 1968.

Hall, R. V., Panyan, M., Rabon, D., and Broden, M.: Instructing beginning teachers in reinforcement procedures which improve classroom control. *J Appl Behav Anal,* 1:315-322, 1968.

Harris, F. R., Wolf, M. M., and Baer, D. M.: Effects of adult social reinforcement on child behavior. *Young Child,* 20:8-17, 1964.

McKenzie, H., Clark, M., Wolf, M., Kothera, R., and Benson, C.: Behavior modification of children with learning disabilities using grades as token reinforcers. *Except Child,* 34:745-752, 1968.

O'Leary, K. D., and Becker, W. C.: Behavior modification of an adjustment class: token reinforcement system. *Except Child,* 33:637-642, 1967.

Thomas, D. R., Becker, W. C., and Armstrong, M.: Production and elimination of disruptive classroom behavior by systematically varying teacher's behavior. *J Appl Behav Anal,* 1:35-45, 1968.

Wolf, M. M., Giles, D. K., and Hall, R. V.: Experiments with token reinforcement in a remedial classroom. *Behav Res Ther,* 6:51-64, 1968.

Wolf, M. M., Risley, T. R., and Mees, H. L.: Application of operant conditioning procedures to the behavior problems of an autistic child. *Behav Res Ther,* 1:305-312, 1964.

Zimmerman, E. H., and Zimmerman, J.: The alteration of behavior in a special classroom situation. *J Exp Anal Behav,* 5:59-60, 1962.

Chapter 20

THE TIMER-GAME: A VARIABLE INTERVAL CONTINGENCY FOR THE MANAGEMENT OF OUT-OF-SEAT BEHAVIOR

MONTROSE M. WOLF
EDWARD L. HANLEY
LOUISE A. KING
JOSEPH LACHOWICZ
DAVID K. GILES

ALTHOUGH THE ABILITY to maintain an orderly classroom does not necessarily result in the achievement of academic goals, orderliness is often considered to be a prerequisite for effective teaching. Thus, it is not surprising that the management of classroom behavior has become a focus of applied behavioral research (Wolf, Giles, and Hall, 1968; Barrish, Saunders, and Wolf, 1969; Madsen, Becker, and Thomas, 1968; Hall, Lund, and Jackson, 1968; Thomas, Becker, and Armstrong, 1968; O'Leary, Becker, Evans, and Saudargas, 1969; Osborne, 1969).

Wolf, Giles, and Hall (1968) described an experimental remedial classroom for low achieving sixth grade children in which academic behavior was supported by a token reinforcement system. One classroom problem was a moderately high rate of out-of-seat behavior, a common problem characterized by apparently aimless wandering, extended stays in the lavatory, prolonged pencil sharpening, and more visiting than is considered desirable. A technique was introduced for managing the out-of-seat behavior. It involved the occasional ringing of a kitchen timer that was set by the teacher to ring after intervals of varying durations, averaging about 20 minutes. Every student who was in his seat when the timer rang avoided the loss of tokens. While it seemed that the timer game was effective in reducing out-of-seat behavior, no objective data was presented. The present study describes an empirical evaluation of the effects of the timer game.

Experiment I

Method

SUBJECTS AND SETTING. A group of sixteen low-achieving children from a low-income, urban elementary school attended a remedial class every day after school. Fourteen of the children were fourth graders and two were third graders. The children met each afternoon for three hours. They were instructed to complete homework and remedial assignments. Tokens (points), which were given for correct answers, were supported by backup reinforcers such as snacks, candy, clothes, and field trips. The physical setting, token reinforcement contingencies, remedial education program, and materials have been described in detail elsewhere (Wolf et al., 1968).

RESPONSE DEFINITION. The out-of-seat behavior of the students was recorded by an observer. The one-hour session was divided into 30-second intervals. During each 30-second interval the observer would look at each student in a predetermined order and count the number who met the criterion for being out of their seats. The response definition required that "the seat portion of the child's body not be in contact with any part of the seat of the child's chair."

The out-of-seat behavior was independently measured by a second observer during two sessions. The number of instances of agreement about the presence or absence of the response in each 30-second interval for each student was calculated. The two sessions yielded agreements of 93 and 94 percent between the two observers.

EXPERIMENTAL CONDITIONS. There were three conditions. Baseline rate of the out-of-seat behavior was first obtained for each child for seven sessions. The timer-game was then introduced. On the average of once every 20 minutes the timer rang. (The range of intervals between rings was zero to 40 minutes.) Every student who was in his seat when the timer rang earned five points. Five points was a very small proportion of the average student's accumulation of approximately 400 points per day.

The timer-game was continued for six sessions. The baseline condition was then reinstated for seven sessions.

Results

As Figure 20-1 shows, the timer-game was effective in reducing the out-of-seat behavior. Each dot corresponds to the number of intervals a particular student was out of his seat. The heavy line indicates the average amount of out-of-seat behavior for the entire class each day under each condition. On the average, seventeen intervals containing out-of-seat behavior per child were recorded per session during baseline. The introduction of the timer game reduced the average to about two intervals per child. A return to the baseline condition resulted in an increase in the number of the out-of-seat responses to an average of seventeen intervals per child.

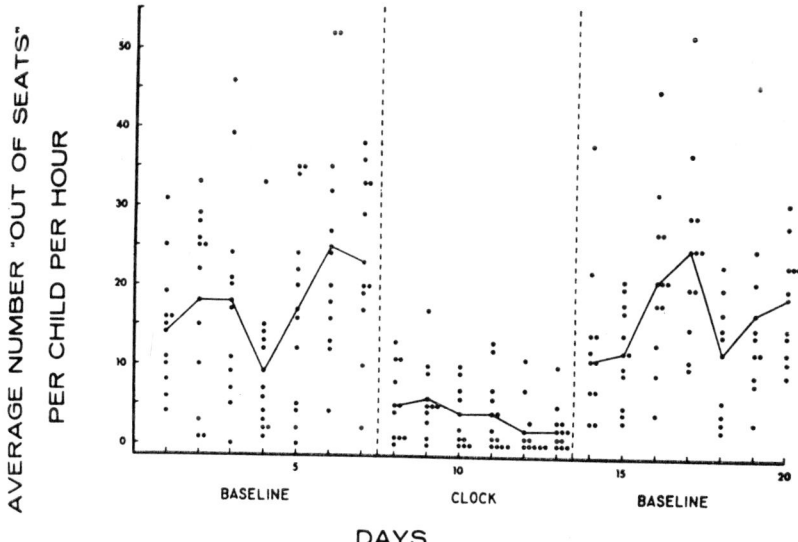

Figure 20-1. Experiment I. The heavy line represents the average number of 30-second intervals containing out-of-seat responses during a daily one-hour observation period. The individual dots represent the number of intervals containing out-of-seat responses for each of the children.

Experiment II

Method

SUBJECT AND SETTING. One of the students (Sue) in Experiment I whose behavior was not greatly modified by the timer-game was the subject of this study. The classroom procedures and token reinforcement system were the same as in Experiment I. Out-of-seat behavior was recorded by an observer for 1½ hours each day using the same response definition as in Experiment I.

INDIVIDUAL POINTS CONDITION. Sue's out-of-seat behavior was observed under the baseline condition and two slightly different contingency conditions involving the timer-game. Under the first contingency condition Sue was told that she would have an opportunity to earn extra points by playing the timer-game. A 9 x 3 inch piece of construction paper was attached to the wall. The numbers 10, 20, 30, 40, and 50 were drawn on the paper with a marking pen. Sue was told that she would be given 50 points at the beginning of each session but that she would lose ten of these points each time she was out of her seat when the timer rang. In such instances, the teacher would cross off the highest number on the paper, indicating the number of Sue's points that remained. The timer was set to ring after varying intervals but on an average of every ten minutes.

PEER POINTS CONDITION. In the second contingency condition Sue and the other students were told that the rules of the game would be changed slightly so that more children could play. The new rule was that Sue would still be able to earn points for herself, but that she would also earn points for the four students who sat closest to her. At the end of the session the points remaining from the original 50 would be divided equally among Sue and her four peers. For example, if 40 points remained, Sue and the others would earn eight points each.

Results

Figure 20-2 shows that the individual points condition resulted in an immediate decrease in the amount of out-of-seat behavior that occurred during the no points condition. However, the peer

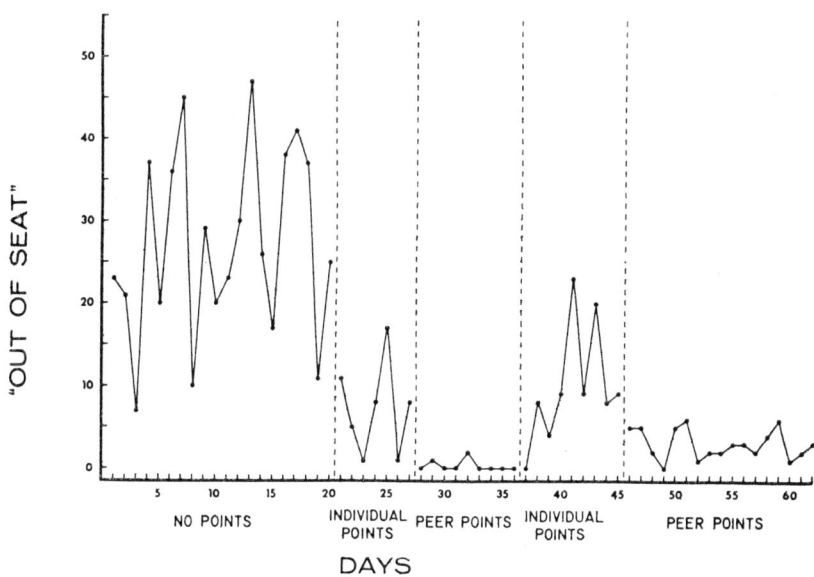

Figure 20-2. Experiment II. The number of intervals containing out-of-seat responses made by Sue throughout several experimental conditions.

points condition resulted in even greater suppression although Sue earned only one-fifth as many points as she did under the individual points condition.

Discussion

The timer-game was an effective technique for decreasing the out-of-seat behavior of the students in the remedial classroom. It was also practical since it did not require continuous monitoring by the teacher. The teacher needed to observe only the out-of-seat behavior that occurred when the timer rang. The purpose of the variable interval contingency rather than a fixed interval contingency was to reduce the likelihood that the students would discriminate the time when the bell was about to ring. The bell was just as likely to ring after having just rung as to ring only after a very long interval.

The peer points condition resulted in more control over Sue's out-of-seat behavior than the individual points condition. Exactly what the peers contributed to the effect must await further analysis. Our impression was that they provided a number of consequences and other functions for Sue. For example, if she stood up, she was immediately reminded to sit down. If she broke her pencil, which she often did, one of the four peers would volunteer to sharpen it for her. If she went to the lavatory, she was reminded to hurry. However, the extent of their attending behavior was not determined.

The results of the peer points condition correspond to the results of a peer contingency in a classroom setting described by Patterson (1965) where he modified the hyperactive behavior of a second-grade child. Patterson arranged for the child to earn M&M's at the rate of one every ten seconds when he was attending appropriately. The M&M's were then shared with all the members of the class. Patterson reports that while it was difficult to evaluate the roles of both the M&M's and the peers, his opinion was that the peers had some influence in reducing the hyperactive behavior. Since in Experiment II of this study the role of points for the individual student was analyzed independently of the effects of points for the peers, it was clear that the peers did make a contribution beyond the points themselves. The question of how the peers made their contribution remains for further analysis. Other researchers (Graubard, 1969; Sloane, 1969) have reported success in adapting the timer-game to a variety of classroom situations.

It is likely that Sue's reaction to the peer condition may not be common to all students. There may very well be students for whom the peer attention generated by the peer points condition would serve to strengthen the out-of-seat behavior rather than reduce it. But the experimental conditions imposed here seemed to insure at least some degree of success in modifying out-of-seat behavior with the timer-game.

REFERENCES

Barrish, H. H., Saunders, M., and Wolf, M. M.: Good behavior game: Effects of individual contingencies for group consequences on disruptive behavior in a classroom. *J Appl Behav Anal*, 2:119-124, 1969.

Graubard, P.: Yeshiva University, New York City. Personal communication, 1969.

Hall, V. R., Lund, D., and Jackson, D.: Effects of teacher attention on study behavior. *J Appl Behav Anal, 1:*1-12, 1968.

Madsen, C. H., Becker, W. C., and Thomas, D. R.: Rules, praise, and ignoring: Elements of elementary classroom control. *J Appl Behav Anal, 1:* 139-150, 1968.

O'Leary, K. D., Becker, W. C., Evans, M. B., and Saudargas, R. A.: A token reinforcement program in a public school: A replication and systematic analysis. *J Appl Behav Anal, 2:*3-14, 1969.

Osborne, J. G.: Free-time as a reinforcer in the management of classroom behavior. *J Appl Behav Anal, 2:*113-118, 1969.

Patterson, G. R.: An application of conditioning techniques to the control of a hyperactive child. In L. P. Ullmann and L. Krasner (Eds.): *Case Studies in Behavior Modification.* New York, Holt, Rinehart & Winston, 1965, pp. 370-375.

Sloane, H.: University of Utah, Salt Lake City. Personal communication, 1969.

Thomas, D. R., Becker, W. C., and Armstrong, M.: Production and elimination of disruptive classroom behavior by systematically varying teacher's behavior. *J Appl Behav Anal, 1:*35-45, 1968.

Wolf, M. M., Giles, D., and Hall, R. V.: Experiments with token reinforcement in a remedial classroom. *Behav Res Ther, 6:*51-64, 1968.

SECTION V
FUTURE CONSIDERATIONS

Chapter 21

BEHAVIOR MODIFICATION: WHERE DO WE GO FROM HERE?

THOMAS LOVITT

ONE OF THE OUTSTANDING characteristics of those who measure directly and continuously—whether they are called behavior modifiers or precision teachers—is their enthusiasm. As a group and as individuals, they have an energetic and positive outlook. One reason for their optimism is their conviction that any behavior can be changed if the environment can be arranged in an appropriate way. Another factor that may account for their exuberance is that they measure continuously, thus obtaining immediate feedback about a student's progress and the effectiveness of their teaching instead of having to wait for results of an experimental treatment.

People dedicated to continuous measurement and contingency management are positivistic in their approach toward education and change, and indeed, as Forness and MacMillan* illustrate, there is ample evidence to validate much of their enthusiasm. This notwithstanding, one might ask how behavior modification will influence the educational process in the future.

Undoubtedly, in the next few years more individuals from those disciplines concerned with the management and treatment of children will begin to use behavior modification techniques. As reported in this issue, these methods have been adopted by audiologists, speech therapists, regular, remedial, and head start teachers, and teacher consultants. Previous reports have described the use of behavior modification techniques by nurses, school psychologists, teacher aides, rehabilitation personnel, and occupational therapists, and it is anticipated that direct and continuous measurement will increase in use.

The widespread acceptance of behavior modification proce-

---

* See Forness & MacMillan, pp. 93-100.

dures could result in a common assessment and training framework. A multidisciplinary diagnosis, then, could result in more than a pedantic debate. Perhaps if a social worker, for example, obtained direct information about a student by observing him in his home rather than acquiring indirect hints by a telephone conversation with his parents, and perhaps if a school psychologist collected data expressly related to a pupil's math or peer relationships instead of depending on standardized test results or questionnaires, the two professionals could by their common technique establish better rapport with one another and, more importantly, with the pupil's teacher. Were all therapeutic personnel to measure behavior in a like manner, the jargon or mystique currently associated with each discipline would be eliminated.

Apart from this foreseen accelerated use of behavior modification practices and the resultant ease of communication, certain trends can be seen, based on the investigations in this issue and other recent reports.

Measurement and Change

One trend which is becoming apparent is that behavior modifiers and other concerned individuals are beginning to discriminate between measurement and change. In the past, most operant conditioners and behavior modifiers have acted in accord with their titles, conditioning and modifying, by concentrating solely on change. They assessed a behavior only long enough to obtain a stable baseline, rearranged the environment in some way to alter the behavior, and then observed the effects. Perhaps the reason for this strategy was that the behavior modifiers traditionally dealt with people whose behaviors desperately needed to be changed; either noxious behaviors needed to be extinguished or fundamental behaviors had to be generated. Many behavior modifiers would have felt unfulfilled if they had only obtained baseline data without attempting a behavioral alteration.

Meanwhile, others committed to direct and continuous measurement occasionally discovered that, although a behavior was measured, modification efforts did not always ensue. That modification plans are not necessarily subsequent to baseline measurement could come about because either the behavior occurred at a normal rate, or the behavior was not amenable to modification with the techniques available.

Most behavior modifiers are disinclined to believe that once a behavior had been described it cannot be changed. The correctness of this conviction, however, can only be ascertained after millions of behaviors have been measured and attempts made to change them. But even if behaviors do exist which cannot at present be altered, measurement could still be warranted. Scientists measure many phenomena that are not currently subject to manipulation, such as typhoons, hurricanes, tornadoes, and earthquakes. By continuously measuring these events, scientists have predictive information concerning when and to what extent certain hazardous conditions will occur. A similar strategy ought to prevail in regard to human behavior: If "unchangeable behaviors" are discovered, particularly important ones, measurement should be obtained.

Many behavior managers do measure behaviors that could probably be altered, yet they make no attempt to do so. Their interest is simply to discover the current status of a behavior. Some investigators, for example, are obtaining data on performances of normal individuals, a key motive being to determine norms in order to help those individuals who deviate. For unless the extent to which an individual's performance veers from normal standards is known, the rehabilitation process could be too long or too short. Following treatment, a patient could be returned to his original environment undercured or supercured.

A second reason to obtain measurement on performance which is normal and does not require remediation is to *prevent* abnormality. This emphasis on assessment of normal development parallels similar approaches in medicine or dentistry. These professions recommend, and sometimes provide, diagnostic services that can detect mildly developed symptoms of serious medical conditions, thus preventing the further development of these maladies.

In education, serious measurement has traditionally been used when performance has been defective, and, therefore, it is often associated with failure and frustration. In practice, the degree of a pupil's maladaptive behavior can often be ascertained by the weight of his diagnostic dossier. If teachers continuously monitored important behaviors of children, they could detect minor deviations from the norm and quickly arrange the slight remediation tactic called for. Moreover, if teachers would intervene when the deviation of a pupil's behavior was minor, modification would be less expensive than the massive treatment required after the problem had increased, and this procedure would be far healthier for the pupil being treated.

Academic Measurement

A second and extremely noteworthy trend in the work of some behavior modifiers is their interest in academic performance.* For some time continuous measurement and contingency management tactics have been used to establish discipline and order in classrooms. Several investigations (Becker, Madsen, Arnold, and Thomas, 1967) have been published describing how behaviors such as talk-outs, out-of-seats, and hitting others have been successfully dealt with by operant or behavior modification procedures.

More recently, other investigators have begun to measure academic behaviors such as words read, problems answered, and sentences written. Not only have reading, writing, and arithmetic been measured, but data have been obtained in such areas as music and creative writing, activities once considered by some unmeasurable.

Important as the assessment and control of disruptive behaviors may be, the teacher's primary responsibility is to teach. He is obligated to assist youngsters to acquire greater skills in the subjects taught. It is therefore important for the teacher to define these skills and to measure the extent to which pupils acquire them.

---

* See Gaasholt, pp. 129-135; McKenzie, Egner, Knight, Perelman, Schneider, & Garvin, pp. 137-143.

The teacher interested in obtaining academic data must immediately deal with two curriculum problems. One is the matter of definition—deciding what to count. The teacher must first describe a response class, for example, additional facts where the sums are 0-9, or reading words of one syllable which begin with a consonant and have a medial short vowel. A second problem in obtaining academic measures is to locate materials which pertain to specific skills. Few commercial programs specify which tasks or behaviors they deal with, or progress from one skill to another in a coherent manner. In some math books, for example, one page may contain computation problems, the next story problems. Before useful academic data can be obtained, the teacher must be certain that the materials the student is expected to use are coherent in sequence and equivalent in type. Often these materials must be developed by the teacher.

In time, the continuous measurement of curriculum materials could answer three of the most controversial issues plaguing educators: (a) how can educational techniques and procedures be evaluated, (b) how can the identification and arrangement of behaviors in a given process be evaluated, and (c) how can proficiency or mastery levels be determined?

In regard to the first point, teachers are eager to have data on the effectiveness of their procedures. Many are curious about the effects of seating arrangements, room displays, and teaching devices on child performance. If continuous measurement of pupil performance is obtained prior to an environmental alteration, and if data continue to be gathered while the alteration is in effect (and, in some cases, when the alteration is removed), the effects of various changes will be discernible.

The data will also serve as the basis for communicating with the public. People in the community want to know how their tax monies are used. Such information is being requested more and more by the public; no longer can educators simply ask for large sums of money without furnishing tangible evidence of their accomplishments. Today is the age of accountability.

The second controversial issue, sequencing skills, is of great concern to all involved in human development. Notions about the specification of behaviors within a process and their subsequent arrangement have been, to a great extent, less than empirically derived. This is particularly true when the problem is to describe how a complex cognitive process, such as receptive and expressive language, is developed. Similar difficulties arise when attempts are made to plan the most efficient route toward reading or creative writing.

The Brickers* and others seem to be working toward the establishment of a network of requisite behaviors leading to the acquisition of language. By first delineating the requisite behaviors for language development, then logically arranging these behaviors, researchers will be in a position to evaluate the function of such a program. When behaviors are first defined and then arranged and when data regarding individual interactions with such a schema are obtained, researchers can be influenced either to alter the list of requisite behaviors or to rearrange their sequencing.

In reference to the third point, the determination of mastery levels, Gaasholt† presents methods for establishing proficiency rates and discusses how, once established, these criteria can signal when children should be promoted from one skill level to another. Her suggestion for setting proficiency levels in mathematics is to have each child write numerals, and that writing rate will serve as a referent from which to evaluate performance on problems of varied difficulty. To establish proficiency rates in writing for children, she suggests that one-half the adult writing rate be used.

Certainly other strategies can be employed to establish criterion performance. One way is to obtain rates from a norm group. If, for example, a kindergarten teacher wants his pupil least proficient in letter recognition to perform that skill like an average student, he can obtain data from the entire class and use the median rate as the criterion rate. Another way of arriving at proficiency levels is to gather data from an advanced group. A

---

* Bricker & Bricker, pp. 101-111.
† See pp. 129-135.

first grade teacher can obtain various data from second graders, and use these facts to set proficiency levels for his first graders.

Although current efforts to sequence skills and to establish proficiency levels are naive approximations, continued research aimed at refining such work can assist not only in the development of educational programs for children, but in the evaluation of teachers. For in the future, if proficiency levels are established for the various skills children are expected to acquire, and if more is known about the sequencing of materials, it will be possible to evaluate teachers on the basis of their instructional skills rather than on irrelevant attributes. Teachers could be judged according to the number of skills they taught their pupils; their assessment would not be based on whether they merely acted or talked like teachers.

Multiple Measurement and Change

Some educators are critical of many operant or behavior modification studies because of their simplicity and apparent disregard for the complete individual. Admittedly, most investigations have focused on the measurement and manipulation of one isolated behavior which often represents only a small part of a child's total behavior repertoire. A notable exception is the classic study of Dicky by Wolf, Risley, and Mees (1964) where several behaviors were measured one at a time and subsequently changed.

It is anticipated that future behavior modifiers will be interested in measuring a wide range of children's behaviors. One way to accomplish this is recommended by Allen, Everett, and Turner*: "Modification of only one or two of a child's behaviors at a time is essential to a successful program. A teacher's responses may become scattered and unsystematic if too many contingencies must be kept in mind...."

An alternative to this ordered approach would be to simultaneously measure a number of behaviors, using an environmental change with only one at a time. Investigators then could assess

---

* See pp. 119-127.

not only the direct effects of an environmental change on a specific behavior but also the side effects of the variable.

Such generalized effects are suggested by McKenzie and his colleagues.* Coincident with the improved arithmetic performance of a boy, the boy's mother noted a positive change in his attitude and his reading teacher, a favorable change in his reading. Had measurements in the boy's attitude and his reading been obtained, along with the measurement in math, and if all rates improved when a contingency was imposed only on math, the speculations of the mother and reading teacher could have been verified.

Agriculture and medicine have discovered that the simplistic cause and effect notion of environmental relationships—when a variable is directed toward one behavior and effects are anticipated on only that behavior—is a naive concept. Agricultural researchers have found that when an insecticide is used to control one pest, that pest may be controlled, but others may also be affected. When a new drug or rehabilitation procedure is used in medicine, the consequent side effects must be studied as well as the intended effects.

Certainly, parallel situations exist in education; when an event is programed to change one behavior, not only that behavior is affected, but so are related and even unrelated behaviors. This in no way suggests that the Freudian advocates who warn of symptom substitution are correct—that as one behavior decelerates, another accelerates. Their homeostatic concept of behavior is as unsophisticated as that of the behavior modifiers who argue that only the behavior they are attempting to change will be altered while all others will remain unchanged.

Some investigators (Philips, 1968; Birnbrauer, 1968) have measured multiple behaviors while associating an environmental contingency with a single behavior, but the results of these studies are far from conclusive. Certainly, future investigators must attend to the dimensions of the important topic of generalization.

---

* See pp. 137-143.

The process of teaching is largely based on principles of generalization. Once a specific skill is developed, that behavior will assist in the acquisition of related, but more complex behaviors. When skills are arranged for pupils in a logical but unscientific manner, teachers often assume that generalization will occur. When, however, transfer does not take place, teachers are often disappointed.

A more realistic approach would be to arrange circumstances whereby the process of generalization can be scientifically measured. When serious efforts are scheduled to assess generalization, the data may reveal that skills previously considered unrelated do, in fact, share certain commonalities—when one behavior is learned, other behaviors develop. For example, a pupil's performance in discriminating shapes and sounds, in recognizing letter names and sounds, and in saying and writing certain trigrams is measured. Of these, if only shape discrimination has been taught, and yet the pupil's competence in the other behaviors accelerates, this resultant generalization would attest to the efficiency of such a grouping of skills.

Contrary findings could also emerge from systematic generalization studies. They may reveal that many prerequisite activities are, in fact, superstitious—that when an initial behavior is developed a subsequent behavior does not necessarily follow. It may be discovered that although a youngster is taught to discriminate a variety of symbols, visually and aurally, he has difficulty in understanding certain phonetic relationships. Or, once these phonics skills have been taught, the pupil may experience great difficulty in attacking new sight words.

Parametric or Component Analyses

Baer, Wolf, and Risley (1968) in a recent methodological report regarding the state of behavioral experimentation noted that, "At this stage in the development of applied behavior analysis, primary concern is usually with reliability, rather than with parametric analysis or component analysis." They also noted that many applied investigators, in their attempts to manipulate behavior, neglect to precisely analyze either the dimensions of the independent variable or its elements. However, considering the recent use of systematic behavioral principles in field settings, this lack of refinement is not too alarming, for it is first necessary to discover independent variables, albeit imprecisely explained, which will serve to alter behavior. If, however, behavior modification is to advance from a technology to a science, methodical parametric or component analyses must be undertaken.

Many experimenters have manipulated, for example, teacher praise or attention, and their reports assert, for the most part, that this variable generally influences pupil performance. Teacher praise or attention is, however, an extremely complex independent variable; it is a combination of many personality traits and dimensions, including the sex, size, facial features, and vocal characteristics of the manager. The researcher concerned with the effects of precise social variables would do well to isolate these personality characteristics and analyze each component separately.

The study of Wolf, Hanley, King, Lachowicz, and Giles* is indicative of current efforts to isolate more carefully the variables that influence behavior. In one of their experiments they discovered that when points were withdrawn contingent on a girl's getting out of her seat, the rate of that behavior decelerated. The conditions of this project—the numerals written on the board, the periodic ringing of the timer, the girl's being in or out of her seat, the crossing out of the numerals, the total points earned—were clearly visible to other members of the class. It was, therefore, possible that the effectiveness of this contingency was due as much to peer influence as to the tokens themselves. The investigators, in subsequent experimental phases, attempted to distinguish between token and peer effects. When the number of points was held constant across conditions, and when conditions where peers received or did not receive points were manipulated the data suggested that peers were more influential than points.

---

* See pp. 113-117.

As the authors mentioned, the specific behaviors or traits of the peers which influenced the girl's behavior were unknown. One of several elements of the peer condition could have controlled her actions—peer prompts to remain in her seat, peer consequences if she got out of her seat, peer consequences when they received points, her being motivated by being liked or recognized by her peers, and/or her being able to assume the role of a benefactor. Although further research could be scheduled to obtain more definitive information about the components of an independent variable, the authors began to explore systematically certain properties of a controlling variable.

Just as few studies to isolate the components of certain experimental variables have been conducted, few reports are available on the parametric analysis of a variable. Ordinarily, when food or free time has been used to affect a behavior, subsequent studies have not analyzed precise values of these variables; that is, the effect of 2 cc's of food compared to the effect of 6 cc's, or the effect of ten minutes free time versus 20 minutes.

O'Leary and his colleagues* demonstrated how a tactic commonly used to decelerate behavior can be experimentally investigated, and equally important, parametrically assessed. By alternately scheduling different amplitudes of the same variable, reprimands, they were able to analyze the comparative effects of two intensity levels on disruptive behavior. Their data, revealing that soft reprimands are generally more effective, serve to point out that varying strengths of the same independent variable may in turn differentially affect the measured behavior.

Again, as in the Wolf study, these authors stress that further analyses are required, for although loud and soft reprimands initially appear to differ only in terms of intensity, other situational differences may arise. Proximity is affected when loud or soft admonitions are dispensed—the teacher is generally nearer the pupil when soft reprimands are given. Correspondingly, as intensity lessens and proximity increases, the scolding shifts from public to private: the nearer and softer, the more private

---

* See O'Leary, Kaufman, Kass, & Drabman, pp. 145-155.

the receipt of the reprimand. Further investigation is required to understand more completely this often used but complex variable.

Future investigators might profitably follow the leads of Wolf and O'Leary and conduct experimental analyses of the components and dimensions of certain influential occurrences. If such studies were carried out in special and regular classrooms, clinics, and other field settings, the credibility of applied behavior analysis would be increased, allowing more widespread acceptance of its principles.

Pupil Management

A final trend is the interest in training pupils to manage their own behaviors. Obviously, if classroom teachers are expected to obtain daily measures of 30 children in three or four subject areas, their patience, zeal, and ingenuity will soon be exhausted. Recent reports,* however, show that it is not necessary for teachers to assume all the measurement duties since children are capable of handling some of their own data keeping. Future research could describe procedures for teaching pupils to manage their own routines and follow up the effects of this increased responsibility on academic performance.

In some instances (Lovitt and Casperson, 1969) children have been taught to calculate their time spent on certain programs, to total accurately their correct and error responses, and to divide these frequencies by the time spent on a program in order to obtain performance rates. In fact, some children have learned to plot their rates graphically, to evaluate their performance, and to explain the whole data process to other students. When children learn to correct, count, chart, and evaluate themselves, not only will the teacher be freed of a great deal of clerical work, but the pupils will benefit. Many aspects of self-recording—counting, adding, dividing, and telling time—are related to pupils' mathematics programs.

Also, the pupil learning these skills is developing the basics of

---

* See Gaasholt, pp. 129-135.

self-management, one of the goals of contemporary education. In the past, operant conditioners and behavior modifiers have been severely criticized for controlling behaviors, the basis for the argument being that the free will and creativity of individuals is denied. In some instances these critics are correct; if a behavior modifier manipulates an individual's behavior merely to demonstrate his clinical acumen, he has only partially fulfilled his responsibility. A manager may have assisted the individual to make a complicated discrimination, but that person may not be prepared to arrange for himself similar productive situations. The teaching strategy used by behavior modifiers should be the same as that advocated by others involved in training. The manager must wean the client from his external support by instructing him to manage himself.

Future researchers could explore more complex dimensions of self-management than those discussed in this issue. Pupils could be taught not only to count and chart, but to specify their own objectives, to design their own programs, to schedule their activities, to evaluate their performances, to provide their own feedback, and finally, to design their own contingency systems.

Were schools committed to pupil management as an integral feature of their curricula, the probability of producing unique, independent, motivated students would be increased. The principles of behavior modification—direct observation, continuous measurement, and systematic manipulation—offer a promising route toward the realization of this commitment.

REFERENCES

Baer, D. M., Wolf, M. M., and Risley, T. R.: Some current dimensions of applied behavior analysis. *J Appl Behav Anal,* 1:91-97, 1968.

Becker, W. C., Madsen, C. H., Jr., Arnold, C., and Thomas, D. R.: The contingent use of teacher attention and praise in reducing classroom behavior problems. *J Spec Educ,* 1:287-307, 1967.

Birnbrauer, J. W.: Generalization of punishment effects—A case study. *J Appl Behav Anal,* 1:201-211, 1968.

Lovitt, T. C., and Casperson, B.: Instructing self-management skills to second graders. Unpublished manuscript, University of Washington, 1969.

Philips, E. L.: Achievement place: Token reinforcement procedures in a home-style rehabilitation setting for "pre-delinquent" boys. *J Appl Behav Anal,* 1:213-223, 1968.

Wolf, M. M., Risley, T. R., and Mees, H. L.: Application of operant conditioning procedures to the behaviour problems of an autistic child. *Behav Res Ther,* 1:305-312, 1964.

INDEX

A

A-B-A design, 25
Abramovitz, Arnold, 129, 133
"Accelerating consequences" of behavior, 32
Allen, K. Eileen, 14, 23, 36, 217, 218, 220, 229, 263
Allowances, as reinforcers, 201-214
American Psychological Association, 87
Anderson, R. C., 201
Armstrong, M., 231, 247
Arnold, C., 17, 168, 260
Artuso, Alfred A., 79, 148, 194
Ausubel, D., 47, 51
Autistic children, 13, 15-16
Aversive conditioning (punishment), 50-51, 53
Ayllon, T., 12, 33, 52
Azrin, Nathan H., 10

B

Baer, D. M., 10-11, 12, 20, 36, 48, 81-82, 213, 217, 229, 231, 265
Baldwin, A., 50
Bandura, A., 13, 46, 47, 49, 50, 51
Barrett, B., 33, 52
Barrish, H. H., 247
Becker, Wesley C., 17, 90, 91, 92, 101, 104, 142, 151, 152, 153, 154, 155, 168, 169, 201, 202, 216, 231, 247, 260
Behavior
 generalization of, 264-265
 high vs. low frequency (probability), 39, 78
 maladaptive (see Maladaptive behavior)
 measurement of, 23-25, 58, 62-68, 232-233, 258-265
 by students, 268-269

Behavior modification
 ancient Greece and Rome, 5
 benefits of, 52-53
 common characteristics of, 22-23
 component analysis of, 265-268
 defined, 5
 fundamental principles of, 23, 26
 goals of, 79-80
 limitations of, 78-87
 morality of, 71-76
 origins of, 5-17
 trends in, 257-269
Behavior modification techniques
 desensitization, 7-8, 11, 52, 120, 121, 127, 132n
 discrimination learning, 13, 51-52
 "emotive imagery," 120-127, 133
 extinction, 11-12, 46, 53
 partial reinforcement, 46, 47, 53
 positive reinforcement, 11, 47-48, 53, 84-86
 precision teaching, 57-68
 punishment, 50-51, 53
 reprimands, 168-185, 267-268
 shaping, 222-225, 228
 social modeling, 8, 13, 48-50, 53
 staging, 36-37
 time-out, 53
 token reinforcement (see Token reinforcement)
Behavior therapy, defined, 53
Behavioral principles, 32-33
Benson, Cedric, 141, 231
Bentler, P., 52, 129
Bernard, C., 26
Bijou, S. W., 12, 20, 32, 77, 81-82, 84, 90, 143, 144, 158, 213, 220
Birnbrauer, J. S., 14, 90, 141, 142, 143, 144, 154, 158, 159, 166, 167, 231, 264

Bonner Springs Junior High School (Bonner Springs, Kansas), 232
Brackbill, Y., 52
Brady, 32
Bricker, D., 262, 262n
Bricker, W., 262, 262n
Broden, Marcia, 231, 232
Brooks, B., 33
Bruner, J., 30
Buckley, N. K., 58, 168
Buell, J. S., 14, 23, 36, 217, 218
Burnham, W., 7
Bushell, D.

C

California Achievement Test (CAT), 146, 148, 189, 192
Casperson, B., 268
Chalfant, J., 44, 45
Children's Rehabilitation Unit (University of Kansas Medical Center), 17, 36, 39
Chimpanzees, 30
Church, R., 51
Clark, Marilyn, 141, 142, 146, 201, 203, 231
Classroom behavior, modification of (see Autistic children; Behavior modification techniques; Emotionally disturbed children; Language, acquisition of; Maladaptive behavior; Mentally retarded children; Phobias; School phobia; Token reinforcement; Underprivileged children; and Table of Contents)
Cognitive dissonance, theory of, 82-83
Combs, C. F., 81
Cooperation, conditioned, 10, 109-115
Council for Exceptional Children, 29n
Cruickshank, W. M., 202, 203

D

de Baca, 39
"Decelerating consequences" of behavior, 32, 33
Delinquency, 15
DeMeyer, M. K., 13, 77
Denny, M., 128

Deprivation-satiation conditions, 10-11
Desensitization, 7-8, 11, 52, 120, 121, 127, 132n
Discrimination learning, 13, 51-52
Disruptive behavior, coding systems, 92, 171
Dropouts, 146-147
Dunlap, K., 9
Durrell Analysis of Reading Difficulty, 204

E

Ebner, M., 187
Eddy, E. M., 80
Eliciting effect, 49
Emotionally disturbed children, 14, 31, 37-38, 44-46, 144, 148, 151-152, 159, 187-199, 232
    capacity to learn abstract ideas, 31
"Emotive imagery," 120-127, 133
    defined, 121
Engelmann, 216
Engineered classroom design (Santa Monica Project), 188-191
Engineered Learning Project (ELP), 58-65
English, W., 7-8
Erikson, 80
Evans, M. B., 168, 247
Evans, Richard I., 71
Everett, Paulette M., 263
Experimental Education Unit (University of Washington), 17
Extinction, 11-12, 46
    defined, 53
Eysenck, H., 33, 128

F

Fear, conditioned, 6-7, 8
Ferster, C. B., 13, 28, 30, 31, 32, 48, 77, 85, 128
Festinger, L., 82-83, 84
Finley, 33
Flavell, J. H., 81
Forness, Steven R., 257
Franks, C., 45, 48
Freedom, defined, 75-76

Freitag, G., 16, 77
Fuller, P., 9

G

Gaasholt, Marie, 262
Gagné, R. M., 81
Gallagher, J., 44, 45, 152, 154
Garvey, W., 52
Gates McKillop Diagnostic Reading Tests, 58, 147
Generalization of behavior, 264-265
Gerwirtz, J., 10
Giles, David K., 145, 201, 231, 247, 266
Girardeau, F., 12
Glossary of terms, 53
Gold, V. J., 77
Grades as reinforcers, 141-142, 201-214
Graubard, P.
Grossberg, J., 42, 45

H

Haberman, J., 7
Hall, R. Vance, 145, 168, 201, 231, 247
Hanley, Edward L., 266
Haring, Norris G., 17, 32, 39, 77, 86, 144, 147, 187, 216
Harlow, H., 83, 84
Harriet Tubman House, 110
Harris, Florence R., 14, 23, 36, 217, 218, 220, 229, 231
Harris, M., 45
Hart, B. M., 14, 23, 36, 217, 218
Hauck, M., 147
Haughton, E., 12, 33, 65
Hawkins, R. P., 220
Hayden, A. H., 216
Head Start children, 216-229
Hegrenes, J., 52
Henke, L. B., 217, 229
Henry, G. W., 5
Henry, J., 80
Hero-images, 121
Hewett, Frank M., 15, 17, 33, 48, 77, 79, 84, 148, 188, 189, 194
High vs. low frequency (probability) behavior, 39, 78

Hively, W., 77
Holland, J., 33
Holmes, F. B., 8, 52, 120
Homme, 39, 40
Houser, J. E., 149, 154, 155
Hulten, W. J., 219
Hunt, J. McV., 82
Hunt, W., 198
Hutson, A., 50
Hyperactivity, 15, 16, 149, 150-151

I

Imitation (see Social modeling)
Incentives for positive reinforcement, 205-206
Inhibitory effect, 49
IS Description, 60-62, 68
Itard, J., 5-6

J

Jackson, D., 168, 231, 247
Jensen, A. R., 84, 85
Jersild, A. T., 8, 52, 120
Johnston, M. K., 217, 220
Jones, Mary C., 7, 8, 120, 120
Jones, R., 149
Journal of Abnormal and Social Psycology, 109n
Journal of the Experimental Analysis of Behavior, 116n
Journal of Mental Science, 120n
Journal of Special Education, 44n
Juniper Gardens Project (Kansas City), 17
Juvenile delinquency, 15

K

Kassorla, I. C., 77
Kelley, C. S., 217
Kendler, Howard, 87
Kidder, J. D., 90, 141, 143, 144, 158, 231
Kinder, B., 16
King, Louise A., 266
Klein, J. W., 216
Kothera, Richard, 141, 231
Krasner, L., 5, 20, 21, 46, 79

Krasnogorski, N., 8
Kuhlmann-Anderson IQ Tests, 159
Kunzelmann, H. P., 65, 144, 187, 219
Kupers, C., 50
Kuypers, David S., 142, 152, 153, 155

L

Lachowitz, Joseph, 142, 201, 203, 266
Landes, R., 80
Language, acquisition of, 15-16, 225, 262
LaRue D. Carter Memorial Hospital, 116
Lawler, J., 14, 90, 142, 154, 158
Lazarus, Arnold A., 11, 52, 120, 129, 132, 137
Levin, G., 38, 77, 198
Levin, H., 51
Levinsky, D., 150, 154
Levitt, E. E., 44
Lewis, W., 46
Lindsley, Ogden R., 10, 14, 32, 33, 52, 57, 61, 128
Loud vs. soft reprimands, 168-185, 267-268
Lovaas, O., 16, 51, 77
Lovinger, E., 128
Lovitt, Thomas C., 17, 77, 268
Lund, D., 168, 231, 247
Lupton, A., 52

M

Mabry, J., 20
McCauley, B. D., 20
McCloskey, M. L., 201
Maccoby, E., 51
McKenzie, Hugh S., 141, 147, 231, 264
MacMillan, Donald L., 257
McQueen, Marjorie, 17, 151, 158, 187
Madsen, C. H., 17, 168, 247
Maladaptive behavior
 baby-talk, 118-119
 coding systems, 92, 171
 drop-outs, 146-147
 hyperactivity, 15, 16, 149, 150-151
 juvenile delinquency, 15
 obscene conduct, 149-150
 out-of-seat, 37
 socially maladjusted, 152-153
 stammering, 9
 stuttering, 10
 tantrums, 11-12, 35, 46, 92, 118-119, 159, 220-221
 thumb-sucking, 36
Mann, L., 78
Marshall, H., 50
Martin, I., 126
Maslow, A. H., 83
Mattson, R., 58
Mees, H. L., 48, 163, 240, 263
Mentally retarded children, 6, 9, 14-15, 142-144, 149-150
Merrell, D., 128
Metropolitan Achievement Test, 182
Meyer, W., 51
Michael, J., 31, 52
Minke, 33
Modeling (see Social modeling)
Modeling effect, 49
Moore, G. A., 80
Moral values, modification of, 13
Motivation, 41, 81-84
Multiple measurement and change of behavior, 263-265
Murphee, O. D., 109

N

Negative reinforcement, defined, 53
Neurosis, developed under laboratory conditions, 8
Nimnicht, G., 216
Nolen, P., 144, 187, 216, 219
Northeast Johnson County Cooperative Program in Special Education, 202
Nurnberger, 32

O

Offenbach, S., 51
O'Hara, J., 52
O'Leary, K. Daniel, 90, 91, 92, 101, 104, 142, 151, 152, 153, 154, 155,

Index

168, 169, 201, 202, 231, 247, 267, 268
Orlando, R., 77
Osborne, J. G., 247
Out-of-seat behavior, 37, 152

P

Panyan, M., 231
Parametric analysis of behavior modification, 265-268
Parsons State Hospital (Kansas), 12
Partial reinforcement, 46, 47
  defined, 53
Patterson, G. R., 16, 77, 128, 149, 150, 151, 154, 187, 252
Pavlov, I. P., 6
Peabody Picture Vocabulary Test (PPVT), 143, 144, 149
Peer reinforcement, 266-267
Penny, R. O., 52
Perline, I. H., 150, 154
Peters, H. N., 109
Peterson, R. F., 220
Philips, E. L., 264
Phillips, L., 32, 39, 78
Phobias, 7, 11, 52, 120-127, 128-138
Piaget, J., 13, 80, 81, 82, 84
Point system used in token reinforcement, 237-240
Positive reinforcement, 47-48
  defined, 53
  desensitization, 11
  variables of, 48
Precision teaching, 57-68
  method of, 58-59
  steps of, 57
Premack, D., 39, 78
Proficiency levels in math, 62-65, 262
Proficiency levels in writing, 65-68
Psychiatric ward and token reinforcement, 12
Punishment, 50-51
  benefits of, 51
  defined, 53
  limitations of, 50

Q

Quay, H., 17, 48, 151, 158, 159, 187, 198

R

Rabon, D., 231
Rachman, S., 129
Rainier School (Washington), 14-15
Raven Matrices Test, 149
Rayner, R., 6
Razrun, G., 85
Redl, F., 44, 51
Reese, Ellen P., 73, 75
Reinforcement, 84-86
  negative, 53
  peer, 266-267
  positive, 11, 47-48, 53
  self, 84
  token (*see* Token reinforcement)
Reinforcers
  analysis of, 13
  arbitrary vs. natural
  available at school, 205-206
  social, 10-11
Reprimands, loud vs. soft, 168-185, 267-268
Response facilitation effect
Retarded children, 6, 9, 14-15, 142-144, 149-150
Reversal design, 25
Reynolds, N. F., 217, 229
Risley, T. R., 48, 163, 240, 263, 265
Roeland School District #92 (Shawnee Mission, Kansas), 202
Rogers, Carl, 75
Ross, D., 50
Ross, S., 50

S

Santa Monica City Schools Project, 17, 187-199
Saskatchewan Hospital, 12
Saudargas, R. A., 247
Saunders, M., 247
Schaeffer, B., 16
School phobia, 125, 128-138

Schweid, E., 220
Schwitzgebel, R., 15
Sears, R., 51
Seguin, E., 6
Self-evaluation by students, 268-269
Shaping, 222-223, 224-225, 228
Sheehan, J., 10
Shores, R. E., 152
Sidman, M., 25, 154, 166-167
Siegel, S., 210
Sight Vocabulary Program, 143
Simmons, J., 16, 38, 77, 198
Skinner, B. F., 9, 10, 32, 33, 42, 71, 75, 76, 109, 111n, 113, 128
Skyline Elementary School (Shawnee Mission, Kansas), 202
Slack, C., 48
Sloane, H. N., 20, 252
Social modeling, 8, 13, 48-50
  defined, 53
  effects of, 49-50
Social reinforcers, nature of, 10-11
Society for the Experimental Analysis of Behavior, Inc., 116
Solomon, R. L., 51, 169
South Bay Union of Boston, Mass., 110n
Spontaneous remission, 46
Spradlin, J., 12
Sprague, R. L., 17, 151, 158, 187
SRA Achievement Tests, 204
SRA Reading Series, 204
Staats, W., 33
Stachnik, T., 20
Stafford, R. R., 81
Staging, 36-37
Stammering, 9
Stanford Achievement Test (SAT), 145, 146
Stanford Diagnostic Arithmetic Test, 58
Stevenson, H., 52
Stuttering, 10
Sullivan Placement Test, 148
Sulzbacher, S. I., 149, 152, 154, 155
Systematic desensitization, 7-8, 11, 52, 120, 121, 127, 132n

T

Tague, C. E., 90, 141, 143, 144, 158, 231
Tantrums, 11-12, 35, 46, 92, 118-119, 159, 220-221
Teacher's presence as a reinforcer, 37-38
Thomas, D. R., 17, 168, 232, 247, 260
Thorndike, E. L., 6
Thumbsucking, 36
Time-out, defined, 38
"Timer-game," 247-252
Token reinforcement, 12, 14-15, 90-105, 141-156, 158-167, 201-214, 234-245, 247-252, 266
  point system, 237-240
  problems of, 201-202
Tokens vs. teacher attention, 143-144
Tosti, D., 40
Treating behavior vs. treating its roots, 41, 42, 44-46
Turner, Keith D., 263

U

Ullman, L. P., 5, 20, 21, 46, 79
Ulrich, R. E., 20
Underpriveleged children, 145-146, 248
University of California at Los Angeles, 15, 16
University of Kansas, 203
  Medical Center, 17, 36, 39
University of Oregon, 58
University of Washington, 17

V

Valett, R., 77
Verbal behavior, differential reinforcement of, 225
"Verbal confirming response" (V_c), 84-85

W

Walker, H. M., 58, 168
Walters, R. H., 46, 47, 169
Warren, A., 46

Watson, J., 6-7, 8
Wechsler Intelligence Scale for Children, 189
Weickart, 216
Weir, M., 52
Werry, J. S., 17, 151, 158, 187
Whelan, R. J., 17, 77, 86, 187, 201
White, M., 45
White, R. W., 83, 84
Whittier, J., 149
Wilcoxon, F., 114n
Wilcoxon Matched Pairs Signed Ranks Test, 210, 211
Williams, C. D., 11-12, 46
Witwatersrand University (Johannesburg, South Africa), 128n
Wolf, Montrose M., 14, 24, 33, 36, 48, 90, 141, 142, 143, 145, 158, 159, 163, 166, 167, 201, 203, 217, 218, 231, 240, 247, 263, 265, 266, 267, 268
Wolpe, J., 11, 52, 120, 127, 128, 129, 132, 135
Wolpe's Reciprocal Inhibition Principle, 120
Wood, F. H., 80
Wright, M. A., 149
Wrobel, P. A., 201

Z

Zigler, E., 52
Zilboorg, G., 5
Zimmerman, C., 57
Zimmerman, Elaine H., 14, 34, 35, 46, 78, 231
Zimmerman, J., 14, 34, 35, 46, 78, 231

DISCHARGED DISCHARGED
NOV 28 1988
OCT 22 1977
DISCHARGED
         JUN 25 1984
DISCHARGED

DISCHARGED

MAY 0 5 1993

DISCHARGED

RESERVE